W. P. Strickland

The pioneer bishop

The life and times of Francis Asbury

W. P. Strickland

The pioneer bishop
The life and times of Francis Asbury

ISBN/EAN: 9783742836687

Manufactured in Europe, USA, Canada, Australia, Japa

Cover: Foto ©Andreas Hilbeck / pixelio.de

Manufactured and distributed by brebook publishing software
(www.brebook.com)

W. P. Strickland

The pioneer bishop

THE PIONEER BISHOP:

THE LIFE AND TIMES OF

FRANCIS ASBURY.

BY

W. P. STRICKLAND.

WITH AN INTRODUCTION BY NATHAN BANGS, D.D

ENGLISH EDITION:

WITH AN INTRODUCTION BY

THE REV. S. W. CHRISTOPHERS,

OF MANCHESTER.

MANCHESTER:

DAVID KELLY, 53, MARKET STREET,

LONDON:

SIMPKIN, MARSHALL AND CO.,

1860.

INTRODUCTION.

SOME families have grown into nations, and have gained an imperishable name, without preserving any distinct memory of a single patriarch belonging to the parent house. Religious institutions, too, now and then make the world feel their power, though it is never certainly known to whom the honour of their birth is due. The genealogy of such cases is not an agreeable study. At all events, it would scarcely be chosen by those who think it wise to abstain from an excitement of their curiosity when there can be no sure promise of satisfaction. He who has toiled up to the highest peak of a mountain range, that he may note the point at which some noble river begins its course, will hardly believe that the pleasure of his upward journey has balanced his labour, if, after all, he finds that the object of his pursuit is covered with impenetrable mists. But there is a joy in clearly tracing the beginning of great things. No one can realize the full grandeur of such social and religious movements as have swayed the destinies of a continent, without a pleasant sense of awe; but the feeling becomes more rich and happy when, at the same time, it is possible to turn and look in upon the first conceptions and experimental efforts of those leading spirits with whom the vast movements began. Let the reader, for instance, call up before his mind the gigantic proportions of that religious system which now takes a chief part among the very many which are doing so much to christianize every department of life in the United States; and then, in the light of the great fact, let him look back upon the first workers, or on the "Life and Times" which are pictured in the present volume, and a single glance will be enough to convince him that the world never saw small beginnings more interesting in themselves, or gathering more significance from the breadth and power of their result.

A hasty review of the leading religious sections as they arrived and took their places on the Western Continent, and a rapid observation of the colonial provinces on the eve of their revolutionary outbreak, agreeably prepare the mind for an introduction to the "Times" of the "Pioneer Bishop." How the Methodist Preacher of the Old World became a Bishop in the New, John Wesley himself explains, in a letter which Mr. Strickland has given in his seventh chapter. In that letter, the writer's judgment admits a principle which his feeling, as a Churchman, would not let him act upon in his choice of terms. Hence the one whom he allows to be truly a Bishop, he cautiously denominates Superintendent. He was not fast enough for his "Brethren in America." They had a notion that those who really were Bishops should be called so. Asbury had already caught the rising spirit of the far west; and it is amusing to find his old friend and spiritual superior startled at his mode of "going ahead." "There is indeed," says Wesley, in a letter from London, "a wide difference between the relation wherein you stand to the Americans, and the relation wherein I stand to all the Methodists. You are the elder brother of the American Methodists; I am, under God, the Father of the whole family. * * * But on one point, my dear brother, I am a little afraid both the Doctor (Coke) and you differ from me. I study to be little; you study to be great. I creep; you strut along. I found a school; you a college! Nay, and call it after your own names! O, beware, do not seek to be something! Let me be nothing, and 'Christ be all in all!' One instance of this, of your greatness, has given me great concern. How can you, how dare you, suffer yourself to be called Bishop? I shudder, I start at the very thought! Men may call me a knave, or a fool, a rascal, a scoundrel, and I am content; but they shall never, by my consent, call me Bishop! For my sake, for God's sake, for Christ's sake, put a full end to this! * * * Thus, my dear Franky, I have told you all that is in my heart." To which soever of the parties such a rebuke more properly belonged, those who relish a smart bit of letter writing will, perhaps, be tempted to think that it was better for a young bishop even to suffer a little undeserved pain, than for the world to lose so characteristic an epistle. But who will say that Asbury does not deserve the title of Bishop? Let the reader follow him, with giddy speed, round and round his circuit of thousands of miles, and mark the rise of living churches, while he catches, here and there, a curious insight into the American Methodist's style of thought and expression. The "Pioneer" will be found equal to every demand, either on his outer or his inner man. His wilderness-born companions seemed, at times, to admire or envy him for "as fair, and as clear, and as thin a skin as ever came from England;" but they never found him shrinking from the course of duty, whatever there was of hard fare, rough lodging, vermin or filth, flood or storm, mountain or swamp. Truly, he was a Bishop of all work. Now he is reading his Hebrew Bible or his Greek Testament amidst vast solitudes; now, in some Conference, he is ruling those who supposed, it may be, that they were ruling him. Now he is teaching the squatter's wife to keep her log-cabin clean, and now conversing with General Washington. At one time, he is showing a smart western girl how to leap her horse over a chasm; and at another is in cozy chat with his clergy, and helping them to settle the destinies of Europe by the light of prophecy. By turns, he tries to keep Methodism from the process of entanglement in the question of slavery, gives Quakers lessons on zeal, apologizes for his own celibacy, or proclaims his fear that "women and the devil would get all his preachers." The good man always appears to know his calling. Nor can it be anything but pleasant to watch him gathering around his own person, as their common centre, benevolent societies, college corporations, Sunday schools, missionary societies, and, in fact, everything that can bless the land which he now called his own. He has beautifully pencilled his own character in a single sentence dropped towards the close of his long, romantic, adventurous, but truly evangelic career: "If I can only be instrumental in the conversion of one soul in travelling round the Continent, I'll travel round till I die!" But, now, the reader himself must travel with "The Pioneer Bishop."

S. WOOLCOCK CHRISTOPHERS.

Manchester, Dec. 21st, 1859.

INTRODUCTION TO THE AMERICAN EDITION.

A LIFE OF BISHOP ASBURY has long been a desideratum among the biographies of the Church ; I say the *Church*, meaning to comprehend the entire Christian community. For though he was a minister of a sect, and a bishop of the Methodist Episcopal Church, yet his labours made a most salutary impression upon the Christian community at large, and tended to mould the minds and hearts of all that came or shall come within their influence into the image of Christ. He may therefore be presented as an exemplar of every minister of the Lord Jesus, as exhibiting that spirit of catholicity which ought to possess and actuate the hearts and heads of all who are inducted into the sacred office. Such a biography, well written, cannot do otherwise than exert a hallowing influence on all who examine its pages with a right spirit, in leading them forward in the path of obedience, faith, and love, and inducing them to make the sacrifice needful to enable them to fulfil their ministry with persevering diligence, that they may finally finish their " course with joy."

One fault of many biographers is the mingling up of every incident, however remotely connected with the person concerned, that may have occurred during his lifetime, interweaving into his biography events and things with which he had little or nothing to do, thus making him responsible for things and events over which he had little or no control. This method belongs more properly to general history, instead of the history of an individual. It has been adopted, I have often thought, to make up for the barrenness of the subject by the introduction of matters quite foreign to, or at least but remotely connected with, the person whose character and conduct are delineated. There are, to be sure, certain great characters which have appeared upon the stage of human existence and action, which have stamped their character upon the world—

such as Alexander, Bonaparte, and Washington, among warriors and statesmen, Luther, Arminius, and Wesley among Christian ministers and reformers—with whose lives are linked cotemporaneous events and characters that must be noticed, in order to give a full and comprehensive view of what they did, and of the influence they exerted on society. And if an apology could rightfully be made for this kind of biography for any public man, it might be made for Bishop Asbury, for certainly he stood up before the community as a giant in intellect, and as a saint of the first magnitude, having professed and exemplified the "heights and depths" of "perfect love," and displayed the zeal and diligence of an apostle in the work of the Christian ministry.

Dr. Strickland, however, has not availed himself of this privilege, but has confined himself strictly to the life and labours of Bishop Asbury, calling him, very appropriately, the "pioneer bishop." Such indeed he was, for he was the first Protestant bishop that ever trod the American soil, and he was the only bishop that followed the example of the apostles and primitive evangelists by itinerating through the length and breadth of the land, visiting alternately the cities and villages, the older settlements, and traversing the wilderness in search of the lost sheep of the house of Israel, carrying with him the light of truth and the love of God and man wherever he went. I say the biographer confines himself strictly to the life and labours of Bishop Asbury, but nevertheless embracing those cotemporaneous events which necessarily connected themselves with him, or which were produced by his active and energetic labours. This was necessary to make the portrait complete; for, wherever the bishop moved he moved others, and they others, and thus his circle of influence was continually enlarged, so that the little one "soon became a thousand, and a small one a strong nation." The work of reformation spread in every direction; ministers and people were raised up, through his instrumentality, to praise the Lord. A man thus distinguished as a leader of "God's sacramental host" must necessarily cluster around him many others, some of them nearly equal to himself, others of an inferior grade, all of whom must be noticed with greater or lesser particularity, in order to render the portraiture full and perfect in all its parts.

Dr. Strickland has already evinced his competency to the task of writing the life of Bishop Asbury, in other departments of literature, such as the History of the American Bible Society, History of the Missionary Society of the Methodist Episcopal Church, and other works of equal merit, and it is hoped and believed that his reputation as an author will suffer nothing in the present under-taking. His plan is calculated to insure success, by bringing the facts into as small a compass as the subject would permit, and thus presenting the life of Bishop Asbury full and complete, in a style of popular eloquence, to readers of all classes, tastes, and attainments.

Those who were acquainted with Asbury, as was the writer of this Introduction, cannot but remember his dignified appearance, his manly eloquence, and the solemn and commanding manner in which he administered the sacred ordinance to those on whom he laid his hands, while he said, "Receive the Holy Ghost for the office of an elder in the Church of God, now committed unto thee by my hands and prayer." Generally this impressive act and these solemn words were attended with an " unction of the Holy One," which rested upon the recipients of this holy office, and ran through the assembly of God's people like electricity. Though I can well remember those seasons of solemn grandeur and holy delight, yet I find it difficult to describe them, there being a secret something arising from a consciousness of the Divine presence which renders it indescribable, or, as St. Paul expresses it, " unspeakable and full of glory." We felt indeed that Christ spoke through his servant, and realized

> " The solemn awe which dares not move,
> And all the silent heaven of love."

The influence of the life of such a man, with its prominent features fully brought out, upon those who read it with attention, with faith and prayer, must be great and salutary. Some biographies, to be sure, possess nothing interesting, being made up of common-place re-marks, possessing no traits of character, experience, or conduct, but what may be found in every individual of their class, and therefore are dull and prosing, and soon pall upon the mental appetite. Not so the life of Bishop Asbury. He possessed strong points of cha-racter. His experience of Divine things was deep and genuine, glorying in nought but " Jesus Christ, and him crucified," saying, "I rejoice continually in the perfect love of God." His labours were great, his travels extensive, and his constant moving from place to place brought him into all sorts of company, the rich and the poor, the learned and unlearned, so that in reading a faithful record of those things we have a panorama spread out before us filled with a variety of figures, all of an interesting character, all instructive and edifying.

I could write much upon these topics, but I will not anticipate the biography before me. Let it be circulated and read, and then the reader will be fully acquainted with the birth, education, conversion, and sanctification of FRANCIS ASBURY, and will, I doubt not, praise God for raising up and qualifying him for the work of the ministry, and then putting him into the bishopric of the Methodist Episcopal Church, in which office he exemplified, in an eminent degree, the graces of humility and firmness, of patience and perseverance, and those commanding talents which enabled him rightly to divide the word of truth, and give to every one his " portion of meat in due season."

N. BANGS.

New-York, Aug. 26, 1858.

CONTENTS.

CHAPTER I.

CHAPTER II.

CHAPTER III.

CHAPTER IV.

CHAPTER V.

CHAPTER VI.

CHAPTER VII.

CHAPTER VIII.

CHAPTER IX.

CHAPTER X.

CHAPTER XI.

CHAPTER XII.

CHAPTER XIII.

CHAPTER XIV.

CHAPTER XV.

CHAPTER XVI.

CHAPTER XVII.

CHAPTER XVIII.

CHAPTER XIX.

CHAPTER XX.

CHAPTER XXI.

CHAPTER XXII.

CHAPTER XXIII.

LIFE AND TIMES

OF

FRANCIS ASBURY.

CHAPTER I:

The Relation of Childhood to Manhood—Province of Education—Diversity of Mind—Basis of Distinction—Asbury's Birth—Parentage—Native Character —Influence of Religion—Death of his Sister—Its Effect on his youthful Mind—His Early Conversion—School Days—Cruel Treatment—Change of Residence—An Irreligious Family—Trials—Returns Home—Learns a Trade —Course of Reading—Importance of Right Kind—Pernicious Principle— Hears of the Methodists through his Mother—Attends their Preaching—His Impressions—Religious Enjoyment—Holds Prayer Meetings—Opposition— Meetings for Prayer and Exhortation in his Father's House—Extends his Sphere of Labour—Souls Converted—Licensed to Preach—Early Labours— Appointed to a Circuit—Conference at Bristol in 1771—Volunteers as a Missionary to America, and is accepted.

" THE child is father to the man." Perhaps, more properly speaking, it may be said the child is the model of the man. Rarely does it happen that distinguishing traits of character are found to exist in persons whose early life and training have not been marked with distinctive peculiarities. The practised eye of the botanist can detect in the germ of the acorn the quality and size of the future oak, and the laws of nature are not more invariable in their operation than are the laws of mind. Inspiration gives prominence to the fact that there is an important relation between right training and character, and has assumed it as an axiom in human development, and the experience and history of the world most clearly attest its truth.

That the child stands related in a most important and significant sense to the future man, is a natural fact current and patent to all

B

nations, and recognized in all religions and forms of instruction. We readily admit that education sustains an important place in the formation or cultivation of the mind, but it cannot impart a quality to mind. Quality is native and inborn; and to affirm that all minds possess the same type, is to affirm what is not true, and what is contradicted by all history and experience. To be sure, mind is mind, just as marble is marble; but there are different casts in the former, just as there are different qualities and shades in the latter. Endless variety characterizes all the works of creation, and this variety pervades the world of mind as well as the world of matter. What wonderful varieties of mind are found in children even of the same parents, and how strikingly is the fact illustrated! Were all minds alike, then it is perfectly obvious that the same training under the same circumstances would produce the same results. Every day's experience, however, shows that this is very far from being the case.

It is a common remark, made in relation to a portion of mankind, that they are " cast in nature's finest mould ;" and we hear the equally common remark of others, that " they are rough specimens of humanity." Why this diversity exists, it is not our province to know. God, who " has made of one blood all nations of men upon the earth," and has " fixed the bounds of their habitation," has made us to differ ; but the reasons for this diversity are among the mysteries of his works, which are beyond the reach of man.

Whatever is essential to mind, however, is common to all minds, just as what is essential to matter is common to all matter ; but the possession of these essential attributes is compatible with the most endless variety in formations, orders, and classes. We assign to rocks certain formations ; to animals, certain orders ; to plants, certain species ; and to minds, certain classes. Nothing is more common than to speak of a class of minds, and to assign them a place in the world of intellect. This latter remark, however, is predicated of quality, and not of anything acquired. Education only develops the latent powers of the mind, and disciplines the native forces of the intellect to action. Perception, imagination, judgment, and consciousness are no more the product of education than the mind itself, and where either of these are absent or defective in the original quality no education can impart them.

We have pursued this train of thought further than we intended, and yet we think it is worthy of more consideration than has generally been given to it. What we designed in our preliminary remarks was simply to reiterate the generally acknowledged fact, that great eminence and distinction in the world come not from chance, nor yet from any particularly favourable circumstances, though these must, to some extent, exist, but from an original quality inhering in the mind itself as the basis thereof.

Francis Asbury was born on the 20th of August, 1745, near the foot of Hempstead Bridge in Staffordshire, a short distance from Birmingham. His father's Christian name was Joseph, and his mother's Elizabeth. His parents, we are told, were "amiable and respectable." How much is embraced in these two words! With the parents of young Asbury amiability was not a feigned but real possession. The basis of their gentleness was in their hearts, and added to it were the genial influences of religion. Grace has wonderful power to soften and refine the manners, as whatsoever is "lovely and of good report" is produced by its operation.

But what is more, the parents belonged to the better class of England's population. By this we do not mean that they were allied to the nobility, but they were of what we would consider the real aristocracy of England, occupying a middle position between the idle, effeminate, and vicious of the upper classes, and the ignorant, degraded, and sunken of the lower. Virtue, morality, and religion, as well as patriotism and true loyalty, in every country enlightened and refined, have always been found among the middle classes to a far greater extent than among the higher. It was from this class young Asbury sprung. But what is more than all this, and what in the language of Addison constitutes the highest style of humanity, they were Christians. From such a parentage we may well look for children of the right stamp. These godly parents were blessed with but two children, Francis and a lovely daughter, who, like a fair and beauteous flower, bloomed a few short summers by their side, and was transplanted in a more genial clime. The transit from earth to heaven of the loved one preyed heavily upon the youthful heart of the bereaved brother, and gave to his ardent affections a heavenly turn; and thus to the many examples of youthful piety furnished in sacred and profane history, was added another prominent one in the conversion of Francis at the early age of seven.

The father of young Asbury, though not wealthy, was in comfortable circumstances; and being desirous of giving his son all the advantages of education, he placed him early in school to one Auther Taylor, at Sneal's Green, in the vicinity of Barr, whither he had removed. When between the age of six and seven Francis commenced reading the Bible, and he says, in his short biography, of himself, that he "was greatly delighted in the historical part of it." At this school another kind of discipline awaited him, different from that of a mental character. His teacher, he informs us, was cruel and tyrannical, and vented his spleen upon the children committed to his care. Being a child of God, even such a discipline was made to work for young Asbury's good. The sufferings he endured from this pedagogue of "brief authority" were borne submissively by the child and carried to a throne of grace. In his own expressive language, "God was very near to him," and proved, "a very present help in time of trouble." He knew his father's anxiety about his education, and this, doubtless, had its effect in prompting him to bear longer than he otherwise would the unkind treatment he received. The very presence of such meekness and submission in the child, instead of assuaging the wrath of the tyrant, seemed only to whet his tigerlike appetite, and his cruelty became so great that it was no longer endurable. The result was that Francis was taken from school, and thus snatched from the clutches of the teacher as the prey from the mouth of the destroyer.

It was evident that God was preparing him for a great and important work in the world, and as the Israelites were not allowed to enter Canaan until after forty years' suffering in the desert had prepared them for the promised inheritance, and as our divine Lord himself entered not into glory until he passed through the severe discipline of a sorrowful life and an ignominious death, and as his followers generally are "made perfect through suffering," so the future zealous, self-sacrificing, and devoted preacher was called to the trial of his faith. From school he was removed to another part of the parish, and became an inmate of one of the wealthy and fashionable families of that neighbourhood. In this house God was not known, as it seems its inmates were of those who "called not upon his name."

We may stop here to ask what is wealth, position, and influence among those who are denominated "the first families," and who move in the highest circles of genteel society, and claim an alliance with the nobility of the land, if the blessing of God rests not upon them? As that nation in the highest sense is a "royal nation," and that people "a peculiar people," who are allied to Jehovah as their King, so that family rises in dignity and importance which walks in the fear of the Lord and the light of his countenance. His stay with this family, surrounded as he was with the blandishments of fashionable society, and the constant example of a vain and frivolous course of life, proved a much sorer trial of his faith than any through which he had passed. The afflictions he endured at school drove him near to God, and kept him humble; but the circumstances by which he was surrounded in this irreligious family had a tendency to draw him from the Lord. His faith, however, though severely tried, proved adequate to the test, and though, to use his own language, he "became somewhat vain," having naturally a light and joyous disposition, "he did not become openly wicked."

After remaining some months with this family he returned to the paternal roof. He was now in his fourteenth year, and it became necessary for him to make choice of some branch of business. Having made a selection of a trade suited to his judgment and taste, he entered upon it and prosecuted it with all diligence. While engaged in this business he became the inmate of a kind family, who, he says, treated him like a son. His religious feelings, which had met with a temporary interruption, very soon returned to him, and he recommenced prayer morning and evening, being, as he says, "drawn by the cords of love as with the bands of a man." His faith was strengthened and his enjoyments heightened by frequent attendance at Bromwich church, where he heard Ryland, Stillingfleet, Talbott, Bagnall, Mansfield, Hawes, and Venn, some of whom were among the most distinguished ministers and ornaments of the English pulpit.

At this time he devoted himself more particularly to reading and study. Among the books he read was Whitfield's Sermons. The course of reading in which he took most delight was of a religious character, and the department under this head embraced mostly those books of a practical and experimental description. How important in the formation of a religious character is it that the right kind of books be read; for, whatever may be the experience in after life, the religious faith will take its tone and colouring in a great degree from the mental aliment. Those who in early life are indoctrinated in the Westminster Confession of Faith, the Augsburgh Confession, or the Thirty-nine Articles, and works which fall in the line of these doctrines, no matter what may afterward be their Church relations, will find it difficult to divest themselves entirely of their early impressions. Hence it is of the greatest importance that our youth have the right kind of books brought in contact with their minds in the forming stage of their religious character. The principle adopted by some parents is of the most latitudinary character. They say, "Let the children alone in their choice of books, and also in their choice of a Church, until they grow up and are able to judge for themselves." Such advice we regard as infidel, and pernicious in a high degree. If it be right to act upon this principle in regard to a question of such vital moment, and one involving happiness for time and eternity, as the question of a right faith does, then is it equally right, nay, more so, to allow them the largest liberty in regard to all their choices.

Fortunately for young Asbury, his religious tastes led him to seek the right kind of spiritual food, and those books only were read which were adapted to his religious habitudes and feelings. The opportunity which he enjoyed of hearing sermons from pious and distinguished divines, and of reading books of a religious character, greatly sharpened his appetite for spiritual things, and it is not to be wondered at that he was on the alert for anything of interest that might come up in the religious world around him. Until now he had not heard of the Methodists. Like Fletcher, who in the early part of his religious career was ignorant of them, the sect everywhere denounced as the wildest fanatics was to him unknown. He had, however, tasted of the spirit of Methodism, for the piety which still lingered in the old Church of the Reformation was baptized by that name wherever it was found. If any were suspected, either among Churchmen or Dissenters, of being more than ordinarily prayerful or devotional in spirit or practice, they were at once branded as Methodists. It may have been that young Asbury's studious and prayerful habits first introduced him to the name. But be that as it may, it came to his ears, and as soon as the opportunity presented itself he asked his pious mother who the Methodists were, and where they could be found. He doubtless felt a desire kindred to that of Fletcher to behold this strange religious sect, whose zeal for God and religion had given them notoriety. From his mother he received a most favourable account, and besides, she directed him to a person who could give him all the information he desired about them. That person he soon found, and it was not long before he availed himself of the opportunity of accompanying him to a neighbouring town to hear them for himself. When they arrived at the place of meeting he was surprised to find that it was not a church. The service was probably held in a private house, or a barn, or perhaps in the open field ; as regards this Asbury does not inform us ; but he does enter minutely into a description of the people and their exercises, the latter of which were different from anything he had ever witnessed before, and made an impression which was never erased. Though the people had not assembled in a church, with its tower, and bell, and organ,

         " And storied windows, richly dight,
           That cast a dim religious light,"

yet he entered where the congregation "sat together in heavenly places," and "worshipped at the very gate of heaven." To use his own simple, nervous language, "It was better than a church, the people were so devout; men and women kneeling, and all saying amen." After prayer, "with the spirit and understanding, they all united in singing a hymn of praise." The soul of the worshippers was in the sound, and it was more sweet and entrancing than any that had ever fallen upon the young stranger's ear. But how was his astonishment increased to find that the prayer which had been offered was not dictated by a prayer-book. Could it be possible that so wonderful a prayer could come out of untaught lips. Wonders began, but wonders were not to cease with his first introduction to the Methodists; stranger sights were to be presented to his eyes, and stranger sounds were to fall upon his ears than he had yet seen or heard. The preacher rose and took his text, but he had no manuscript before him; and if he had, there would have been no velvet-cushioned pulpit on which to place it. The sermon was plain, practical, pointed, full of unction, and attended with the demonstration of the Spirit and power to the hearts and consciences of all.

Prepared as was young Asbury for the scenes he witnessed, notwithstanding the astonishment they created, he soon partook of their spirit, and commenced, "after the way others called heresy, to worship the God of his fathers." Several times he attended these meetings, and at every time with increasing interest, and in "the fellowship of kindred minds" he made rapid progress in spiritual life. Though his joy was not so full as that of some others, who would becloud his faith by telling him that "a believer was as happy as if he were in heaven," yet he "was happy, free from guilt and fear, and had power over sin, with the possession of great inward joy."

Feeling that it was his duty to hold prayer-meetings in the neighbourhood, he united as many with him as he could of like faith, and commenced religious services in the house of a friend. These meetings were largely attended. Multitudes, attracted by the voice of praise and prayer in places where these sounds were before unknown, came to the meetings; many from idle curiosity, but more were prompted by a spirit of opposition, as appears from the fact that the friends at whose houses the meetings were held, fearing an outbreak, were unwilling to have them continued. Opposition, however, could not daunt or damp the zeal of the young soldier of the cross; and though obliged to desist from holding meetings at these places, he was favoured with another sanctuary,

and that was home.   In his father's house he resumed the meetings for prayer, and, unmolested, exhorted, with fervency and
power, the multitudes who came there, to flee the wrath to come
and be saved from their sins.   He also extended the sphere of his
labours to Sutton-Cofields, where he was greatly encouraged and
strengthened in his work by witnessing the conversion of several
souls.   He went to Bromwich-Heath several times for the purpose
of attending class-meeting, a means of grace which he much enjoyed, and which he ever after availed himself of when opportunity presented.   He also attended band-meeting at Wednesbury,
the place where he first heard Methodist preaching, as above described.   These last means of grace formed distinctive peculiarities
in the Wesleyan connection, though the latter has been abandoned
in America, more, however, on account of their disuse than from
any want of confidence in their importance in promoting the piety
of those who attended them ; and class-meetings are perhaps more
effectual in keeping up the life and power of religion, and advanc-
ing personal holiness, than any other prudential means devised by
the Church.   It is a matter of general observation that attendance
on class-meetings in any particular charge is perhaps the surest indication of the tone of piety.

The fervency and eloquence which characterized his prayers and
exhortations excited the wonder of all, and when he first appeared
and took part in Methodist meetings, the preachers, as well as the
people, were surprised at his wonderful gifts.   The question was,
Where did he acquire such self-possession, such readiness of utter-
ance, such fluency and appropriateness of language ?   Had they
known how faithfully he read his Bible, and with what avidity
he devoured sermons and religious books within his reach, but,
above all, the fact that his mother was accustomed to take him
with her regularly to a female meeting for the purpose of reading
and expounding the Scriptures and giving out the hymns, they
would not have been at a loss to conjecture from whence the youth
obtained his furniture of mind and his facility in religious exercises.   It was not long before the society became convinced that
one who had such gifts and grace, and whose labours had been
blessed to the awakening and conversion of souls, was called of
God to enter upon the work of the ministry proper.   He was
impressed not only with a sense of its importance, and the duty of
giving himself wholly to the work, but the voice of the Church,
as the voice of God, concurring therewith, deepened and strengthened that impression, and determined his future course.   From
the preacher in charge of the circuit he received license as a local

preacher, and he was accordingly soon introduced to Methodist chapels, in which he held forth the word of life to "wondering, weeping thousands." Multitudes were attracted by his extreme youth, not being more than seventeen years of age. He sustained a local relation for several years, though, in fact, he was a travel-ing preacher; and visiting various places in Derbyshire, Stafford-shire, Warwickshire, and Worcestershire, he preached the Gospel to the crowds who attended his ministry. Besides his Sabbath labours, he preached during the week three or four times, and often five times. Thus he continued, in season and out of season, preaching far and near until he was twenty-one years of age, when he was received into the Wesleyan Conference, and appointed to labour on a circuit, according to the Wesleyan form. He was now engaged in the work to which he was called, and he gave himself up exclusively to it, and as an obedient son in the Gospel he went from appointment to appointment. After travelling circuits for about five years he attended the Conference held at Bristol on the 7th of August, 1771. He was now in the twenty-sixth year of his age, and had been engaged in the work of the ministry for nine or ten years; studious, devoted, self-sacrificing, and faithful in the discharge of all his duties, he had acquired a standing in the Con-ference which commended him to the confidence and esteem of all his brethren, both senior and junior. He not only had made him-self acquainted with the doctrines and discipline of Methodism, but he cherished for them the warmest affection, and conscientiously reduced them to every-day practice.

Asbury went to this Conference with peculiar feelings. He had for some time been strongly impressed with a desire to go as a missionary to America. The more he thought and prayed about it, the more deep and powerful became the impression. The difficulties and dangers attending the voyage were great, and the increasing conviction that it was his duty to volunteer his services for that then distant land preyed heavily upon his mind. He was subjected to sore trials, and called to pass through a severer dis-cipline of affliction than he had experienced before in his ministerial life. The Lord was evidently preparing him by this discipline for the great undertaking he had in contemplation. The Wesleys and Whitefield had been in America years before. A few Methodist emigrants had settled in New York, Philadelphia, and parts of Maryland, and Wesley had sent over missionaries in the persons of Richard Boardman and Joseph Pilmoor but two years before. These missionaries had entered upon their work of feeding the flock of Christ in the New World. When at this Conference Mr.

Wesley called for volunteers for the work in America, among the first that responded was Asbury. He had prayerfully considered the matter, and being satisfied that it was the will of God he should enter upon the work, he "conferred not with flesh and blood," but accepted the call, and from that moment his heart was in America.

CHAPTER II.

Asbury returns Home—Encounters Trials—His Mother—Visits the Scenes of his early Labors —Parting with Parents—Bristol Outfit—Richard Wright— Embarkation—Sickness—Preaching on board by Wright—Self-examination —Motives—Reflections—His first Sermon at Sea—Advantage of Trials— Books read on the Voyage—Study of the Bible—His Heart bound to America—Personal Religion—Full Consecration to his Mission—Last Sermon on Shipboard—Gale—Sight of Land—Voyage ended—Reception in Phila-delphia—Preaching by Pilmoor—Progress of Methodism—Encouragement— The Soldier Preacher.

HAVING consecrated all upon the altar of American missions, Asbury left the seat of the Conference and turned his face homeward. Already he had passed through severe conflicts, which served as a discipline to prepare him for the great work to which he had devoted himself; but other and yet severer trials awaited him. How he should communicate the intelligence to his kind and gentle-hearted mother, that he had entered into an engagement to leave the home of his youth, perhaps never to return, was a question that greatly perplexed him. Difficult and trying as was the task, he was enabled, however, to accomplish it, and she who had trained him for God and his cause in a spirit of genuine self-sacrifice, not only calmly, but heroically gave him up. Like the mother of the Wesleys, who, when asked if she was willing to give up her son John to go to the wilds of America as a missionary among the savages of Georgia, replied, "If I had twenty sons I would cheerfully give them all to God as missionaries," so the mother of Asbury gave up her only son with Christian resignation, and cheerful acquiescence in the leadings of Providence.

Prior to taking farewell of his parents, and bidding a final adieu to home and friends, he started out on an itinerant tour for the purpose of visiting the scenes of his early labors. He preached in Staffordshire, Warwickshire, and Gloucestershire, and enjoyed much life and power in his ministrations. Wherever he went he announced his determination to go out as a missionary, and excited no little wonder among his friends, though none of them attempted to dissuade him from so noble and glorious an undertaking. Some were so impressed with its importance that they were constrained to speak in warm terms of the purpose he had formed, and regretted that they could not accompany him.

At length the hour arrived when he was to take his leave of fond parents and make preparations for his departure. Tears were shed, but they were the tears of sanctified affection and hopeful trust in God, who had called the parents to give up their son, and the son to go to a land of strangers to preach the Gospel. He arrived at Bristol, near which he was to take shipping for America, in the latter part of August. His outfit was of the slenderest kind, consisting of a few pounds and a small amount of clothing. At Bristol he met Richard Wright, a young man who had been in the itinerant connection but one year, but who, impressed with the importance of the missionary work, had volunteered to accompany him.

On the 4th of September they embarked and were soon fairly out at sea. That vexatious accompaniment of a voyage, seasickness, Asbury did not escape, and such sickness, to use his own language, as was unequalled by any he had ever experienced. When the Sabbath came his colleague preached on deck to the crew, who were attentive listeners to the word of life. After recovering from his illness, in a calm and thoughtful mood he went into a thorough self-examination in regard to the motives that prompted him to engage in the missionary work. As if mistrustful and afraid of the deceitfulness of the human heart, he instituted a most searching analysis, and was enabled to arrive at the following result : namely, that his visit to the New World was not to gain honor or emolument, but clearly and simply to devote himself to the service of God, and incite others to the same hallowed consecration.

He was by no means ignorant of the religious condition of the people among whom he was going to labor, but had acquainted himself with the state of the Churches, and all the religious movements of the country. He had studied the means connected with the revivals in America, and also the causes of their decline, as they had been exhibited in the reports which came to England ; and from what he knew of the effects attending the preaching of the Gospel by the Methodists, and the discipline as administered by them, he felt impressed with the fact that, as well in America as in England, these agencies were peculiarly adapted to the awakening and conversion of souls, and the training of the Church to a holy life.　The signal success which had crowned the labors of Wesley and his coadjutors in England, he felt assured would attend the labors of the missionaries in America, if faithful to their high and responsible trust.　He had determined, in this view of the case, if God did not own and bless his labors after having made a full and fair trial, that he would not remain in America, but return to England.

The second Sabbath at sea having arrived, Asbury preached his first sermon to the sailors from Acts xvii. 30 : "But now God commandeth all men everywhere to repent."　He had a strong and irrepressible desire that the hardy sons of the ocean might be brought to repentance, and that before he reached his destination he might behold some fruit of the labors bestowed.　He felt willing to do or suffer anything if he could only be instrumental in saving souls, hence he bore cheerfully the privations and hardships of the voyage.　Having no beds, and being obliged, with his colleague, to sleep on hard boards, he realized the importance of possessing much courage and patience, and was not a little comforted by the thought that if others could undergo hardships for mere temporal interests, he surely should not complain where eternal interests were involved.　His trials had a tendency to increase and fasten the impression that he was, to use his own words, not running before he was sent ; and hence, as these trials increased, he became more and more convinced that he was acting in accordance with the Divine will.

Regularly as the Sabbath returned he preached to the ship's company.　His subjects were adapted to his audience, and were treated in the most plain and pointed manner.　The sailors all seemed to give great attention to the word, but whether any were converted during the voyage was not known to him who labored with all zeal and fidelity to bring them to a saving knowledge of the truth.　During the passage he spent much of his time in reading, meditation, and prayer.　The books which he read were Sellon's Answer to Elisha Cole, which he thought no one could read and be a Calvinist ; De Renty's Life, Norris's Works, Edwards on the Work of God in New England, Wesley's Sermons, and the Pilgrim's Progress.　The Bible, however, was his constant companion, and this he studied with increasing interest, pouring out his soul in prayer to the Father of lights that he might have a clear vision of those wondrous truths which it contains, and be able to interpret it in such a manner that all who heard might receive a portion adapted to their condition.

While shut up in his cabin he felt his heart strangely drawn out for America, and he realized a wonderful sympathy and union of spirit with those who to him as yet were strangers. The spirit of sympathy which exists in all who realize a love for souls, and which constrains them to encounter toil, privation, and hardships for their salvation, was felt by Asbury in an extraordinary degree. As a true evangelical preacher, he was not a stranger to that love which prompted the Saviour to give his life a ransom for man ; and now that it no longer remained a question in regard to his call to preach the Gospel in America, the people to whom he was going to minister, and for whose salvation he was about to labor, became endeared to him by the strongest and tenderestties. Associated with this was a deep and earnest desire, accompanied by incessant prayer, that he might be "complete in all the will of God, and holy in all manner of conversation, as He that had called him was holy." Every day he realized an increasing singleness of purpose in regard to the object of his mission ; and as the vessel approached the American shore, he was conscious of a consecration to God and his cause more full and satisfactory then he ever experienced before.

On the 13th of October he preached his fifth and last sermon on board. The wind was high, and the ship tossed exceedingly, rendering it difficult for one to stand on deck. Determined, however, to lose no opportunity of preaching to the sailors, he fixed himself against the mast, and discoursed with warmth and freedom from 2 Corinthians, v. 20 : "Now then we are ambassadors for Christ, as though God did beseech you by us : we pray you in Christ's stead, be ye reconciled to God." In alluding to this, his last sermon on board, he says "he felt the power of truth in his own soul, though he saw no visible fruit of his labors."

After a voyage of eight weeks, during which many privations were encountered and hardships endured, the joyous intelligence that they were in sight of land was received gratefully by the missionaries. Though another Sabbath intervened between his last sermon and their entry into port at Philadelphia, yet Asbury gives no account of the manner in which it was spent. The tedious voyage at length was brought to a close, and it was with emotions of profound gratitude to God for that providence which had guided them safely through the deep, that he and his colleague placed

their feet on the American shore. How was that gratitude
increased when on landing they were received with the utmost
kindness, and introduced to the largest hospitality! In referring
to their reception, Asbury says: "The people looked on us with
pleasure, hardly knowing how to show their love sufficiently,
bidding us welcome with fervent affection, and receiving us as the
angels of God."

The first evening spent in Philadelphia was at the old St.
George's Church, where they listened to a discourse from Joseph
Pilmoor, who came to America with Boardman in 1769, the first
missionaries sent over by Wesley. The arrival of Asbury and
Wright as a re-enforcement to the clerical ranks of the infant
Church in America was hailed with joy, and the large congregation
assembled were greatly quickened and refreshed in their spirits by
their presence. Though but five years had elapsed since the introduction of Methodism into the country through the labors of Embury,
Webb, and Strawbridge, yet considerable societies had been formed
in New York and Philadelphia, and in different parts of New
Jersey, Maryland, and Virginia. In that short space "the little
one had become a thousand;" and so wonderfully did the word of
God grow and prevail through the instrumentality of these pioneers
of Methodism, that the highest hopes were encouraged of the most
abundant success.

To Captain Webb, the soldier-preacher, is perhaps to be ascribed
the honor of introducing Methodism into Philadelphia. After he
had removed from Albany to Long Island he extended his labors
to Philadelphia, where he preached with success, and was the first
to write to Mr. Wesley urging him to send preachers to America.
Be this as it may, one thing is certain, that in New York and
Philadelphia, as well as several points on Long Island, the captain,
by his zeal and devotion to the cause of God, and the material aid
which he afforded to the infant societies, was of vast service to the
Church, and deserves to be ranked among its pioneer worthies.

CHAPTER III.

BEFORE resuming the thread of personal narrative in the biography of Asbury, it may not be amiss, as we contemplate a sketch of the times as well as the life of that remarkable man, to call the attention of the reader to the condition and circumstances of the American colonies at the time of his arrival in this country. But one year before the landing of Asbury great joy prevailed in London on the reception of the intelligence that commercial intercourse was about to be resumed between England and the United States. Merchants of New York consulted those of Philadelphia on agreeing to a general importation of all articles, tea only excepted. The proposition was favorably received by the Philadelphians, and would doubtless have been agreed to but for the reception of a letter from Franklin, urging them to persevere on their original plan. Some leading merchants in New York, however, resisted concession; but others went from ward to ward to take the opinions of the people, and it was ascertained that a large majority were disposed to confine the restrictions to tea alone. The Philadelphians were incensed at this decision, and when the packet sailed with orders for all kinds of merchandise except tea, they said to the New Yorkers: "Send us your old Liberty Pole, as you can have no further use for it." The students at Princeton burned the letter of the New York merchants by the hands of the common hangman. Boston tore it to pieces, and threw it to the winds; South Carolina, whose patriots had just raised the statue to Chatham, read it with scorn.

It was not long, however, before the colony of Massachusetts was proclaimed by the king to be under martial law. The harbor of Boston was made a rendezvous for all ships stationed in North America, and the fortress which commanded it was given up to be garrisoned by regular troops. Castle William was taken from the governor, and remained in possession of England for upward of five years. Franklin, who then held the office of deputy postmaster general under the crown, was selected as the agent of the assembly to redress their grievances, and be their mediator with the mother country. He was now in the sixty-fourth year of his age. The authorities of the king took care to negative all appropriations for his salary, and determined not to recognize him as an agent.

Such being the condition of things in the East, we now turn to the West. The inchoate title of all that vast territory in the Mississippi valley had been received from the Six Nations. The people of Virginia and others were exploring and surveying the richest lands on the waters of the Redstone, Monongahela, Ohio, and Kanawha, and each year they were penetrating further south and west. Washington had descended the Ohio in a canoe, and made selections of the richest lands for the soldiers and officers who had served with him in the French war. At the same time Boone, the pioneer hunter, was exploring Kentucky, and the "Long Hunters" had found their way down the Cumberland to Limestone Bluff, where Nashville now stands. Trappers and restless emigrants had crossed the country from Carolina to the Mississippi, while others descended from Pittsburg to Natchez; and James Robertson, from the home of the Regulators in North Carolina, had explored Tennesse. He was followed by others from the same region, and became their guide and protector. The Regulators had become a formidable body, and when they were not allowed peaceably to possess their lands, which they explored, but were oppressed by lawyers, proprietors, and landjobbers, they resolved on seeking redress. They accordingly appeared at court, determined to have justice done, and that without the interference of any attorney save the king's. They elected a representative to the House, but he was voted a disturber of the peace, and put in prison. A riot act was gotten up, declaring it illegal for more than ten men to remain assembled together after it was read, and if any were found guilty of its violation they were tried in the Superior Court, and if condemned forfeited their lives, with all their property.

The Regulators gathered together in the woods on hearing that their representative was expelled and imprisoned and they themselves threatened with death as outlaws. Their number had increased to five hundred, and they demanded his release, which was reluctantly granted. A battle afterward occurred between them and the king's troops on the Alamance River, in which twenty of them were killed and several wounded. Of the king's troops, nine were killed and sixty-one wounded. One of the Regulators who was taken prisoner was hanged on a tree; then followed a proclamation excepting from mercy outlaws and prisoners, and promising it to none but such as would take the oath of allegiance, pay taxes, submit to the laws, and deliver up their arms. Six more of them were afterward taken and hung. At length they sought the far-off wilderness, where no lawyers could follow them or governors lord it over them, and there they took up their abode on the romantic banks of the Nolichucky. Before them spread away an immense forest abounding in game, and possessed of a rich and fertile soil.

In 1771, the year that Asbury landed in America, Great Britain commenced the work of centering in itself power over the colonies, by the double process of making all civil officers dependent for support solely upon the king, and giving to arbitrary instructions an authority paramount to the charter and laws. Taxation unjust and unequal was forced upon the colonists until forbearance ceased any longer to be a virtue. Samuel Adams protested in the House against this unrighteous usurpation in the following words: "We know of no commissioners of his majesty's customs, nor of any revenue his majesty has a right to establish in North America; we know and feel a tribute levied and extorted from those who if they have property have a right to the disposal of it." Wise men saw the event that was approaching, but knew not that it was so near. "Out of the eater came forth meat," said Cooper, the clergyman; and Franklin foretold a bloody struggle, in which America, growing in strength and magnitude, would obtain the victory. Instructions were drawn up by Samuel Adams to the agent of the House, avowing broadly the principle that colonial legislation was free of Parliament and of royal instructions. That sturdy patriot had declared long before at a town meeting: "Independent we are and independent we will be." Things were approaching a crisis. In August Boston saw drawn up in her harbor twelve vessels of war, carrying more than two hundred and sixty guns. In the West the same resistance showed itself against the concentration of colonial power in England, and the rights of freemen were as loudly demanded on the prairies of Illinois as on the heights of Boston.

The governor, in his annual proclamation for the festival of

c

thanksgiving, which was customary to be read from every pulpit, sought to ensnare the clergy of Boston by enumerating as a cause for thanksgiving that "civil and religious liberties were continued," and trade enlarged." The deception was too transparent, and all the ministers, except Pemberton of the Old South Church, refused to read it ; and when he, of whose Church the governor was a member, began confusedly to do so, the patriots of the congregation turned their backs on him, and marched out of the church with intense disgust and indignation. Nearly all the clergy agreed on Thanksgiving Day to implore of Almighty God the restoration of their lost liberty.

This last event occurred just one month after Asbury put his foot in the streets of Philadelphia, and the reader will see what was the precise condition of the country synchronical with the advent of him who was to take so large a share in its ecclesiastical as well as general history. The rough and rapid outline which we have given of the colonial history at that time is important, more from the light which it will throw upon the subsequent life, character, and acts of Asbury, than from any design to present it as a part of the history of the times. There are other matters, however, deserving attention, and which must not be omitted.

The inhabitants of Virginia were oppressed by the central authority on a subject of still more vital interest to them and their posterity. Their halls of legislation had resounded with eloquent denunciations against the terrible evil of slavery. Again and again had they passed laws restraining the importation of negroes from Africa, but all their enactments on this subject were disregarded. How to prevent the Virginians from protecting themselves against the increase of this evil was debated by King George in Council, and on the 10th of December, 1770, he issued a proclamation under his own hand, commanding the governor "upon pain of the highest displeasure, to assent to no law by which the importation of slaves should be in any respect prohibited or obstructed." This rigorous order was solemnly debated in the Assembly of Virginia. They felt the necessity of an act to restrain the introduction of a race, the number of which already in the colony gave them just cause to apprehend the most alarming consequences, and they felt impelled by the circumstances of the case to seek some means by which not only their increase would be prevented but diminished. The interest of the country, they declared, "manifestly required their total expulsion." Jefferson, like Richard Henry Lee, had begun his legislative career by resisting the slave-trade. To the mind of Patrick Henry, the thought of slavery darkened the picture of the future, even while he cherished faith in the ultimate abolition of an evil which was opposed to the welfare of the country. Instead of laying their grievances before Parliament, they presented their appeal directly to the King. Their language was : "The importation of slaves into the colonies from the coast of Africa hath long been considered a trade of great inhumanity, and under its present encouragement we have too much reason to fear it will endanger the very existence of your majesty's American dominions. We are sensible that some of your majesty's subjects in Great Britain may reap emoluments from this sort of traffic ; but when we consider that it greatly retards the settlement of the colonies with more useful inhabitants, and may in time have the most destructive influence, we presume to hope that the interest of a few will be disregarded when placed in competition with the security and happiness of such numbers of your Majesty's dutiful and loyal subjects. Deeply impressed with these sentiments, we most humbly beseech your majesty to remove all those restraints on your majesty's governors of this colony which inhibit their assenting to such laws as might check so pernicious a commerce."

In this manner Virginia led the way in the condemnation of the slave-trade. Thousands in Maryland and New Jersey were ready to adopt a similar petition, and so also were the Legislatures of North Carolina, Pennsylvania, New York, and Massachusetts. There was no conflict of opinion on this subject in the colonies. Virginia harmonised all opinions, and represented the moral sentiment and policy of all. Franklin roused the attention of the people and ministers to the subject through the press. The king, however, was inexorable ; and while the courts of law adopted the axiom that as soon as a slave sets his foot on English ground he is free, the monarch stood in the path of humanity, and made himself the pillar of the colonial slave-trade.

Having glanced at the political and civil condition of the country, it may be considered of equal, and perhaps of greater importance, that illusion be made to its religious condition. This we have as yet but barely hinted at, and shall, as far as the materials at our command will allow, present the reader with an outline sketch of the condition and circumstances of the various denominations in the land.

The first religious sects that came to this country were the Episcopalians, the Puritans, and the Lutherans. Sir Humphrey Gilbert was the first who directed his attention to this country from religious considerations, if we except the Jesuit missionaries, who had, with a courage and constancy so characteristic of that order,

braved the dangers of the ocean, and penetrating the far-off wildernesses of the north, and west, and south, planted the cross and established missions among the native inhabitants. Among the
motives presented to Queen Elizabeth by Sir Humphrey, for founding religious sentiments, were "honour for God, compassion on
poor infidels captivated by the devil, and the relief of sundry people
within that realm distressed." The letters patent received from the
queen proceed upon the supposition, that "the spread of the Christian faith among the natives justified such settlements," and he
was "granted full power and liberty to discover all such *heathen lands*
as were not actually possessed by any Christian prince or people."
He was authorised to enact laws over two hundred leagues of settlement, provided they did not conflict with the laws and policy of
England, and were not against the true Christian faith professed in
the Church of England." Associating with himself his relative,
Sir Walter Raleigh, an expedition was sent out in 1584, and the
glowing description of the country made to the queen induced her
to bestow upon the whole country the name of Virginia. The
following year one hundred more colonists were sent out. In 1606
a new company applied for and obtained from James I. a charter
for the settling of Virginia. The charter expressly provided that
the colonists should "secure the true service and preaching of the
word of God, and that it should be planted and used according to
the rites and doctrines of the Church of England, not only in the
said colonies, but among the savages bordering upon them, and
that all persons should kindly treat the savage and heathen people
in those parts, and use all proper means to draw them to the true
service and knowledge of God." The expedition sailed in December, 1606, and landed at Cape Henry, in Virginia, April, 1607.
It was accompanied by the Rev. Robert Hunt, their minister, who
administered the holy sacrament on their arrival on the shores of
James River. Rev. Mr. Whitaker followed soon after and joined
the Colonial Church, and was denominated the Apostle of Virginia.
This minister was the first Protestant who baptised an Indian convert, and that first convert was Pocahontas. Subsequently, in
1679, a grant was given by Charles II. for erecting a church in
Boston, which was called the King's Chapel. In 1784 the Episcopal Church became independent of the English, and assumed the
name of the Protestant Episcopal Church in the United States,
and Rev. Drs. White, of Philadelphia, and Provoost, of New York,
were consecrated by the Archbishop of Canterbury the bishops of
that Church in 1787.

The next denomination in the order of time that was introduced into the country was the Puritans, or Congregationalists. This people sought these shores as an asylum for conscience. A large number, after braving the dangers and rigors of a wintry ocean, landed at Plymouth, in Massachusetts. On the Sabbath of the 22nd of December, 1620, they went on shore, and held Divine service. In 1629 a Church was organised at Salem ; one in Charles' town in 1630 ; one in Duxbury in 1632 ; and others soon after in Connecticut. Emigrants who arrived from England from time to time, differed from them in their theological views and polity ; but as they wished to have Church matters consolidated, after several councils an arrangement was made to unite them in the general principles of Congregationalism. Their early efforts in the cause of learning are worthy of all praise. They founded Harvard College, at Cambridge, in 1635.

The Rev. John Eliot, one of their early ministers, became the pastor of the church in Roxbury in 1646, and was the first Protestant missionary to the Indians. His whole life was spent in labours for their conversion. He was emphatically the apostle to the Indians, and many were converted through his instrumentality. He translated the Bible into native Indian, and it was the first Bible printed in this country—the New Testament in 1661, and the Old in 1663. Churches were organised in New Hampshire, New York, and other parts of the country. To Harvard has been added Yale and other colleges, the pride of the land. No Church has ever been blessed with more learned or pious ministers than has the Congregational. The number of churches gathered in Massachusetts from 1670 to 1680 was twenty.

Next we notice the Lutherans. The earliest settlement of this denomination in this country was made by emigrants from Holland to New York, soon after the first establishment of the Dutch in that city in 1621. The cause of this emigration was the intolerant decrees of the Synod of Dort in 1648. While the territory yet belonged to Holland, the few Low Dutch Lutherans were compelled to hold their worship in private ; but after it passed into the hands of the British, in 1664, liberty was granted them by all the successive governors to conduct their public worship without any obstruction. Thus we see that the establishment of the Lutherans in New York was but a short time after that of the Puritans in Massachusetts. The Rev. Jacob Fabricus was their first minister, and was very successful. Though they spread and increased in various parts of the country, yet it is somewhat remarkable that they never made much progress in New York, where they commenced. In 1748 there were eleven Lutheran ministers in the

United States; the number of congregations was about forty, and the Lutheran population was estimated at sixty thousand.

The Associated Baptists next claim our attention. Some of the first emigrants who planted New England were Baptists. Roger Williams arrived at Nantasket in 1631, and from his energetic piety was soon invited to become assistant minister at Salem. Not long after he was accused of "embracing principles which tended to Anabaptism," and was at length driven from the colony, and sought refuge among the Indians in Rhode Island. In 1638 he was baptised, with ten others, and they unitedly formed the first Baptist Church at Providence. A few years previous to his baptism, though unknown to him, a distinguished Baptist minister from London arrived in Boston, where he remained some time, diffusing Baptist principles. He subsequently took charge of the church in Dover. The attempt to organise a Baptist Church in Weymouth was resisted by the court of Boston. Several of the members were fined, imprisoned, and disfranchised by the Puritans. In 1644 a poor man became a Baptist, and was complained of to the court for not having his child baptised, and because he refused was tied up and whipped. Three men of Lynn were complained of for being Anabaptists, and were fined. In 1761 a Church was organised in Ashfield, Massachusetts, and the Rev. Ebenezer Smith was ordained over them. The Baptists were taxed for the support of the Puritan Church, and their lands were sold to pay the taxes. A Church was organised in Swansey, R. I., in 1663; another at Welsh Tract, in Delaware, in 1701; another in Prince George County, Virginia, in 1714; and still another in New York in 1762. Subsequently Churches were organised in other states, and the Baptists spread rapidly.

In 1664 the Sabbatarian, or Seventh-Day Baptists organised Churches in Rhode Island. In 1708 the Seventh-Day German Baptists organised a Church in Germantown, Pennsylvania, and elsewhere.

The Reformed Protestant Dutch Church was among the earliest organised in the country. The Dutch from Holland first discovered the rivers Hudson and Connecticut in 1609, and shortly after they erected cabins on Manhattan Island, where New York now stands. The town, which was called New Amsterdam, increased in size and importance from year to year as fresh emigrants arrived. Educated as the inhabitants were in the national Church, they brought with them strong religious prejudices. A Church was gathered in New York in 1619, and there was one at Albany at an earlier period. The first regular minister of the Gospel settled at New York was Rev. Everardus Bogardus, and the Dutch language was exclusively used in the churches until 1764, when Rev. Mr. Laidlie, a Scotch minister from Flushing, in Holland, connected himself with the Dutch Church, and was invited to New York to commence service in the English language. The Dutch Church extended to New Jersey, Connecticut, and elsewhere ; but though it required strength and influence in New York, it made little progress in other places,

We have not space in this chapter to enumerate all the denominations that had an existence in this country prior to the introduction of Methodism ; but we cannot close without noticing the Presbyterian Church, which dates back to an early day. Scotch and Irish Presbyterians came to this country as early as 1640, and according to Cotton Mather four thousand Presbyterians arrived in New England. At a later period Londonderry, in New Hampshire, was founded by a hundred families of Irish Presbyterians, who brought their pastor with them and organised a Church. Another Church was formed in Boston in 1729, and it remained such until 1786, when it became Congregational. In the year 1737 five hundred arrived from Scotland and settled in New York, and subsequently Scotch and Irish colonists settled in Ulster county, and also at Orange and Albany. New Jersey, and particularly the eastern part of it, became the home and possession of the Presbyterians, and they maintain it to a considerable extent to this day. The largest emigration, however, was to Pennsylvania, where, it is said, in 1729 nearly six thousand arrived, and from that time up to the middle of the century as many as twelve thousand came over every year. From Pennsylvania they emigrated in large numbers to Maryland, Virginia, and North Carolina, and in 1773 no fewer than sixteen hundred from the north of Ireland settled in South Carolina. Georgia too was partly colonised by Scotch and Irish Presbyterians.

Maryland was largely settled by English Roman Catholic families brought over by Lord Baltimore, and the Roman religion for many years exerted a predominant influence upon the population. This state has been regarded as the stronghold of Romanism, and had that Church possessed the vitality of Protestant Churches, it might have spread more extensively than it has in the United States. Roman Catholic voyagers and priests were the first to cast eyes upon this vast inheritance, the first to explore its mighty rivers and broad prairies, and the first to plant the cross and break the silence of the wilderness with the voice of prayer and praise. It was doubtless reserved under God to be the fortress and stronghold of a Protestant Christianity, offering an asylum to the oppressed of every clime, and holding up, by the example of freedom of conscience, a beacon of hope.to the persecuted of all lands.

A report was sent to the Bishop of London in the year 1761, which presents the numbers of the different religious denominations, embracing the Jews and Catholics. The number given amounted in all to one million eighty-four thousand, only sixty thousand short of the entire population. Where was ever such an exhibit presented to the world in modern times? This, however, was merely a nominal membership.

CHAPTER IV.

Colonial Period—Colonists in a State of Rebellion—Church and State—Religious Denominations—Persecutions—The "Great Awakening"—Decline in Religion—The Wesleys—Their Labours in America—Methodist Emigrants—Philip Embury in New York—First Meeting—Subsequent Meetings—Incidental Remarks in relation to Local Preachers—The Value of their Labours in early Times—First Methodist Preaching in America—The little Band in Barrack-street Workshop—Secret of the Success of the early Preachers—Embury as a Preacher—Conversion of an English Officer—Becomes a Local Preacher—Ordered to America and stationed at Albany—Visits New York and preaches for the Methodists—Multitudes attracted—Place too small—Larger Room obtained—Opposition—First Methodist Church built—Reinforcement of Preachers sent over by Wesley—Pilmoor's Letter to Wesley—Strawbridge in Maryland—Boardman in Philadelphia—Letter to Wesley.

THE period about which we have been writing, denominated the Colonial Period, was peculiarly marked. Many events of a striking and interesting character had transpired which cast their significant shadows into the future, indicating a crisis which could not long be delayed. It required not the ken of a prophet to see that the great privations, toils, and sufferings of the colonists would serve as a discipline, in the exercise of which they would be enabled to work out their salvation. The oppression by the Government of Great Britain, which sought by its unrighteous exactions to crush out the spirit of liberty and independence, had evidently reached that point in human endurance when patience exhausted would give place to resistance, and when, instead of feeling it to be a duty to obey the reigning power, the subjects would be as strongly impressed with a sentiment if not quite as loyal, at least as patriotic and right, that "Resistance to tyrants is obedience to God."

At the time our sketch of Asbury's arrival in America commences, the colonists were in a state of rebellion, and just on the eve of a revolution. Up to this period there was a union of Church and state, as well as a union with the British Government. They had yet to learn the practicability of a Church without a politico-ecclesiastical government, and also that of a state without a king. We have already seen that the denominations of the Old World were pretty thoroughly represented in the provinces of the New. It must, however, always be an occasion of regret, that while most of them had been driven to this land, or at least exiled themselves on account of the persecutions which they suffered, they should so soon forget the rock from whence they were hewn, and the bondage from which they had been delivered, as to bear away with them to the land of their exile the spirit of their oppressors. It may have been that, in consequence of being so long under the influence of oppression at home, they had caught the contagion and brought it to this land. Certain it is, whatever may have been the cause, the oppressed were not long in the enjoyment of the rights of conscience before they became oppressors themselves. The very Puritans, of whom it is said by the poet,

"They left unstained what here they found,
Freedom to worship God,"

were not exactly what the poet represented. If it could be said that they left all men to the enjoyment of freedom of opinion and the rights of conscience, they were particularly careful to have that freedom of opinion to quadrate with their own notions in respect to religion. In other words, every man was perfectly free to think as they should dictate. His thoughts might flow freely, but it must be in the channel which the Puritans had excavated. Their persecutions of the Baptists and the inoffending Quakers must ever constitute a sad and melancholy passage in their history. Nor were they alone in manifesting a persecuting spirit. The Episcopalians in the southern provinces persecuted the Presbyterians, and a rivalry and hostility existed among the sects in all parts of the country to a greater extent, if not more rancorous, than has been exhibited since that day.

The revival of religion which spread over the country, denominated "The Great Awakening," and which was brought about by the faithful labours of Edwards, Prince, Frelinghuysen, Dickinson, Finley, and the Tennents in the northern and middle states, and of Davies and others in Virginia, and the Wesleys in Georgia, together with those of Whitefield, who traversed the continent with heart of fire and tongue of flame calling sinners to repentance, had from various causes, but particularly from the unsettled and distracted state of the country, gone into a sad decline. The churches were in a dead state, and the Spirit of peace, which flies from scenes of strife and confusion, had at least for a season departed.

The Wesleys had returned to England, but still the heart of John lingered on these shores. The love which prompted him to come to this country more than a quarter of a century before, and labour for the perishing in the wilderness, when his mission was looked upon by his fellow ministers of the Established Church as a wild, fanatical, Quixotic undertaking, had not died within him, and when among the emigrants were members of his own societies, his attachments were increased instead of lessened. Of this number, as before remarked, a few had taken up their residence in New York. Becoming acquainted with each other, they soon sought an opportunity of uniting together in religious worship. Their first place of meeting was in the private house of Philip Embury, who had been converted in Ireland, and had heard Wesley preach in that country. His place of residence was in Barrack-street, near the site of the present City Hall. Embury was not only a Methodist, but he sustained the relation of a local preacher in the Wesleyan Connection in Ireland. Being urged to give out an appointment for preaching, he was at length induced to do so, and accordingly a meeting was subsequently appointed in his workshop.

We may dwell here a moment to remark, that local preachers have been of eminent service to the Methodist Church, both in Europe and America. They proved valuable assistants to Wesley, and went everywhere, sharing his labours and reproaches in preaching to the destitute in town and country. Itinerant as was the economy of Methodism, and extensively as did the regular preachers travel from place to place, yet they could not visit all places, and many a section of the country was prepared, through the labours of the local preachers, for the visits of Wesley and his itinerant helpers, as in the case of the labours of Nelson at Birstal and other places. But more especially have their services been valuable in this widely extended country, particularly in early times. When the history of the Church shall have been written up, it will be found that in many of our large cities and towns, and populous neighbourhoods where Methodism flourishes, and is first for numbers and influence among the sister Churches of these places, the seed was sown first by the hand of the local clergy, who laboured in the vineyard of their Master without the hope of fee or reward, except what they looked for in heaven. Unaided and alone, in the midst of sacrifice, toil, hardships, aye, and not unfrequently of bitter persecution, such as would dampen the zeal and slacken the energies of the most of us who have entered into their labours, have they gone up to the high places of sin with the handful of corn whose spreading and multiplying products now "shake like Lebanon." All honour to those noble men who braved the toils and hardships incident to the planting of Methodism in this country! Their "testimony is in heaven, and their record on high;" and when they who sowed and they who reaped shall come together at the angel shout of harvest home, may we all rejoice together. As we write, a host come thronging on our memory. It may be said of many of them, as was said of an earthly warrior :

> "They sleep their last sleep,
> They have fought their last battle ;"

and the sound that shall wake them will be the voice of Him who called them into the field of conflict, and whose Spirit nerved them for the fight. Faithful men, ye "have fought a good fight, have finished your course," and have entered into the rest and blessedness of heaven.

Embury, as we have already said, was a local preacher, and we left him with our readers while we made a short digression to allude to his brethren of the same class in the ministry. His congregation, small in numbers, assembled in his shop and listened to his sermons. These were the first Methodist sermons preached in New York, and the members constituted in 1766 the first Methodist society formed in America. What a theme for reflection is suggested by these last two sentences ! The first sermons in New York to the first Methodist society in America. Not a century has passed away, and what results from this beginning! Now the generic name "Methodist" covers a membership of a million and a half, all springing from the parent stock. For each and every one of that first little band there are now two hundred and fifty thousand. When from the top of the rocks we behold the plains below whitened with the tents of our Israel, well may we exclaim, "What hath God wrought!" and how vain and foolish would be the attempt of any crazy prophet to curse whom God has so signally blessed.

The little band in Barrack-street workshop assembled from

Sabbath to Sabbath, their numbers continually increasing. Their meetings were regarded by the regular clergy of New York as irregular and fanatical proceedings, but they were not of sufficient importance to attract any particular notice. Thus they continued their worship unmolested, and it was not a great while until the shop became too small to hold the people, and they were obliged to seek for a larger place. Embury labored with his hands during the week for the support of his family, and on the Sabbath "laboured in word and doctrine" with the little flock which had committed itself to his care. In this he imitated the Apostle Paul, who wrought at his trade a year and a half at Corinth. We wonder not that some of our early local preachers did not preach better ; the wonder is that they were able to preach at all. Their abilities were limited, and their facilities for theological attainments were less. The success which attended their ministry was to be attributed to their deep experience in the things of God. They were like Carvosso, men of faith and prayer ; and though they could not deliver nicely-adjusted, systematic, elaborate, and eloquent discourses, according to the homiletic model, yet they came before the people with hearts full of love to God and love for perishing souls, and their exhortations went burning to the hearts of their hearers, who realized that the "excellency of the power was of God and not of man." No knowledge of the Bible, however critical, no acquaintance with theology and Church history and government, however extensive, can atone for the want of a personal, deep, and thorough experience in religion. There are some things in religion that hermeneutics cannot interpret nor exegesis unfold. "The natural man knoweth not the things of the Spirit, because they are spiritually discerned." "The Spirit searcheth all things, even the deep things of God," and it is only in this transparent medium that they can be seen. Without this Divine teacher and his illumination, spiritual things can neither be apprehended nor appreciated. That which in its operations is sublime and glorious as God, is often to the unregenerate eye but confusion and folly.

Embury preached "not in words of man's wisdom," but in demonstration of the Spirit and of power. Coming before the people from time to time with a heart full of the love of Christ, and a fresh experience in religious attainment, his word was attended with a divine unction, and commended itself to the consciences of all who heard. Those who came within the reach of the means of grace were graciously benefited by the labours of this local preacher ; but few, however, comparatively speaking, were induced to attend his ministry. The Wesleyans had secured but little respect as yet in England, and if they were even known in this country, it was not to be expected that they would excite enough attention to bring many of those who were in the habit of going to church to visit so irregular and unauthorized a meeting. This state of things, in the providence of God, was not permitted long to remain.

A year before the time of which we are writing, an English officer was induced, in the town of Bristol, England, to follow the crowd which was wending its way to hear Wesley preach. His fame as a preacher had spread far and wide among the masses, and notwithstanding the opposition excited against him by the regular clergy, the multitude were anxious to hear him, and gladly availed themselves of the opportunity to do so. We would not have the reader entertain the idea for a moment that Wesley or Whitefield, who called out the masses in their day, were anything like some of the popular preachers of the present day in England and America. The novelty connected with their preaching did not consist in letting down the language of the pulpit to the slang of the stump, and merging the preacher into the politician. Every truth they uttered was grave and solemn, attended with no lightness of manner, foppish swagger, or artistic air, more benefiting the clown or the stage-player than ambassadors of Christ. "The love of Christ constrained them," and their earnest declaration of the truth "commended them to every man's conscience." They carried the Gospel to the uncared-for masses, and it was this concern for neglected souls which characterized all their labours, that won upon the hearts of the masses, and brought thousands of the destitute to listen to their ministrations.

The English officer, more perhaps out of curiosity than from any religious motive, found himself in the midst of a crowd of earnest zealous worshippers. The word of truth, plainly presented and calmly enunciated, was attended with a power which reached his heart. The result was the conversion of Captain Webb, the officer alluded to, and his subsequent enlistment in the army of Immanuel as a local preacher. He was soon after ordered by his government to America, and subsequently to the post at Albany, New York, where he took up his quarters as barrack-master. It was not long before he heard of the small society of his brethren in New York, and seizing the first opportunity, he descended the Hudson and appeared in their midst in military dress. The suddenness of his appearance, and the strangeness of his costume in their meeting, attracted general attention; but when they learned he was a Wesleyan Methodist preacher the interest was increased a hundred fold. When it was rumoured abroad that a British officer would preach in full military dress, the new room which the society had obtained was by no means capacious enough to contain the crowds that flocked to hear him. Those who were permitted, heard the Gospel from his lips in demonstration of the Spirit and power.

It soon became necessary to seek accommodations adapted to the increasing multitudes, who came out from all parts of the city to hear him. The society accordingly hired a large rigging loft in William-street ; but this did not answer the purpose long, as it was found the place was not commodious enough to accommodate the people. Unmistakeable were the effects of Gospel truth on the hearts of the hearers, and a religious excitement, which always adds interest to a meeting, and increases the number of hearers, was manifested. Until now, as we have already remarked, the Methodists were too few and insignificant to excite attention or much opposition, except to elicit from grave and orthodox divines the admonition to their people to avoid their meetings. But now the opposition became more apparent, and if the regular clergy could well have accomplished it, they would have put a stop to these irregular proceedings. It was all, however, of no avail ; the people would come to meeting, and many were awakened and converted.

To accommodate the society and congregation, as well as to obtain " a local habitation and a name," it was determined to select a suitable site and erect a church. A lot was accordingly obtained in John-street, and a plain, unpretending house of worship erected thereon, which, on the 30th of October, 1768, was dedicated by Embury with appropriate religious services. This was the first Methodist church in America, and a thousand hallowed associations gather round the spot where it stood.

Wesley having heard of the movements of this infant society, addressed them a letter of encouragement, accompanying it with a subscription of two hundred and fifty dollars, and at the same time sending them two preachers in the persons of Richard Boardman and Joseph Pilmoor. These missionaries landed in Philadelphia in 1769, and Boardman proceeded immediately to New York, where, in the city and surrounding country, he entered upon his labours. Captain Webb, in the mean time, like a true evangelist, visited Long Island, preaching the Gospel in several places, and extended his labours as far as Philadelphia, and for the first time many were privileged to hear Methodist preaching. In 1769 Pilmoor addressed a letter to Wesley containing the following : "I have preached several times, and the people flocked to hear in multitudes. Sunday evening I went out upon the Common. I had the stage appointed for the horse-race for my pulpit, and I think between four and five thousand people, who heard with attention still as night. Blessed be God for field preaching!"

About this time Robert Strawbridge, from Ireland, a local preacher of considerable eminence, settled in Frederick County, Maryland, and commenced preaching in his own house with an earnestness and power characteristic of the sons of the Emerald Isle. He was enabled soon to erect a log church, and organize a small society. The companion of Boardman, Mr. Pilmoor, having ministered the word of life to the society at Philadelphia, which numbered one hundred, directed his course to Maryland, and entered into the labours of Strawbridge, greatly to the spiritual edification and comfort of the little flock. He also visited Virginia and North Carolina.

In April, 1771, Boardman addressed a letter from New York to Wesley, giving an account of a revival in which thirty were added to the society, five of whom were converted. He speaks highly of the attainments of the clergy of the English and Dutch Churches of the city of New York, and regarded them as the best in America. His letter concludes by expressing an earnest desire that Mr. Wesley would visit America.

CHAPTER V.

Reception in Philadelphia—Pilmoor—Asbury's first Sermon in America—Visit to Staten Island—New York—Boardman—Asbury's Opinion of the Americans —Visit to the Country—Pilmoor—Asbury in Philadelphia—Appointed Superintendent—Criticism of a Book—An Officious Priest—Quarterly Meetings—Baltimore—New York—Church Worshippers—Philadelphia—Rankin —St. Paul's Church—Rankin's Opposition to Revivals—First Conference— Baltimore—Quarterly Conference—Otterbine—Second Conference—Desire to be sent to Baltimore—Disappointed—Norfolk—Revival in Virginia— Asbury's Opinion of the English Preachers who left the Country—Rumours of War—Warm Sulphur Springs—Wesley and Politics—Conference at Deer Creek—Declaration of Independence—Difficulties about the Sacraments— Retires to Judge White's in Delaware—Trials—Action of Southern Preachers—Asbury's Efforts at Union—Plan proposed—Rejected—Delegates sent to Southern Conference—Successful Result.

ASBURY opened his mission in Philadelphia. We have already alluded to the cordial greeting given to him and his colleague by the members of the society in that city. His elevation of spirits, resulting from such an expression of Christian sympathy in his behalf, was remarkable, and he says in referring to it, "My mind was drawn heavenward; the Lord hath helped me by his power, and my soul is in a paradise." His first meeting with the society, as we have already seen, was on the first evening after his arrival, when he listened in the old St. George's Church, to a Sermon from Joseph Pilmoor, who was then stationed in that city, and interchanged with Boardman of New York. The next meeting he attended was a watch-night meeting, which began at eight o'clock and lasted till midnight. Pilmoor again preached, and the services were continued by a religious conference, during which a large number related their Christian experience. Toward the close of the meeting, Asbury says, "a plain man from the country spoke, and his words went with great power to the souls of the people, so that we may say, 'Who hath despised the day of small things?' Not the Lord our God; then why should self-important man?" We find him the next day engaged in personal labours with individuals who were awakened, and anxiously inquiring what they should do to be saved. His conversation with them and his prayers in their behalf were attended with a blessing not only to them but to himself, and he felt more than ever convinced that in obeying the call which summoned him from his home and kindred to brave the dangers of the ocean, and bear the messages of the Gospel to the inhabitants of this New World, he was in the line and order of Providence.

The first sermon which he preached, though he makes no mention of it in his Journal, was one in which he enjoyed much freedom. He remarked that in speaking to the people he "felt his mind opened and his tongue unloosed." His last sermon during his stay in Philadelphia was preached on the 6th of November, from the text, "He that spared not his own Son, but delivered him up for us all, how shall he not with him also freely give us all things?" The sermon was delivered in the evening, and in describing the occasion he says, "It was a night of power to my own soul and to many others." His first ministrations impressed the Church in that city that he was a minister of no ordinary stamp, evincing by the manner in which he treated his subjects, and the depth and fervor of his feelings, that he was a workman eminently qualified by training and experience to divide the word of truth, and give to saint and sinner their portion in due season.

After remaining ten days in Philadelphia he went to Burlington, where he preached in the court-house to a large and attentive congregation. From thence he directed his course to New York.

Having met on the road a gentleman by the name of Van Pelt, who resided on Staten Island, and being accompanied by him on his journey, he was induced to go to Staten Island, and spend a short time in that place before going to New York. After three days' journey they reached the hospitable mansion of Mr. Van Pelt, where Asbury ever after found a home. As he had made no engagement to be in New York at any particular time he remained a few days on the Island, and preached in the evening at the house of his friend. The kind reception which he met from the people, and the religious enjoyment which he experienced, still further encouraged him in the belief that his mission was in accordance with the ordination of God. On the Sabbath he discoursed in the morning to a large congregation in the house of his friend, and in the afternoon to a much larger one. He preached also in the evening to a large congregation assembled at the house of Justice Wright. On Monday he left for New York, where he met Richard Boardman, who was stationed in the city. In him he found a genial spirit, and was so favourably impressed with the man that he makes the following record in his Journal: " My friend Boardman is a kind, loving, worthy man, truly amiable and entertaining, and of a child-like temper." Boardman, as we have already seen, was Pilmoor's colleague, and between them they had for their field of labour New York and Philadelphia, as well as other points accessible in the country.

Boardman, having left his colleague, Pilmoor, in Philadelphia, the place of their landing, proceeded to New York. On his way he stopped at a large town where a company of soldiers were stationed, through whose influence he procured the use of the Presbyterian Church, where he preached to them and a large number of the citizens. When he arrived at New York he was cordially received. Referring to the congregations that then attended his ministry, he said, "so great was the crowd that attended meeting, only a third part were able to get into the house." He thought the Americans excelled all the people he ever saw in their desire to hear the word.

The year that Asbury arrived the society in New York was blessed with a revival, and such was its extent that Boardman, in his letter to Wesley, describes it as a " great awakening." His zeal in the cause of religion, connected with great urbanity of manners, endeared him to the people, and it was not to be wondered that Asbury found in him a loving companion. He only remained in this country a few years. After his return he laboured as an itinerant in England and Ireland during a period of eight years.

D

He died in great peace at Cork, having preached the night before his death. Mr. Wesley says of him: "He was a pious, good-natured, sensible man, greatly beloved by all who knew him." As though the old adage proved true, "like priest like people," so Asbury found among the New York Methodists a kindred spirit to that of their beloved pastor. He describes them as "loving and serious," and remarked that "there appeared also among them a love of discipline."

His introduction into New York being thus auspicious, he opened his mission with encouraging prospects. His first sermon was preached in the old John-street Church, on Tuesday, the 13th of November, to a large and attentive congregation. His text was well selected, being 1 Corinthians ii. 2 : "I determined not to know anything among you save Jesus Christ and him crucified." The text is illustrative of his settled purpose of mind in entering upon his work in America, and his whole subsequent life gave evidence of the manner in which he adhered to that purpose. If ever, since the days of the apostles, there were any ministers who gave themselves up with exclusive devotion to their work, Asbury was most certainly of that number. His next sermon was on the following day; during its delivery he felt his heart greatly enlarged, and he was convinced that the membership enjoyed the "life and power of religion."

When the Sabbath came he preached again to a large concourse of people, and was much refreshed in spirit at witnessing their zeal and devotion, and felt more strongly attached to them than ever, expressing his belief that the Americans were more ready to receive the word than the English. He was particularly impressed with the sight of so many sable sons and daughters of Africa, who were in the congregation, and who united with the people in cheerful melody to sing the Redeemer's praise.

Unwilling to confine his labours to the city, he resolved on visiting what Boardman in his letter to Wesley called the "back settlements," and accordingly he went to Westchester. At this place his friends waited on the mayor for the use of the court-house to preach in, there being no church, and it was readily granted. On Sabbath morning a congregation assembled, and he discoursed from the text, "Now he commandeth all men everywhere to repent." In the afternoon his congregation increased ; many of the chief men of the town were present, among whom was the mayor. At both these meetings he realized the Divine presence and power. In the evening he preached at West Farms, and the next day again at Westchester, where he was a guest of the mayor. The next Sabbath he preached in New York, and returned to the country, preaching at New Rochelle, Rye, East Chester, and Mamaroneck. Returning to New York he visited Staten Island, and then again we find him on his former round, preaching through the week, and on Sabbaths, as he had opportunity and could obtain places and congregations.

We have been thus particular in our description, because these were the first regular labours of this true-hearted missionary in this country.

To him must be awarded the honour of initiating the first regular circuit work in America. He evidently saw a disposition on the part of the preachers to confine their labours to the cities, and had resolved that he would be an itinerant in every sense of the term. He had thoroughly imbibed the doctrine of Wesley, to "go where the people wanted him the most," and this demand for his services was not to be determined by any particular desire on his part to preach to such as prized his ministrations, nor yet by the desire of the people to hear him, but where there was the greatest need of Gospel preaching, and where the people were in greatest danger of perishing without it. Such are truly evangelical calls; and wherever the minister heeds them, if he have to pass through persecution like Peter, or even through death like Stephen, he will prove himself a true successor of the apostles of our Lord.

He seemed to consider it improper for him to remain in New York while Boardman was there, and hence he says in his Journal: "I remain in York, though unsatisfied with our being both in town together. I have not yet the thing which I seek, a circulation of the preachers to avoid partiality and popularity. However, I am fixed to the Methodist plan, and do what I do faithfully, as unto God. I expect trouble is at hand. This I expected when I left England, and I am willing to suffer, yea, to die, rather than betray so good a cause by any means. It will be a hard matter to stand against all opposition

'As an iron pillar strong,
And steadfast as a wall of brass;'

but through Christ strengthening me I can do all things. My brethren seem unwilling to leave the cities, but I will show them the way. I have nothing to seek but the glory of God, nothing to fear but his displeasure. I have come to this country with an upright intention, and through the grace of God I will make it appear. I am determined that no man shall bias me with soft words and fair speeches; nor will I ever fear the face of man, or know any man after the flesh, if I beg my bread from door to door ; but whomsoever I please or displease, I will be faithful to God, to the people, and to my own soul."

The population of New York was at that time about twenty-five thousand, and was embraced within the limits of that part of the present city bounded by Beekman-street on the north, and the Battery on the south. There were then seventeen churches on the island, of which the Reformed Dutch and the Episcopal had three each, the Lutherans two, the German Reformed one, the Presbyterians two, and the Seceders, Baptists, Moravians, Jews, French Protestants, and Methodists one each. In describing some of the preachers in New York, Boardman, in his letter to Wesley, says : " We have in this city some of the best preachers, both in the English and Dutch Churches, that are in America."

While on his last round before leaving for Philadelphia, Asbury was taken sick at City Island, and, notwithstanding the kind friends with whom he stopped insisted on his remaining until his health was recruited, he left for his appointments, and so determined was he in filling them, that, though he was quite ill, and part of the time in great pain, he preached at all of them before he returned to New York. When he arrived he found Pilmoor, who had exchanged with Boardman ; but the former being ill, he occupied the pulpit in the morning. Pilmoor was quite popular in the city, and attracted large crowds whenever he came. On one occasion he went out, by request, to the race-course. It was Sabbath evening, and the judge's stand was converted into a pulpit. From this he preached to between four and five thousand people, who listened with great attention.

After visiting Staten Island, and preaching at his friend Van Pelt's, Justice Wright's, and at the ferry, Asbury returned to New York, and from thence started for Philadelphia, preaching on the way at Amboy, Burlington, and New Mills.

The preachers having all met in Philadelphia for the purpose of arranging the work for the year 1772, it was agreed among them that Boardman should go to Boston, Pilmoor to Virginia, Wright to New York, and Asbury to Philadelphia. This was his first appointment proper in America, and he expressed himself much pleased with it. The impression which he made on his first arrival was so favourable that the people were equally well pleased with the appointment, and large congregations attended his ministry. Faithful to his purpose not to spend all his time in the city, he went out into the country and preached at Bohemia, Chester, and other places, returning to Philadelphia and preaching on Sabbaths and meeting the society. He also visited Burlington, Wilmington, Greenwich, Trenton, Gloucester, and other points.

After remaining four months on his Philadelphia circuit he was summoned to New York. On his arrival he found that Wright had preached his farewell sermon, and informed the people that he did not expect to see them any more. Asbury thought they had spoiled him by gifts, and he discovered that those very persons who had exerted such a pernicious influence upon him, were among the first to condemn him. At this his spirit was stirred, and he felt aggrieved somewhat both at preacher and people. Being opposed by some of the members for meeting the society at the same time the classes were held, he complained of a party spirit which he thought prevailed. At a meeting held for the purpose of arranging the temporal affairs of the society, and also for considering whatever related to its spiritual interests, sixteen questions were discussed. There was not that harmony among the membership that Asbury desired, and some considerable disaffection existed in regard to what he considered the requirements of the discipline, but he resolved that with calm and determined energy he would carry out the rules and regulations of the Church. In the meantime he extended his labours to Staten Island, Kingsbridge, and elsewhere. Alluding to the "sharp debates" held in the leaders' meeting in New York, he says a member had charged him with ill usage in saying he opposed his meeting the society, and intimated that he had preached the people away, and that he would destroy the work. In the midst of all these trials he, however, swerved not from what he conscientiously believed to be the path of duty, and preserved a conscience void of offence toward God and man.

On the 10th of October, 1772, he received a letter from Wesley, appointing him Superintendent of the societies in America. Among other instructions contained in this communication was one strictly enjoining that none of his books should be reprinted without his consent. It seems that Robert Williams had engaged in the republication of some of Wesley's works. This he did from the purest motives, but from some cause or other Wesley prohibited him from any further publication. Williams came over as a local preacher, and in all probability commenced preaching in New York before the arrival of Boardman. He was afterward admitted into the travelling connection, and was the first to visit some sections in Maryland and Virginia, extending his labours to North Carolina. He was a man of faith and prayer, and his labours were abundantly blessed.

Receiving intelligence that he was expected to spend the winter in Maryland, Asbury proceeded to Philadelphia, stopping on his way at Princeton, a place he had "long wished to see, for the sake of the pious Mr. Davies, late president of the college there." After remaining a short time he left for Maryland, stopping at a place where a work on the non-eternity of future punishment fell into his hands. This he read and criticised after the following manner : "By his arguments," alluding to the author of the work, "we may as well prove the non-eternity of heavenly joys, for if, as he calls it, a ζωὴ αἰώνιος of the righteous arises from a principle of spiritual life derived from Christ, then the κόλασις αἰώνιος of the wicked arises from a principle of spiritual death in them, and the one will come to an end as soon as the other."

While engaged in preaching in Kent county, Maryland, an officious preacher of the Episcopal Church came to one of his appointments, demanding by what authority he preached. Asbury calmly met the insolent demand by telling him who he was. To this the priest of the Church pompously replied :

"I have the sole authority over this people and the care of their souls, and you cannot and shall not preach ; and if you do I will proceed against you according to law."

Asbury gave him to understand that he had no respect whatever for his assumed authority ; that he came there to preach, and preach he would.

"But," said the divine, "you will create a schism, and draw the people from their work."

"Do not fairs and horse-races hinder the people?" asked Asbury.

At this the clergyman wished to know what was the object of his coming.

To which he replied : "To turn sinners to God."

"Cannot I do this as well as you?" said the parson.

Asbury then said : "I have authority from God."

At this the parson laughed and said : "You are a fine fellow, indeed ;" but it was not long before he changed his tone and became enraged.

Not in the least terrified at the threats of the Episcopal parson, he preached and had him for a hearer.

No conferences having as yet been held, all the business pertaining to the spiritual and temporal economy of the Church was transacted at quarterly meetings. One of these meetings was held during his visit to Maryland. After preaching a discourse on the duties of the ministry, the Quarterly Conference proceeded to business. Among the matters discussed were questions relating to week-day preaching, the administration of the Sacrament, and some other items of minor importance. The preachers were stationed, and each one started to his field of labour for the year. By this arrangement Asbury was stationed in Baltimore ; but he did not confine his labours exclusively to that place, as we find him traversing the country, and preaching at all points where Providence opened his way. His course in this respect, so persistently followed, had its effect upon his brethren in the ministry, and the result was that the work of the Lord spread and prevailed in all parts of the itinerant field. On the 3d of January, 1773, he entered fully upon his work in Baltimore, preaching to a large congregation at the house of Captain Patten, at the Point, in the morning, and in the evening in the city. His religious experience at this time may be described in his own words : " Holiness is the element of my soul. My earnest prayer is, that nothing contrary to holiness may live in me."

He had been offered the use of the court-house in the town, but it being judged unfit as a place for religious meeting it was declined, and he preached in a private house, in which he formed a class consisting of male members. The next day he organised a female class. He continued preaching at the Point and in town during the Sabbaths, and through the week extended his labours into the various parts of the surrounding country.

In March, 1773, he attended a quarterly meeting conference on the Susquehanna, which he opened by a discourse. It was a time of peace and harmony among the preachers, and at its close they went out to their respective fields greatly encouraged to work for God. Having received a letter requesting him to visit New York, as his presence was required, he repaired thither at the close of the quarterly meeting. While in New York, in accordance with instructions from Wesley, enjoined on all preachers in connection with him, he attended the Episcopal Church for the purpose of receiving the sacrament. He had, however, but a poor opinion of the spirituality of the Church worshippers, describing them as the most gay and undevout he had ever seen.

On his return to Philadelphia, Asbury for the first time met Rankin. He came over in company with Messrs. Shadford and Yearbry, and Captain Webb, through whose solicitation mainly Mr. Wesley was induced to reinforce the itinerant corps in America. Rankin was considered by Wesley as possessing peculiar gifts for governing the Church ; and as he was Asbury's senior by several years, he constituted him General Superintendent of the societies in America. His arrival was a source of considerable comfort to Asbury, and he was very favourably impressed with the man. After hearing him preach a discourse from the text, " I have set before thee an open door, and no man can shut it," he thought perhaps he would not be much admired as a preacher, but as a disciplinarian he believed he would be qualified for the place assigned him.

The next day they started for New York, where they arrived on the 12th, and were received by a large company of Methodists at the dock where they landed. Asbury preached on Sabbath morning, and in the afternoon, in company with Rankin, Webb, and Wright, went to St. Paul's Church and received the sacrament. In the evening Rankin preached his first sermon in New York. Alluding to his sermon Asbury says : " He dispensed the word of truth with power ; it reached the hearts of many, and they appeared to be much quickened."

Being anxious to know how the societies were prospering in the country, Asbury went to New Rochelle and preached. On his return he found, to his great satisfaction, that Rankin had been successful in settling some of the difficulties which existed in the society. At this time there was a considerable revival in the society at New York, and some of the exercises witnessed by Rankin were not at all pleasing to him.

Rankin had not long been in possession of the government of the Church until it was found that there was an incompatibility existing between his views and opinions and those of the Methodists of this country. Unlike Asbury, who, on identifying himself with America, left all his prejudices and prepossessions behind, he came, however sincere his purposes and aim to promote the cause of Methodism, with all his English ideas of loyalty and government. He sought to effect by authority what Asbury so happily secured by conciliation and moral suasion. What was remarkable in a Methodist preacher, it appears that Rankin manifested an opposition to the spirit of revivals, asserting that they tended to disgrace religion by the destruction of order. In this he was promptly met by Asbury, who, although he conceded that some enthusiasm and extravagance might occasionally exist in time of revival, yet deemed it injudicious to animadvert with severity on those exhibitions of passionate excitement which more or less accompany deep and lasting revivals of religion. The friends of order, he thought, might well allow a poor and guilty mortal to tremble before his God under deep conviction for sin, and the people of God to sing and shout when the Holy One of Israel appears in power and grace among them. To be hasty in plucking the tares might endanger the wheat. We should not venture to reach forth our hand to touch the ark lest we be smitten for sacrilege. In consequence of this, an unpleasant state of feeling sprang up between Asbury and Rankin, and the latter was unwise enough to communicate it to Wesley, who became somewhat prejudiced against Asbury on that account. These differences, however, did not separate these good men in heart, and they finally gave way after more mature reflection.

On the 14th of July, 1773, the first Conference proper met in Philadelphia. At this Conference it was determined to enforce the rules and regulations of the Wesleyan Conference throughout the connection in America. As we have already seen, the sacraments were not to be administered by the preachers, and the people were earnestly advised to receive baptism and the Lord's supper from the hands of the Episcopal clergy. The number of preachers stationed at this Conference was ten, and as it was the first regular Conference held, we think it of sufficient interest to give their names and appointments : New York and Philadelphia, Thomas Rankin and George Shadford ; New Jersey, John King and William Watters ; Baltimore, Francis Asbury, Robert Strawbridge, Abraham Whitworth, and Joseph Yearbry ; Norfolk, Richard Wright ; Petersburg, Robert Williams. The numbers reported in society were one thousand one hundred and sixteen.

Asbury's labours in Baltimore were much blessed, and as he continued the sphere of his operations, he began to realise his heart's desire in seeing the people turned to the Lord. He was greatly cheered in receiving intelligence of a wonderful revival in Virginia. About this time he drew up a subscription, and carried it from place to place, with a view of raising funds for building a church in Baltimore. He received considerable assistance from Mr. Moore, who zealously co-operated with him in the work, and was enabled to report the sum raised by subscription to be more than a hundred pounds. Two lots had been selected as eligible sites for the building, and Asbury was greatly encouraged. This enterprise proved in the end successful, and Light-street Church was in process of time dedicated to the service of God.

In July a quarterly conference was held at Owing's, in Maryland. In referring to this meeting, Asbury says : " All the preachers appeared to have their hearts fixed on promoting the work of God the ensuing quarter, and we consulted together with much freedom and love. On the first day I inquired into the moral character of the local preachers, appointed them their work, and gave them written licences to officiate. The preachers who spoke at this meeting manifested great earnestness and zeal for the salvation of souls, and many of the people were much affected; all was harmony and love. For the next quarter we had our stations as follow : P. Eberd, E. Drumgoole, and Richard Owings in Frederic Circuit; Brother Yearbry and Brother Rawlings in Kent Circuit ; Henry Watters and Brother Wright in Baltimore Circuit ; and myself in Baltimore town."

About this time he received intelligence of a powerful revival in Virginia, in which between five and six hundred souls were converted, the result of which was the formation of five or six new circuits. Having written to Otterbein, a distinguished German minister, in relation to his settlement in Baltimore, he united, in a true catholic spirit, with some friends of the German Reformed Church in drawing up a plan for his settlement. A short time after he met with Otterbein and another minister of the same Church, and was favourably impressed with their Christian spirit.

At the second Conference, which was held in Philadelphia on the 25th of May, 1774, quite a number were added to the itinerant ranks, and the increase in the membership was upward of nine hundred, nearly double what it was the previous year. In alluding to this Conference, Asbury says : " It was attended with great power, and all things were considered in peace and harmony. We agreed to send Mr. W. to England, and all acquiesced in the stations of the preachers. My lot was to go to York." When he reached his appointment he was again greeted by his friends, but he lamented that there were some remaining roots of prejudice in the hearts of a few. Subsequently he felt much aggrieved at the acrimony of a certain individual, who did all he could to injure him, but he patiently submitted his cause to God. Notwithstanding the efforts of what he calls dissatisfied, restless spirits, he was enabled to keep up a close communion with God, and realised that the fire of divine love glowed in his heart ; that his soul was peace, and his affections pure and withdrawn from earthly objects.

During this year he suffered much from sickness, and for many days was closely confined ; but notwithstanding his illness, he preached three hundred times, and rode two thousand miles on horseback. At the close of his year in New York, in consequence of his feeble health, he began to feel some solicitude about his appointment the ensuing year. Rankin had the power of appointing the preachers, and he expressed a desire that he might be saved from going into what he called the " low country." When he went to Philadelphia, in December, he fell in company with Rankin, and opened his mind fully to him on the subject ; but he found that they disagreed in judgment entirely, and he remarked that it appeared to him that to make any attempt to be stationed in Baltimore would be all in vain. "It is somewhat grievous," says Asbury, "that he should prevent my going to Baltimore, after being acquainted with my engagements, and the importunities of my friends there." Several of the preachers, among whom were Webb and Drumgoole, were of the same opinion with the people in regard to this matter. While Asbury was in Philadelphia he was taken quite ill, and for some time was confined to his room under medical treatment. When he recovered, he went to Baltimore, and was greatly refreshed in spirit in meeting his old friends. Large congregations in town and at the Point, as well as in the country where he preached, attended his ministry.

The next Conference was held at Philadelphia in May, 1775. The Church had increased in numbers astonishingly during the past year, and the membership rose to upward of three thousand. Great peace and harmony prevailed. The subject of war was then a prevailing one, and such was the agitated state of the public mind, Conference deemed it proper to appoint a general fast for the prosperity of the work and for the peace of America. Nineteen preachers were stationed. Asbury, as the Minutes show, was stationed, contrary to his wishes, at Norfolk, but he uttered no word of complaint, going with all cheerfulness to his field of labour. After a somewhat disagreeable voyage, he arrived at Norfolk, where he found no place for preaching but an old dilapidated house, which had been formerly used as a theatre. There were but thirty members in society, and they were in a somewhat disorganised state, having no class-meetings. After labouring a few days alternately in Norfolk and Portsmouth, he persuaded the brethren to issue a subscription paper for building a house of worship, which, however, went tardily on for the present. As usual, Mr. Asbury omitted no opportunity of doing good to the souls of the people ; and for this purpose he made frequent excursions into the country, where he generally found a people willing to hear the word of reconciliation. Having been invited to visit Brunswick Circuit, where the Lord was pouring out his Spirit upon the labours of Mr. Shadford, he arrived there, and says : " God is at work in this part of the country, and my soul catches the holy fire." On meeting with Mr. Shadford, he says : " My spirit is much united to him, and our meeting was like that of David and Jonathan." A remarkable revival of the work of God was then prevailing in that part of the country, chiefly through the instrumentality of Mr. Shadford. Trembling and shaking would seize upon sinners under the word, and in some instances they were so affected as to fall helpless upon the floor or upon the ground. These were strange appearances in this country, and some, of course, looked on with astonishment at the manifest displays of the power and grace of God. The consequence of this great and extensive revival was an addition to the societies of upward of eighteen hundred members. Asbury entered into this revival with great spirit, and gives an extended account of it in his Journal.

Mr. Robert Williams, who was among the first Methodist preachers who visited Virginia, had married, and located at a place between Norfolk and Suffolk, where he ended his days in peace on the 26th of September, 1775. His funeral sermon was preached by Mr. Asbury, who says of him that he had been "a very useful man, and the Lord gave him many seals to his ministry. Perhaps no man in America has been an instrument of awakening so many souls as God has awakened by him."

Rankin, finding it impossible to reconcile the war spirit which pervaded the country, with his views of loyalty, and especially the instructions of Wesley on the subject, resolved to return to England, and in a letter to Asbury informed him of that determination. In his reply, indicative of his own views and feelings on the subject, Asbury speaks as follows : "I can by no means leave such a field for gathering souls to Christ as we have in America. It would be an everlasting dishonour to the Methodists that we should all leave three thousand souls who desire to commit themselves to our care ; neither is it the part of a good shepherd to leave his flock in time of danger ; therefore I am determined, by the grace of God, not to leave them let the consequence be what it may."

While absent on one of his itinerant excursions he heard of a dreadful slaughter at Norfolk and Great Bridge, which, added to the war demonstrations which had already been made in the country, gave pretty strong evidence that troublous times were coming, such as would try men's souls. When he returned to Baltimore, which he did in the spring, so great was the consternation arising from the existence of the war that the congregations were small. The presence of a man-of-war in the river excited the greatest commotion. Alluding to this state of things, he makes the following appropriate and beautiful reflections : "I know the Lord governeth the world, therefore these things shall not trouble me. I will endeavour to be ready for life or death, so that if death should come my soul may joyfully quit this land of sorrow and go to rest in the embraces of the blessed Jesus. O delightful felicity ! There is no din of war ; no unfriendly persecutors of piety ; no enchanting world with concealed destruction ; no malevolent spirit to disturb our peace : but all is purity, peace, and joy. Adapting my discourse to the occasion, I preached this evening from Isaiah i. 19, 20 : ' If ye be willing and obedient, ye shall eat the good of the land : but if ye refuse and rebel, ye shall be devoured with the sword : for the mouth of the Lord hath spoken it.' "

After remaining in Baltimore a short time he went to Philadelphia, and visited Trenton and other places. At Philadelphia also the people were alarmed by the rumours of war, tidings having arrived of a battle off Christiana between thirteen row-galleys and the Roebuck man-of-war. Being sick, he was unable to attend the Conference, which was held in May, 1776, in Baltimore, but he received notice from Rankin of his appointment to that city. When his health admitted, he went to his charge and entered upon his labours, but he was so much debilitated that he deemed it advisable to visit the Warm Sulphur Springs in Virginia. That his time might be properly occupied while there, he adopted the following plan : " To read one hundred pages a day, to pray in public five times a day, to preach in the open air every other day, and to lecture in prayer-meeting every other evening." Such recreation as this, at a watering-place, by a minister of the present day, would be considered among the strangest of strange things. While at the Springs, he met a man who had come eighteen miles for the purpose of seeing and hearing a Methodist preacher. His quarters were not the most comfortable, as will be seen by the following description : "The size of the house in which we live is twenty feet by sixteen, and there are seven beds and sixteen persons, besides some noisy children." After remaining there about five weeks, he left, greatly grieved and disgusted at the practices of the many thoughtless visitors. On the day of his leaving he made the following entry in his Journal : "I this day turn my back on the Springs as the best and worst place I ever was in—good for health, but most injurious for religion."

At this time he received a letter from Wesley, and regretted much that this great man had interfered in American politics. He, however, says that the course of that distinguished man manifested his conscientious attachment to the government under which he lived. He thought if Wesley had been in America he would have been a zealous advocate of the American cause.

Alarms of war reached him, and accounts of bloodshed and slaughter in different parts of the country. This was a grief to his soul, and he earnestly prayed that the Lord might disperse those who delighted in war, and thirsted for human blood. "It is well," said he, "that this is not the home of the righteous. They are blessed with a pacific spirit, and are bound for a kingdom of peace, where

> " No horrid alarum of war
> Shall break our eternal repose;
> No sound of the trumpet is there
> Where the spirit of Jesus o'erflows.
> Appeased by the charms of Thy grace,
> We all shall in amity join,
> And kindly each other embrace,
> And love with a passion like thine."

The next Conference was held at Deer Creek, Harford county, Maryland, in May, 1777, and the number of the preachers had increased to twenty-seven, twenty of whom were present. Since the last Conference, which was held in Baltimore, the patriots of the Revolution had assembled in Philadelphia, and declared the colonies free and independent states, thereby throwing off all allegiance to the British crown. The lines were now distinctly drawn, and no loyalist could possibly hope to find any sympathy among the Americans. Some of the English preachers were ill at ease, and being unwilling to enter into the revolutionary spirit, or embrace the American cause, began to make arrangements for returning to England. [1]

But there were other difficulties existing in relation to the Church. The people began to ask for the ordinances, and as they could see no reason why those who ministered to them the word of life should not also administer the sacraments of baptism and the Lord's supper, they became more and more earnest in their demands. That their ministers, as well as themselves, should be obliged to go to the Episcopal clergy and receive the sacrament at their hands, was something they could not, with their knowledge of the authority drawn from the "regular succession," understand. Nor were the people alone in these views and feelings. The preachers at the south pressed the matter upon the attention of the Conference, and there were strong indications of a separation unless the demand was met.

This feeling was held in abeyance for several years, and did not embody itself in any action until 1779. Asbury, like Wesley, was a true son of the Church, and though he had become thoroughly American in his views and feelings, and, as his subsequent history shows, a republican of the Washington stamp, still his love for Wesley, and his desire to remain in connection with him, was such that he laboured hard to allay the feelings of his brethren.

While Asbury was engaged in his work in Baltimore and vicinity in 1777, he was required to take the oath of allegiance to the state of Maryland. Its form, however, was such that he could not conscientiously take it, and the result was that he was obliged to leave the state and go to Delaware, where the state oath was not required of clergymen. He sought an asylum at the hospitable mansion of Judge White, in Kent county, Delaware. He soon found, however, that his retreat was no place of safety. Scarcely had he been a month at the Judge's before he was obliged to leave, and he went out, not knowing whither. He had not travelled many miles when he came to a house, where he stopped and found the neighbours assembled for a funeral. There being no minister, he hesitated not to improve the occasion by an address full of Christian sympathy. He then pursued his weary way until late at night, when he found shelter. Here he intended to rest till Providence should direct his way ; but the next evening he heard of circumstances which induced him to think it prudent to move the next day. Deeply depressed was his spirit. He was three thousand miles from his native home and kindred. All his countrymen associated with him had left him to his fate. He was considered by most persons, who knew not his heart and his motives, as an enemy to the country, and he was, accordingly, liable any hour to be apprehended and abused.

Leaving his resting-place, he went into a wild and dismal swamp, where he lay concealed till night, when a friend kindly took him in and protected him. Under these circumstances of trial he was sustained by the consciousness that he was in the way of duty. He was seeking neither riches nor honour. He was labouring only for the spiritual good, for the salvation of his fellow men. He trusted in Providence, being confident the God of the prophets and of the apostles would protect and relieve him.

In his seclusion he heard that his friend and brother, Rev. Joseph Hartley, had been apprehended and imprisoned in the county of Queen Anne, and that the amiable Freeborn Garrettson had been assaulted, abused, and nearly murdered by his persecutors. After about a month spent in seclusion, he ventured to return to his old home at Judge White's, where he remained till the troubles were past.

It was with the utmost difficulty he could maintain contentment, and resignation in his restricted circumstances. Pent up in the little state of Delaware, he felt straitened and repressed in his very soul. He says his mind was twisted and tortured ; he knew not whether to fight or run ; he was worried by temptations ; everything appeared under a cloud ; and often he was ready to choose death rather than such a life. Yet he had an agreeable home, he was in no immediate danger, and he had the whole state of

Delaware for his prison-bounds. Yet he was unhappy. Nor could it be otherwise, since God had made him for an itinerant, and called him to travel, and designed the whole country, from the Atlantic to the Mississippi, and from the Gulf of Mexico to the St. Lawrence, for his circuit. Had you placed him in a palace in Delaware, and given him an Eden for his rambles, and a magnificent cathedral for his preaching-place, and ten thousand souls for his audience, he still would have been uneasy. He would have pined for the freedom of the whole continent. He would have longed to climb the mountains, and swim the rivers, and face the bleak winds of the plains. His soul would have yearned to carry the Gospel to the frontier settler in his rude cabin, and to gather into the fold of his Master the lost and wandering sons of neglect and the daughters of destitution. The offer of eligible settlements, of desirable alliances, of wealth, of ease, of ambitious promotion, would have been an insult to such a man. But give him enough of Gospel work to do, and room enough to work, and then, and then only, you insure him content and happiness.

He made his home at Judge White's about two years. The first year he went out but short distances from home, and preached but little. In April, 1779, he held a Conference in his secluded place of exile. The preachers of the northern stations were all present, and great harmony prevailed. So unhappy had Mr. Asbury been under his cramped and straitened circumstances through the year, that he determined, at whatever risk, to venture out from his seclusion and perform regular circuit work. Delaware was accordingly made a circuit, and Asbury appointed in charge. No sooner had he left home for some distant part of the state than his spirits began to revive. He still, however, made his headquarters at Judge White's, though he was most of the time absent on some part of his circuit. After having spent two years in Delaware, he went to Baltimore to attend the Conference of 1780. He had become a citizen of Delaware, and returned to Maryland under the recommendation and protection of the governor of Delaware. By this means he avoided all further interruption, and was permitted to prosecute his work without hinderance.

A judicious and conciliatory letter was adopted and sent to the south, in order, if possible, to prevent the threatened division. The letter, however, failed to produce any material effect. At the Conference held in Virginia, a few weeks after the session of the Northern Conference in Delaware, the southern preachers resolved to proceed in the work they deemed so necessary. They accordingly appointed a committee of the most respectable and elderly men among them to ordain the preachers. The committee first ordained themselves and then the other members of the Conference: They then went forth to administer the ordinances among their people.

Mr. Asbury could by no means approve these measures. The proceeding was altogether a violation of Methodist economy. His heart and intellect at once became devoted to unremitting efforts to reclaim the dissenting brethren. He wrote them a long, an able, and an affectionate letter. He endeavoured to persuade the dissenters to be content to receive the ordinances from the hands of the Episcopal clergy. They replied that the Methodist people would not receive the ordinances from the hands of ministers who were confessedly unconverted men, and many of them notoriously immoral in their conduct. Asbury could but acknowledge the force of the objections ; yet still he could not permit a course so irregular as the southern preachers had taken. Fearing a separation inevitable, he yet determined to rescue as many as possible from the disastrous effects of the schism.

A few days before the session of the Northern Conference for 1780, he received a letter from one of the Virginia preachers encouraging him to hope for effecting a reconciliation by conciliatory and prudent measures. When the Conference assembled, the Virginia difficulties became matter of earnest debate. Some were for disowning, at once, all who had presumed to administer the ordinances contrary to the order of the Church of England. Asbury proposed a union, on condition that the dissentients should ordain no more ; that they should not presume to administer the ordinances where there was a decent Episcopal minister ; and that they should consent to hold, with the north, a union Conference. The consent of the Conference could not be obtained to these terms of union, and there seemed no alternative but a final separation. In this extremity Asbury made one effort more. He moved that a committee be appointed to proceed to the Southern Conference, and to propose a suspension of all proceedings respecting the ordinances for one year. He hoped that, through communication with Mr. Wesley, some plan might, in the mean time, be devised to prevent the disastrous results of a separation. To this plan the Conference assented. Asbury, William Watters, the oldest native preacher in the connection, and the amiable and accomplished Freeborn Garrettson, were appointed the committee. With much anxiety, and many fears for the result, the committee proceeded to Virginia.

The Conference met. Asbury, on being desired by the members

E

to open the case, read Wesley's "Thoughts against Separation" from the Church, exhibited his own private letters and instructions from Wesley, and explained to them the sentiments of the Conferences held at Delaware and at Baltimore.   He then preached a public discourse, in which he prudently omitted all allusion to existing difficulties, presenting only a plain exhibition of Gospel truth, accompanied by a warm and affectionate exhortation.

The morning session of Conference thus closed with the prospect of satisfactory adjustment of all difficulties.   In the afternoon when they met it seemed there was little disposition to compromise. Asbury, with his colleagues, explicitly stated the conditions of union, mildly expostulating with the dissenters, and firmly insisting on the terms of compromise as the basis on which he and the Northern Conference could agree.   He then left them to deliberate on the matter.   After an hour the Conference informed him they could not accept the terms of union.   On receiving intelligence of their decision Asbury was overwhelmed with such a cloud of sorrow as never before had settled on his soul.   He wept, his associates wept, and the committee appointed by the Conference to announce their decision wept.   All hope of preventing a final division among the Methodists vanished.   Henceforth the people, who ought to be united in sentiment and in practice, harmoniously labouring to spread Scriptural holiness over the land, would be distracted by dissension, and driven by rivalry into measures of hostile aggression on each other.   With a sorrowful spirit and desponding heart, Asbury kneeled alone in his chamber before the Lord, and poured out his full soul in fervent prayer.   He then called at the Conference room to bid them farewell.   Great was the joy of his heart on learning at the door that the Conference had yielded.   The terms of compromise were adopted, the conditions of union accepted, and the Methodists were one again.   After mutual congratulations, the eloquent William Watters delivered a sermon on that appropriate text, "Come thou with us, and we will do thee good; for the Lord hath spoken good concerning Israel."   After preaching they held a love-feast.   It was an affecting, a glorious time. Preachers and people talked, and wept, and sung, and shouted. The spirit of dissension was effectually laid.   The Methodist community throughout America was yet one and inseparable.

CHAPTER VI.

THE gloomy clouds which hung bodingly over the horizon of the infant Church having been dispersed, Asbury started from the Conference with a light and joyous heart. His first visit was to Petersburg, and from thence he passed through the country, preaching from house to house everywhere, spreading abroad the savor of peace and union. There were then but few churches in the country, and he held forth the word of life in barns and cabins, and in the woods wherever a congregation could be collected. An extract or two from his Journal will show how hard was his service and how poor his fare : " We set out," he says, " for Crump's, over rocks, hills, creeks, and pathless woods. The young man with me was heartless before we had travelled a mile ; but when he saw how I could bush it, and sometimes force my way through a thicket and make the young saplings bend before me, and twist and turn out of the way or path, for there was no road, he took courage. With great difficulty we came into the settlement about two o'clock, after travelling eight or nine hours, the people looking almost as wild as the deer in the woods. I have only time to pray and write in my Journal ; always upon the wing ; as the rides are so long and the roads so bad, it takes me many hours, as in general I walk my horse. I crossed Rocky River about ten miles from Haw River. It was rocky sure enough. I can see little else but cabins in these

parts built with poles. I crossed Deep River in a ferry boat, and
the poor ferryman swore because I had not a shilling to give him."
These were every-day occurrences, experienced in many sections of
the country visited by this indefatigable man. From Virginia and
North Carolina he travelled to Pennsylvania, Delaware, and New
Jersey.

On the 24th of May, 1781, Conference convened in Baltimore.
The preachers from the South were present, and all but one of them
concurred in the action of the preceding Conference in suspending
the administration of the ordinances. Great unanimity prevailed
among all the ministers, and they were of one heart and one mind,
possessing the unity of the Spirit in the bond of peace. The large
majority of the preachers set their names to a resolution, that they
would preach the doctrines of primitive Methodism contained in the
standards of the Church, and that they would faithfully enforce
the discipline. At this Conference regulations were adopted relating to local preachers, and certain matters pertaining to the
duty of travelling preachers in reference to the exercise of discipline.

Among the preachers who located at this Conference, was John
Dickins, who, just one year before, according to Asbury's Journal,
drew up the subscription for a Kingswood school in America, which
afterward assumed the more imposing name of Cokesbury College.
About this more hereafter.

Soon after this Conference Asbury wrote to Wesley, and laid
before him in detail the exact condition of affairs in the Methodist
Church. Having settled all matters pertaining to his superintendency, he set out to travel through the bounds of his work.
He directed his course for the south branch of the Potomac, and
travelled through a wild romantic region. After swimming his
horse over the Great Capon river, fatigued and weary he found
rest in the cabin of a friendly settler. His resting place, however,
was on the top of a chest, and his clothes his only covering. This,
however, was better far than he often had. Frequently, when
benighted in the wilderness, he had slept on the ground, or on
rocks, or on some boards in a deserted cabin, with nothing to eat.
Being unable to cross the South Branch, he was obliged, as the
explorers express it, to strike for the mountains. On the summit
of one of these ranges he found a congregation as wild as the
wilderness around them. Here he remained over Sabbath, and
the mountain settlers were summoned far and near to listen to the
word. When the hour for preaching came about two hundred
persons were collected, and the voice of prayer and praise waked
the echoes of the mountain. From hence he went to another

appointment. On his route he had a view of what is called Hanging Rock Castle. The walls of this wonderful structure rise up three hundred feet high, and seem as if built with square slate stones. At his last preaching place he had three hundred hearers. Crossing the South Branch he entered a settlement of Germans, and as he could not preach in that language he expressed a wish that the Methodist Church had German preachers, as he could see by the spirit of the people that a great work might be wrought among them. What Asbury sighed for has since been fully realized, and the Methodist Church embraces in its fold thousands of German members and whole districts of German preachers.

Anon we find Asbury in the valley. Above and around him rose up in their grandeur the Alleghanies, furnishing themes of thought for the loftiest contemplation, and inspiring a mind like his with profound emotions of reverence and love for the hand that had reared them, and covered their summits with living verdure. In crossing the Fork Mountain he found another German settlement, and was much comforted in spirit in striving to preach to them. Near the preaching place was a large spring of great depth and clearness. Within two hundred yards from this source, the quantity of water discharged was sufficient in volume to turn a mill. About half a mile distant was another natural curiosity. Two caves were to be seen about two hundreds yards apart. The entrances to both are narrow, but grow wider and deeper as they are entered, until the explorer finds himself in the midst of wide and lofty chambers, supported by curiously formed pillars. In one of these chambers Asbury, inspired by the scene, sung,

"Still out of the deepest abyss
Of trouble I mournfully cry."

The stalactites, to the mind of the preacher, resembled the pipes of an immense organ, and when struck emitted a melodious sound, the intonations varying according to the size of the stalactites. The walls, which rose up in gloomy grandeur around him, and from which projected galleries, very much resembled an old cathedral. To a mind more romantic in its cast than that of Asbury the scenery in this wonderful chamber might have seemed more grand and magnificent, but it could not have excited profounder love and adoration for the wonderful and beautiful in the creations of God.

Interesting as were the scenes around him, and much as they invited to study, the Master called, and he must away on his errand. Some nights after we find him on the banks of Lost River, sympathizing with and praying for the men who had been drafted for the army. Again we find him benighted in the mountains, sleeping among the rocks, with nothing for his covering but the vaulted sky. Thus on he travelled until he reached Leesburg, where he held a quarterly meeting, and from thence he pursued his way, preaching from place to place, through Maryland and Pennsylvania.

The next Conference was held at Ellis's, in Virginia, on the 17th of April, 1782, and adjourned from thence to Baltimore, May 21. The number of preachers received on trial and into full connection during the sessions of this Conference was twenty, and the whole number sixty-six. The numbers in society had increased to eleven thousand seven hundred and eighty-five. The interchange of the preachers after six months on the different stations, a regulation early adopted, was kept up at this Conference. The appointment of Asbury by Wesley as General Superintendent of the Methodist Church in America was unanimously confirmed by the Conference. The difficulty under which they laboured as unordained ministers, and hence unable according to the canons of the Episcopal Church to administer the sacraments of baptism and the Lord's supper, still continued, and proved a serious embarrassment to them in their labours. They found, however, in the person of the Rev. Mr. Jarratt, a minister of the Established Church, of unquestioned piety and greatly esteemed by all, a friendly coadjutor, and one who was ever ready, as far as possible, to attend the quarterly meetings and administer the sacraments. Impressed with the value of his services, the Conference passed a unanimous resolution expressive of their gratitude for his kind offices, so cheerfully rendered.

Had all the ministers of that Church possessed the same probity and virtue, and the same enlarged Christian benevolence as this man, much unhappy excitement would have been prevented, and much discontent quieted. As it was, the disaffection which existed, as we have seen, was of such a nature as seriously to threaten the disruption of the Church, but through the influence of Asbury's master spirit it was so far allayed as to produce no manifest disturbance or outbreak in the Conference, and the preachers resolved to wait the openings of Providence in relation to their duty in this regard. The Churches under the jurisdiction of the Conference were generally in a prosperous condition, and revivals of considerable interest prevailed in various portions of Virginia and Maryland.

Asbury started out on his eleventh tour refreshed in spirit. He had separated from his brother ministers in all probability never again to see them all in this world, but his benediction rested upon all of them, and his prayers followed them to their different and distant fields of itinerant toil. The first day he rode upward of thirty miles without taking a morsel of food, but, like his houseless and homeless Master, he murmured not. The following day, which was the Sabbath, he preached at Boisseau's Chapel, and in the afternoon in the barn of the beloved Jarratt. This devoted man, like the sainted Fletcher, (whose timely assistance was of great service to Wesley in the early days of Methodism,) had fully partaken of the Methodist spirit, and without fear or reluctance had identified himself with the American itinerants. From hence he rode to Amelia, again without food during the whole of the journey. The next day he rode forty miles, and preached in the Broken-backed church on the Fluvanna circuit. Thus he kept on preaching at various places in Virginia until he reached Baltimore, where the Conference was to continue its session as above mentioned. Great harmony prevailed among all the preachers. The character of each was examined and passed in regular order. At this Conference a plan for publishing books was proposed, but as it was thought the time had not arrived for engaging in this enterprise it was suspended until a future period. During the two weeks' succeeding Conference, Asbury travelled through Maryland and Pennsylvania, a distance of between two and three hundred miles, crossing the mountains on foot and preaching seventeen times in the woods and cabins to the widely scattered inhabitants. From hence he went into Delaware and Virginia, and on the 25th of August, 1783, we find him in New York. From New York he went to New England, and in his travels visited the town of Salem, where the Methodists received liberal assistance from the Quakers in building a house of worship. Finishing his tour in this region, he bent his course southward, and went to North Carolina, and after preaching at different points returned to Virginia. As the Conference was aproaching, he directed his course toward the place of its meeting, which was Ellis's, in Sussex county, from which place, according to a resolution at the previous conference, it was to be adjourned to Baltimore.

As usual on the approach of the Conference, the mind of Asbury was intensely exercised in relation to the general interests of the Church. What perhaps occasioned him greater anxiety than anything else, was the arrangement for the work in the appointments of the preachers. To place himself in the position and stead of all his brethren, and act toward each as he would have them act toward him under similar circumstances, was a work that required a vast amount of thoughtful deliberation, self-examination, and prayer. The still solemn hour of night often witnessed his deep agonizing prayer for that wisdom which was " pure, peaceable, easy to be entreated," and which was " without partiality and without hypocrisy," that he might administer the affairs of the Church with " a conscience void of offence toward God and man." The Conference at Ellis's having lasted two days, closed in peace and harmony, and was afterward resumed in Baltimore.

At this Conference there were reported eighty-two preachers, and thirteen thousand seven hundred and forty members, a large increase over the former year. It seems from Asbury's Journal that a preacher, named William Glendenning, had been devising a scheme to deprive him of the general superintendency, or at least to curtail his powers and prerogatives. The letter, however, which had been received from Mr. Wesley was so clear and decisive on that point that an end was put to all controversy. The letter is dated Bristol, October 3, 1783, and is as follows : —

" 1. Let all of you be determined to abide by the Methodist doctrine and discipline published in the four volumes of Sermons, and the Notes upon the New Testament, together with the Large Minutes of Conference.

" 2. Beware of preachers coming from Great Britain or Ireland without a full recommendation from me. Three of our travelling preachers have eagerly desired to go to America, but I could not approve of it by any means, because I am not satisfied that they thoroughly like either our discipline or our doctrine. I think they differ from our judgment in one or both. Therefore, if these or any other come without my recommendation take care how you receive them.

" 3. Neither should you receive any preachers, however recommended, who will not be subject to the American Conference, and cheerfully conform to the Minutes both of the American and English Conferences.

" 4. I do not wish our American brethren to receive any who make any difficulty on receiving *Francis Asbury* as the general assistant. Undoubtedly the greatest danger to the work of God in America is likely to arise either from preachers coming from Europe, or from such as will arise from among yourselves speaking perverse things, or bringing in among you new doctrines, particularly Calvinism. You should guard against this with all possible care, for it is easier to keep them out than to thrust them out. I commend you all to the grace of God, and am your affectionate friend and brother,

" J. WESLEY."

This was a timely letter, full of that kind of counsel most needed at that time. Had Wesley been a prophet he could not have uttered sayings more truthful, and the subsequent history of the Church shows most conclusively that his predictions were founded in a wise and truthful foresight.

From Ellis's, Asbury started out on his tour, and crossed the mountains, directing his course toward Redstone. Passing Little Meadows he took the Braddock-road, a rough and dangerous way. Finding no accommodations, and being much exhausted by the journey, he was attacked by a fever and suffered much, but still rode on, preaching the next day. Thus he continued his journey until he reached Pennsylvania, and thence proceeded to Maryland. While at Worley's, where he preached to a hundred and fifty people, he heard of the capture of Richard Williams, who was taken by the Indians on the north branch of the Potomac. A few days before Braddock's defeat, it seems that nineteen Indians attacked his father's house, killing both his father and mother and one of his nephews. Williams and his child were taken as prisoners, and carried to Fort Pitt, now Pittsburgh. They tied his hands to a tree every night to prevent his escape. At the fort he was deprived of his child. On the day of Braddock's defeat he was taken across the Ohio river, and sent under guard to Detroit. After remaining there some time he stole a Frenchman's gun and some ammunition, and made his escape, travelling most of the time through the woods. He was pursued by the Indians, who succeeded in heading him, which obliged him to turn out of his course. In crossing a stream the water went over his head and wet his powder. For three days he travelled on without any food, except some roots which he dug as he passed along. Journeying on he came to a river, in the middle of which he saw two canoe loads of Indians. After they passed out of sight he made a raft of logs and crossed over. During all this time he subsisted on what he could pick up by the way. At length he reached the Ohio river, where he was surprised by an Indian who threw a tomahawk at him, but he escaped and succeeded in crossing the river. He was pursued and recaptured by two Frenchmen and five Indians. By these he was again taken to Fort Pitt. Being known as a deserter, a council was held, and he was condemned to be shot. He, however, feigned derangement, and seemed not to understand what was said to him. Again he made his escape, was pursued, seven guns were fired at him in succession by his pursuers, but still he eluded them. Again he was overtaken and fired upon, but again he made his escape. For five days he lived on acorns. One day, while picking some wild cherries, an

Indian rushed upon him with a whoop and seized him, when presently others joined him, and he was again a prisoner. After being in their possession a long time he at length made his escape and reached home, where he found his wife who had been praying for him constantly. Both were faithful members of the Methodist Church, and subsequently preaching was held at their house.

We have related this to show what was the state of the western country, and what the trials of its inhabitants, when Asbury and his fellow-labourers penetrated the wilderness to preach the Gospel to its destitute population.

The next place at which we find Asbury was at quarterly meeting in Philadelphia, whence he went to Burlington, New Jersey, and thence on to New York. Of New York he says : " We found the people alive to God. There are about one hundred in society, and with those in Philadelphia, to my mind, they appear more like Methodists than I have ever yet seen them." He was greatly comforted by this visit, and the members manifested their regard for him by supplying all his necessities. After visiting several contiguous places and preaching, he returned to New Jersey and Maryland. On Sunday, November 14, 1784, at Barratt's Chapel, he met Dr. Coke and Richard Whatcoat. This was his first interview since their arrival in the country. When they made known to him the object of their visit and the powers with which they were intrusted by Wesley, he was perfectly astounded. The idea of his not only having the superintendency, but of his being ordained to that office, was more than he could think of assuming in connection with Wesleyan Methodism ; and he had, to use his own language, come to the determination that if his brethren should unanimously choose him to that office, he would not accept it in the capacity he had hitherto done under Wesley's appointment.

Before the departure of Coke and Whatcoat from England, Wesley had abridged the Book of Common Prayer, and with the assistance of Dr. Coke and Rev. Mr. Creighton, of the Church of England, he set apart by solemn ordination Richard Whatcoat and Thomas Vasey as elders for the Church in America. After this he ordained Dr. Coke as superintendent of the Methodist Church in America, and gave him letters of ordination under his hand and seal, accompanied by a letter, in which he appointed Dr. Coke and Francis Asbury joint superintendents over the Church in America.

The country having declared itself independent of Great Britain, peace having been obtained and commercial relations restored, the question of an independent Church was considerably discussed by the preachers. The prevalent opinion was that the time had arrived for the organization of a separate and distinct Church, free from all ecclesiastical alliance with the British Conference or the Established Church. On the arrival of Dr. Coke with his powers the subject was renewed with greater interest than ever. As the result of a mutual discussion and interchange of opinion among several of the more aged preachers, it was determined to call a General Conference, to meet in Baltimore on the 25th of December, 1784. The Rev. Freeborn Garrettson, who had been early identified with the preachers, and who was a native American, was deputed to go to Virginia and the South and notify the preachers of the intended Conference. As Asbury was desirous of making Dr. Coke acquainted with the preachers and their work, he took him out on a tour from circuit to circuit. At Bohemia they met Vasey, and in company they passed on to quarterly meeting at Deer Creek. Their next appointment was at Gough's. After remaining in this place near a week, they rode to Frederick and held a quarterly meeting, and from thence went to Calvert quarterly meeting. Here Asbury met with Poythress, with whom he had a long and intimate conversation in regard to the contemplated Conference and the new matters which should come before it. The love-feast which was held here was one of great interest and power. The work of religion among the coloured people excited the attention of Asbury much.

It was now within one month of the meeting of Conference, and as the time approached Asbury became more and more absorbed in regard to the momentous questions which would be discussed. He set apart seasons for fasting and special prayer, that he might know the divine will in relation to that point in which he was particularly interested. The preachers and people generally, so far as his knowledge extended, seemed to look upon the contemplated arrangement with favor, and from this he was led to infer the Divine approval. But he was in no way elated with the prospect of advancement to the episcopal office. He was "not high-minded, but feared," as his clear and sagacious foresight assured him that the position would be attended with difficulty and danger. Soon after this he had an interesting conversation with the Rev. Mr. Weems, the subsequent biographer of Washington, on the subject of Episcopal Church government. On the fourth of December he preached in Baltimore, and subsequently at the Point, and from that time he devoted himself almost entirely to preparation for the coming Conference.

CHAPTER VII.

Length of Time in America—His Age—An unordained Preacher—Number of Preachers and Members—Character of the Preachers associated with him—Marsden's Description of Asbury—"Christmas General Conference"—Dr. Coke—Wesley's Letter—An important Occasion—A distinct and separate Organization—Title of Church—Office of Bishop elective—Coke and Asbury elected Bishops—Ordination of Asbury—Ordination Sermon—Ordination of Deacons—Power exercised by Asbury as an Assistant Superintendent under Wesley—Conference defines the Duty of a Bishop—Abuse of Power—Character of the present Episcopacy—Short Obituaries—Asbury's first Sermon as a Bishop—Change in his Journal—Effect of Administration of the Ordinances by Asbury on other Churches—Charleston, South Carolina—Lee—Willis—Conferences—New Circuits—Great Revivals—York—Surrender of Lord Cornwallis—Alexandria—Visit to George Washington—Bath Springs—Preaches in a Theatre—Baltimore—Philadelphia—New York—Heavy Labours—Liberality of New York Methodists—Asbury's first Wagon—Last Wagon.

FIFTEEN years had elapsed since Asbury commenced preaching in America. He was now forty years of age, and more than half of his life had been spent in preaching the Gospel, yet up to this time he was an unordained man. No ordinances of the Church had ever yet been administered by his hands, and he consented with the rest of his brethren in the ministry to receive the sacrament at the hands of the Episcopal priesthood. He had witnessed the progress of the Church in America from a feeble beginning, and had watched over it with the tenderest solicitude. When he entered upon the work there were but eight preachers, and a membership of only about six hundred ; now the number of preachers was one hundred and four, and the membership had risen to fifteen thousand. The preachers associated with him were all men of character, remarkably adapted to the times, and some of them were not a whit behind ministers of other denominations for eloquence and scholarly attainment. If Methodism in England could boast of its Wesley and Fletcher, American Methodism could boast of its Asbury and Coke. They act neither wisely nor justly who, in speaking of our fathers, offer disparaging hints as to their want of education, and their inefficiency on that account. They were not all learned in the schools, perhaps, because such facilities were not afforded them. Nor did they need such learning. They were not as a general thing brought into contact with the learned, but with that stern and sturdy manhood which is the result of an every-day battle with the realities of life. Deep students they were in the things of nature and the mysteries of God. Shut up to their Bibles and communion with the Father of spirits, they obtained an insight into the operations of the human mind and a knowledge of spiritual things which gave them a power over men, and a power with God, such as the closetted theologian, surrounded by his tomes of speculative divinity, never could attain. Often has the remark been made of Asbury that "he could read men," an acquisition, for one whose mission was among the masses, vastly superior to that of an ability to read Sanscrit, or any or all of the languages living or dead. The following, as an illustration of his remarkable penetration and ability to look beneath the exterior, and judge of human character, is related in Cartwright's Autobiography. The incident occurred at one of the Western Conferences : " The Conference had been preceded by glorious revivals of religion, and many of the wealthy, and some of the learned, had joined the Methodist Episcopal Church, among whom were two very learned young men ; one of them the son of a very distinguished, learned teacher, the other the son of a general—a distinguished, wealthy man. Both of these young men professed to have a call to the ministry, and came with a recommendation to the Conference to be received on trial in the travelling connection. They were both present, and Bishop Asbury had narrowly observed their conduct and conversation. At the proper time Brother Learner Blackman, their presiding elder, presented their recommendations. He spoke of them in the highest terms, and considered them a great acquisition to the ministry and the Church. The Conference received them with great unanimity. Bishop Asbury had sat with his eyes nearly shut. After they were received he seemed to wake up. 'Yes, yes !' he exclaimed ; 'in all probability they both will disgrace you and themselves before the year is out.' And sure enough, in six months one was riding the circuit with a loaded pistol and a dirk, threatening to shoot and stab the rowdies ; the other was guilty of a misdemeanor, and in less than nine months they were both out of the Church." Asbury was gifted with a wonderful power of discernment, and rarely failed in his judgment of human character.

The Rev. Joshua Marsden thus describes him : " Bishop Asbury was one of those very few men whom nature forms in no ordinary mould. His mind was stamped with a certain greatness and originality which lifted him far above the merely learned man, and fitted him to be great without science, and venerable without titles. His knowledge of men was profound and penetrating ; hence he looked into character as one looks into a clear stream in order to discover

the bottom ; yet he did not use this penetration to compass any
unworthy purposes ; the policy of knowing men in order to make
the most of them, was a littleness to which he never stooped. He
had only one end in view, and that was worthy the dignity of an
angel ; from this nothing ever warped him aside. He seemed conscious that God had designed him for a great work, and nothing
was wanting on his part to fulfil the intention of Providence.
The niche was cut in the great temple of usefulness, and he stretched
himself to fill it up in all its dimensions. To him the widest career
of labour and duty presented no obstacle. Like a moral Cæsar, he
thought nothing done while anything remained to do. His penetrating eye measured the ground over which he intended to sow
the seeds of eternal life, while his courageous and active mind
cheerfully embraced all the difficulties engrafted upon his labors.
He worshipped no god of the name of *Terminus*, but stretched
'his line of things' far beyond the bounds of ordinary minds. An
annual journey of six thousand miles through a wilderness would
have sunk a feebler mind into despondency; but nothing retarded
his progress, or once moved him from the line of duty. He pursued
the most difficult and laborious course as most men do their
pleasures ; and although for many years he was enfeebled by
sickness, and worn with age and infirmity, two hundred thousand
persons saw with astonishment the hoary veteran 'still standing in
his lot,' or 'pressing his vast line' of duty with undiminished zeal.
The Methodist connection in united America gloried in having
such a man to preside at their head, and few of the preachers ever
spoke of his integrity, diligence, and zeal, without imputing to
themselves some worth in having him as their bishop. To all that
bore the appearance of polished and pleasing life he was dead ; and
both from habit and divine grace had acquired such a true greatness
of mind, that he seemed to estimate nothing as excellent but what
tended to the glory of God. Flattery, of which many great minds
are highly susceptible, found him fortified behind a double guard
of humility, and opposition but served to awaken those energies of
mind which rise with difficulties and surmount the greatest. He
knew nothing about pleasing the flesh at the expense of duty ;
flesh and blood were enemies with whom he never took counsel ; he
took a high standing upon the rugged Alps of labour, and to all that
lagged behind, he said, 'Come up hither.' He was a rigid enemy
to ease ; hence the pleasures of study and the charms of recreation
he alike sacrificed to the more sublime work of saving souls. His
faith was a 'constant evidence of things not seen,' for he lived as a
man totally blind to all worldly attractions. It is true that his

self-denial savoured of austerity, and yet he could sympathize with another's weakness. Some great and good men have had their sportive moments, and without committing 'half a sin,' have both smiled themselves and been amused with others. But, although I have been in his company upon a variety of occasions, I never saw him indulge in even innocent pleasantry ; his was the solemnity of an apostle ; it was so interwoven with his conduct that he could not put off the gravity of the bishop either in the parlour or dining-room. What, on account of levity, was once said of a popular preacher, that he should either never go in or never come out of a pulpit, could never be applied to him. Wisdom is not more distant from folly than his conduct was from anything akin to trifling. He had stated hours of retirement and prayer, upon which he let neither business nor company break in. Prayer was the seasoning of all his avocations ; he never suffered the cloth to be removed from the table until he had kneeled down to address the Almighty ; it was the preface to all business, and often the link that connected opposite duties, and the conclusion of whatever he took in hand. Divine wisdom seemed to direct all his undertakings, for he sought its counsels upon all occasions ; no part of his conduct was the result of accident ; the plan by which he transacted all his affairs was as regular as the movements of a time-piece, hence he had no idle moments, no fragments of time broken and scattered up and down ; no cause to say with Titus, 'my friends I have lost a day.' Pleading with God in secret, settling the various affairs of the body over which he presided, or speaking ' to men for their edification' in the pulpit, occupied all time.

"As a preacher, although not an orator, he was dignified, eloquent, and impressive ; his sermons were the result of good sense and sound wisdom, delivered with great authority and gravity, and often attended with Divine unction, which made them as refreshing as the dew of heaven. One of the last subjects I heard him preach upon was union and brotherly love ; it was the greatest I ever heard upon that subject."

One who was intimately acquainted with him said to the writer : " Asbury was the only preacher I ever heard who preached *to* his text. He never preached *from* it, as many do who select a passage as the mere theme of a discourse, the discussion of which would be as applicable to an axiom of Coleridge as to the text, but he would start a proposition, and in its elaboration would come directly *to* the text. With him, proposition, argument, illustration, incident, everything was either immediately drawn from or directly connected with the subject of discourse."

The Rev. Joseph Travis, of the Memphis Conference, says of him: "Any one of discernment and judgment who has heard Bishop Asbury preach could not but notice his chaste though plain style, his grammatical correctness, without the redundancy of rhetorical figures. In argumentation he abounded in *enthymemes* without the circumlocution of logical propositions. Indeed, he was a learned man, and in science of theology had but few equals if any superiors."

The 25th of December, 1784, at length arrived, and Baltimore witnessed the gathering of sixty out of the whole number of preachers to the annual convocation. Dr. Coke was present at the Conference, and gave great satisfaction by his urbanity, and the impartial manner in which he presided.

The first thing brought before the body was the letter of Wesley, which was subjected to a calm and thorough deliberation. As this letter presents Wesley's reasons for acting as he did, and at the same time is an unanswerable defence of the subsequent action of the Conference, we give it entire.

BRISTOL, *September* 10, 1784.

"To Dr. COKE, MR. FRANCIS ASBURY, AND OUR BRETHREN IN NORTH AMERICA:

" 1. By a very uncommon train of providences many of the provinces of North America are totally disjoined from the British empire, and erected into independent states. The English government has no authority over them, either civil or ecclesiastical, any more than over the states of Holland. A civil authority is exercised over them partly by the Congress, and partly by the state assemblies. But no one either exercises or claims any ecclesiastical authority at all. In this peculiar situation some thousands of the inhabitants of these states desire my advice, and in compliance with their desire I have drawn up a little sketch.

" 2. Lord King's Account of the Primitive Church convinced me many years ago that bishops and presbyters are the same order, and consequently have the same right to ordain. For many years I have been importuned from time to time to exercise this right by ordaining part of our travelling preachers, but I have still refused, not only for peace' sake, but because I was determined as little as possible to violate the established order of the national Church to which I belong.

" 3. But the case is widely different between England and North America. Here there are bishops who have a legal jurisdiction. In America there are none, and but few parish ministers, so that for some hundred miles together there is none either to baptize or to administer the Lord's Supper. Here, therefore, my scruples are at an end, and I conceive myself at full liberty, as I violate no order and invade no man's right by appointing and sending labourers into the harvest.

"4. I have accordingly appointed Dr. Coke and Mr. Francis Asbury to be joint superintendents over our brethren in North America, as also Richard Whatcoat and Thomas Vasey to act as *elders* among them by administering baptism and the Lord's Supper.

"5. If any one will point out a more rational and Scriptural way of feeding and guiding those poor sheep in the wilderness, I will gladly embrace it. At present I cannot see any better method than that I have taken.

"6. It has, indeed, been proposed to desire the English bishops to ordain part of our preachers for America. But to this I object, (1.) I desired the Bishop of London to ordain one only, but could not prevail. (2.) If they consented, we know the slowness of their proceedings ; but the matter admits of no delay. (3.) If they would ordain them now they would likewise expect to govern them, and how grievously would this entangle us. (4.) As our American brethren are now totally disentangled, both from the state and the English hierarchy, we dare not entangle them again either with the one or the other. They are now at full liberty simply to follow the Scriptures and the primitive Church. And we judge it best they should stand fast in that liberty wherewith God has so strangely made them free.   "JOHN WESLEY."

Never before had the preachers met on so important and solemn an occasion. Fifteen years had passed away since Wesley's first missionaries, Boardman and Pilmoor, arrived in America. Fourteen Conferences had been held, and again the toiling itinerants had assembled from their different and distant fields of labour and conquest to congratulate each other on the success which had attended their ministrations. After the necessary action had been taken by which they constituted themselves and fellow members a distinct and separate Church, the question came up in regard to the title by which they should be designated. At this crisis John Dickins, a man of varied learning, sound sense, and sterling piety, than whom none of the entire Conference commanded greater respect, rose and proposed *The Methodist Episcopal Church*, which was adopted without a dissenting voice.

The first act of the Conference, therefore, was to adopt a decla-

F

ration that the Methodist societies are free and independent, and organise them into a body ever after to be known as *The Methodist Episcopal Church in the United States.* The next act was to declare the office of bishop elective, after which a unanimous vote was cast in favour of Dr. Thomas Coke and Francis Asbury as bishops of this church.

Asbury, being up to his election unordained, was first ordained a deacon and then an elder. After this ceremony of consecration, Dr. Coke, assisted by several elders, set him apart by the imposition of hands as Bishop of the Methodist Episcopal Church. The following is the certificate of his ordination :

"Know all men by these presents, That I, Thomas Coke, Doctor of Civil Law, late of Jesus College, in the University of Oxford, Presbyter of the Church of England and Superintendent of the Methodist Episcopal Church in America, under the protection of Almighty God, and with a single eye to his glory, by the imposition of my hands and prayer (being assisted by two ordained elders) did, on the twenty-fifth day of this month (December) set apart Francis Asbury for the office of a deacon in the aforesaid Methodist Episcopal Church. And also on the 26th day of the said month did, by the imposition of my hands and prayer (being assisted by the said elders) set apart the said Francis Asbury for the office of elder in the said Methodist Episcopal Church. And on this twenty-seventh day of the said month, being the day of the date hereof, have, by the imposition of my hands and prayer (being assisted by the said elders) set apart Francis Asbury for the office of Superintendent in the said Methodist Episcopal Church, a man whom I judge to be well qualified for the great work. And I do hereby recommend him to all whom it may concern as a fit person to preside over the flock of Christ.

"In testimony hereof, I have hereunto set my hand and seal this twenty-seventh day of December, in the year of our Lord 1784.

THOMAS COKE."

A sermon was preached by Dr. Coke on the occasion from Rev. iii. 7-11. The sermon was vindicatory of the action of the Conference in its assumption of an episcopal form of government, and entered somewhat elaborately into the argument of succession, concluding with the qualifications necessary for a Christian bishop.

The office of deacon and elder being made elective, as well as that of bishop, the following twelve were elected and ordained elders : Freeborn Garrettson, William Gill, Le Roy Cole, John

Haggerty, James O. Cromwell, John Tunnel, Nelson Reed, Jeremiah Lambert, Reuben Ellis, James O'Kelly, Richard Ivey, Beverly Allen, and Henry Willis. One of these was ordained for the Island of Antigua and two for Nova Scotia. John Dickins, Caleb Boyer, and Ignatius Pigman were elected and ordained deacons.

The ordination of Asbury to the office of bishop, though it conferred upon him a new title, did not increase his power or his usefulness. His determination to submit to the will of a majority, and his unwillingness to exercise any power not delegated to him by his brother preachers, deprived him of the power he exercised under the appointment of Wesley as General Superintendent or assistant. Acting as he did in Wesley's stead, his power was almost, if not quite, absolute in the Conference, and the right was conceded to him at any time to stop discussion on any subject, and decide the question when in his judgment enough had been said on both sides. From this decision there was no appeal. His acts in deciding questions, as well as in stationing the preachers, were peremptory and final. At this Conference, however, under the question, "What is the duty of a bishop?" the following answer is given : "To preside as moderator in our Conferences, fix the appointments of the preachers for the several circuits, and in the interval of the Conference to change, receive, or suspend preachers as necessity may require ; to travel through as many circuits as he can, and to direct in the spiritual business of the societies, as also to ordain bishops, elders, and deacons." In 1789 was added : "The bishop has obtained liberty by the suffrages of the Conference to ordain local preachers to the office of deacons, provided they obtain a testimonial from the society to which they belong, and from the stewards of the circuit, signed by three travelling preachers, three deacons, and three elders (one of them being presiding elder), the names of those nominated being read in the Conference previous to their ordination."

It was doubtless an abuse of the power exercised by Rankin as superintendent which brought him in collision with the preachers, and induced him at one time to complain of Asbury to Wesley ; and it was doubtless the experience of Asbury in regard to the operation of this part of the machinery of Church government that prompted him to take the course he did in refusing the episcopate without the unanimous concurrence of his brother preachers, and also, no doubt, to him is to be ascribed the moderate episcopacy which has ever since characterised the Church.

Our bishops now rarely, if ever, speak in Conference on any subject not immediately connected with their office, and never ad-

vance an opinion unless solicited by the action of the Conference,
much less presume to decide questions of debate. We have even
known them voted down when in the exercise of the only right
they have in deciding questions of order. Their decisions of law
are subject to quadrennial revision, and may be wholly set aside
by the General Conference. They have not even the right which
is allowed to every president and moderator of any and every
ecclesiastical assembly with which we are acquainted, to vote on
any question, no matter how vital to Methodism. They have
never in any instance transcended their powers, but, as those who
have been placed by the Holy Spirit in the position of overseers,
have always commended themselves by their holy lives, and their
zeal and self-sacrificing devotion to all the interests of the Church.

We find in the Minutes of this memorable Conference two short
obituaries under the question "Who have died this year?" This
was the first time this question appeared in the Minutes. Death
had not before invaded the ranks of the regular itinerancy, and
hence no memorials of his doings were to be found on the records
of the previous Conferences. We transcribe these memoirs because of their remarkable brevity and point, and as admirable
specimens of biography. The first answer to the question, "Who
have died this year?" reads, "Caleb B. Pedicord—a man of sorrows, and, like his Master, acquainted with grief; but a man dead
to the world, and much devoted to God."

A writer, in describing Pedicord, says :—"There was one for
whom Asbury looked in vain, one who had been his companion in
many a long and dreary journey, one whose eloquent voice had
often made the hearts of listening thousands

> ' Thrill as if an angel spoke,
> Or Ariel's finger touch'd the string.'

Pedicord, the gentle spirited, the generous minded, the noble
souled, the silver-tongued Pedicord, had fallen, had fallen in his
youth, fallen in his opening glory and abundant promise. Asbury
looked for him and he was not. The grave had closed over his
body, and his spirit had passed to the land where only spirits so
refined, so sensitive, so ethereal as his find congenial sympathy and
rest."

The second answer is as follows : "George Mair—a man of
affliction, but of great patience and resignation, and of excellent
understanding."

These brief, comprehensive memoirs are more expressive than
lengthened eulogy. There is something so remarkable in these

obituaries that the reader will pardon us if we add a few more, as they are found in succeeding Minutes of the Conferences.

"Jeremiah Lambert—an elder, six years in the work ; a man of sound judgment, clear understanding, good gifts, genuine piety, and very useful, humble, and holy ; diligent in life and resigned in death ; much esteemed in the connection, and justly lamented. We do not sorrow as men without hope, but expect shortly to join him and all those who rest from their labours."

"James Thomas—a pious young man of good gifts, useful and acceptable, blameless in his life, and much resigned in his death."

"Henry Bingham—a native of Virginia, four years a labourer in the vineyard, serious, faithful, zealous, humble and teachable, and during part of the last year more than commonly successful ; fervent in exhortation during his sickness, and resigned in death."

"William Gill—a native of Delaware, an elder in the Church, and a labourer in it for about twelve years ; blameless in life, of quick and solid parts, sound in the faith, clear in his judgment, meek in his spirit, resigned and solemnly happy in his death."

"John Cooper—fifteen years in the work ; quiet, inoffensive, and blameless ; a son of affliction, subject to dejection, sorrow, and sufferings, often in want, but too modest to complain till observed and relieved by his friends. He died in peace."

"James White—a native of Maryland, about eight years in the work ; a simple-hearted man and a lively preacher ; afflicted, yet active and laborious ; soft and kind in his affections, patient in suffering, well received and much esteemed, successful in the work of God, resigned in his death."

"Francis Spry—a pious man, skillful and lively in his preaching, sound in judgment, holy in his life, placid in his mind, of unshaken confidence and patience in his death ; four years a labourer in the vineyard."

"John Tunnell, who died of a consumption at the Sweet Springs in July. He was about thirteen years in the work of the ministry, a man of solid piety, great simplicity, and godly sincerity ; well known, and much esteemed both by ministers and people. He had travelled extensively through the States, and declined in sweet peace."

After the session of Conference on Monday, Asbury preached his first sermon since his ordination. It was very evident that the imposition of hands communicated no new grace or gift, for according to his own experience he "was unsettled in mind and low in his own testimony." The next day he travelled on horseback fifty miles through frost and snow to Fairfax, Virginia. The day following he rode forty miles further, and thus continued until the Sabbath, when he halted for labour not for rest.

We now discover a change in the entries made in Asbury's Journal. Previously he gave a simple statement of his preaching, associated with the exercises of his mind, and the incidents connected with his travelling. Now, in addition to these, he records. his acts in administering the ordinances. Hence, at his Sabbath appointment he writes : " We read prayers, preached, ordained Brother Willis deacon, and baptized some children." As a part of his experience, he adds : " I am sometimes afraid of being led to think something more of myself in my new station than formerly." From Virginia he went to North Carolina. In his journey he records the usual incidents of long fatiguing rides over rough roads, crossing rivers and rugged mountains, sleeping in comfortless quarters, frequently three in a bed, and hard fare. He remarks in one place where he administered the ordinances, that "nothing could have better suited the old Church folks than the late step the Conference had taken in regard to ordination ; to the *catholic* Presbyterians it also gave satisfaction ; but the Baptists were not at all pleased with the movement, and in some instances they presented difficulties in the way of infant baptism, unsettling the minds of some." From hence he went to South Carolina, preaching at every place on the route where congregations could be collected. In reference to Charleston he says : " The Calvinists are the only people here who appear to have any sense of religion, and they are much alarmed. Yesterday (Sunday) we had small congregations in the morning and at noon, but at night we were crowded. In the evening, while Brother Lee preached, the people were a little moved." After remaining in Charleston during another week, preaching frequently through opposition from the ministers of the place, who misrepresented the doctrines of Methodism to the people, he departed on his journey. Willis, who had been ordained an elder, and accompanied Asbury and Lee to Charleston, was left to labour in the place, and, if possible, raise up a Methodist society.

During this year Asbury attended three Conferences, at which all the important business of a local nature was transacted. Five new circuits were added : Santee and Pedee in North Carolina, Newark in New Jersey, and Kentucky in the State of Kentucky. The stations in Antigua (in the West Indies) and Nova Scotia were placed on the Minutes. Great revivals prevailed in Maryland and other parts of the country, and upward of five hundred had been converted and joined the Church on Talbot Circuit alone. The membership rose to eighteen thousand, and the number of travelling preachers to one hundred and four, being an increase, in round numbers, of three thousand in the former, and of twenty-one in the latter.

On May 12th, he was at Yorktown. The inhabitants, he says, "are dissolute and careless. I preached to a few serious women at one o'clock, and at the desire of the ladies at four. I lodged in the poorhouse." After visiting other places in Virginia and Maryland, he reached Alexandria on the 25th, and on the following day, in company with Dr. Coke, dined, by invitation, with Gen. Washington, who treated them with great courtesy and respect, and expressed his concurrence in their views against slavery. For Washington, Asbury ever had the greatest regard and admiration, as will be seen in the subsequent pages of this book. While on a visit to the Bath Springs, Virginia, he preached in the theatre, and lodged under the same roof with the play-actors. Some who would not hear him preach at their respective homes, made in this new and strange place a part of his audience. His spirit was much grieved while beholding the vanity displayed by the fashionable frequenters of this watering-place. From Bath he went to Baltimore, and from thence to Philadelphia, where he had a large congregation. From Philadelphia he rode to New York, and preached on three successive days. We note his labours in this city for one Sabbath. He says : "Notwithstanding I was very unwell I preached three times, read prayers twice, and held a lovefeast." Such labours would have been abundant for a well man, but Asbury often preached while labouring under various forms of disease. Such were the necessities of the case that "his zeal consumed him." The society in New York had increased in numbers and in grace since his last visit, and the congregations were also much larger. Again was he refreshed in spirit, and comforted by the liberality of the New York Methodists in supplying his temporal wants. The next Sabbath we find him at a quarterly meeting on Morris river. In this neighbourhood he purchased what he called his first waggon, for which he gave forty pounds, but anticipated trouble in travelling and getting horses.

While the writer was stationed in Marietta in 1838, he visited a friend on Duck Creek, in Washington County, who took him into his yard and exhibited some of the remains of Asbury's "last waggon." Though he is no worshipper of relics, such was his respect and reverence for the pioneer bishop of Methodism, that he asked for and obtained a portion of this waggon from which he had a cane manufactured. This carriage had borne the bishop

around the continent again and again, but here it reached the end
of its journey, and "its weary wheels at last stood still." What
a biography could be written of that waggon! How precious has
been its freight! what adventures, incidents, and accidents could
it relate! Enough to fill a volume.

CHAPTER VIII.

John Dickins—Description of, by Asbury—Subscription for "Kingswood
    High School in America"—Claims of, presented by Asbury—Dr. Coke's
    Sympathy with the Enterprise—Suggests the Propriety of founding a College
    —Adopted by the Conference—Plan drawn up accordingly—Rules and
    Regulations—Abingdon selected as the Site—Beauty of Situation—Laying
    the Corner-Stone of Cokesbury College—Asbury's Sermon on the Occasion—
    Dedication—An ominous Text—First Faculty of the College—Rules and
    Regulations—Asbury and College Finances—Its Management a source of
    great Anxiety—Its History—Destruction by Fire—The Subject of Rebuild-
    ing agitated by Dr. Coke—A building suited to the Purpose purchased in
    Baltimore—College re-opened—Faculty—Regulations and Course of Study—
    Destroyed by Fire—School for Charity Boys in Georgia—Bethel Academy—
    Seminary in New York—Progress of Education in the Church—Remarks of
    Hon. Edward Everett.

THE name of John Dickins is early associated with education in the
Methodist Episcopal Church. While Asbury was travelling in
North Carolina in the spring of 1780, Dickins was his companion.
He occasionally preached, but labored under a bronchial affection
to such an extent that he almost entirely lost his voice. In
describing him, Asbury says: "He is a man of great piety, but he
reasons too much. He has great skill in learning, drinks in Greek
and Latin swiftly, yet prays much and walks close with God. He
is a gloomy countryman of mine, and very diffident of himself."
At this time Dickins drew up a subscription for what Asbury
called "a Kingswood School in America," and which he "hoped
would be for the glory of God and the good of thousands." Thus
the first movement toward education in the Methodist Episcopal

Church took its origin in the minds of Asbury and Dickins upward of seventy years ago. The mind of Asbury became wholly absorbed in the enterprise, and in his intercourse with the people and preachers in different parts of the country he urged its importance and presented its claims. As soon as he met Dr. Coke, after his arrival in this country, he made him acquainted with his plans. With the doctor, of course, the views and purposes of Asbury found sympathy. The design of Asbury was, however, simply the founding of a school similar to that of Kingswood, the idea of an institution having collegiate powers never having entered his mind.

When the subject was brought before the Conference, in 1785, Dr. Coke advocated the propriety of founding a college, and succeeded in securing the adoption of a resolution favoring that view, and providing the incipient measures for the establishment of such an institution.

After due consultation and deliberation the site for the college was selected in the town of Abingdon, about twenty-five miles distant from the city of Baltimore. The spot commanded a magnificent view, extending for twenty and even fifty miles. The valley of the Susquehanna spread out in beauty on either side of the river, forming a most charming landscape. In the distance was to be seen the broad and beautiful bay of the Chesapeake, stretching away as far as the eye could reach. The eminence upon which it was proposed to erect the college buildings seemed to have been formed by the God of nature as a place for the erection of a temple of science.

Through the labors of Coke and Asbury nearly five thousand dollars had been raised by donations and subscriptions for the purpose of erecting the buildings; and at length the workmen laid out the grounds, and commenced laying the foundation of an edifice one hundred and eight feet in length and forty in breadth. On Sabbath, the fifth day of June, 1785, a large concourse of people were assembled on the eminence to witness the ceremonies connected with the laying of the corner-stone of Cokesbury College, for such was the name given it by the Conference in honor of its founders. Asbury had been selected as the speaker for the occasion. Attired in his long silk gown, and with his flowing bands, the pioneer bishop of America took his position on the walls of the college and announced for his text the following : "The sayings which we have heard and known, and our fathers have told us. We will not hide them from their children, showing to the generation to come the praises of the Lord, and his strength, and his wonderful works that he hath done. For he established a testimony in Jacob, and appointed a law in Israel, which he commanded our fathers, that they should make them known to their children : that the generation to come might know them, even the children which should be born : who should arise and declare them to their children : that they might set their hope in God, and not forget the works of God, but keep his commandments." The Spirit of the Lord was with him as with Elijah at the school of the prophets at Bethel. As he dwelt upon the importance of a thorough religious education, and looked forward to the effects which would result to the generations to come from the streams which would spring from this opening fountain of sanctified learning, his soul enlarged and swelled with rapturous emotion.

The work thus auspiciously begun was carried forward to a successful completion, and those who witnessed the laying of the corner-stone also witnessed the raising of the capstone to its place with the shouts of triumphant success. On the 8th, 9th, and 10th days of December, 1787, the college was opened by religious exercises, Bishop Asbury preaching each day in the college building. The dedication sermon proper was preached on Sabbath from those singular, and what afterward proved to be ominous words, and it would seem premonitory of the fate of the college: "O man of God, there is death in the pot." The institution began with twenty-five students. The Rev. Mr. Heath was called to the presidency of the college, and his assistants in the faculty were Jacob Hall, A.M., Patrick M'Closkey, and Charles Tite.

A plan of education was adopted embracing not only a course of study, but rules and regulations for the internal arrangement which, though they might be regarded as somewhat singular at the present day, are worthy of consideration, and some of which might be wisely adopted by our colleges. The design of the institution was to educate the sons of the elders and preachers of the Methodist Church, as well as poor orphans, and the sons of its patrons and other friends, the latter of whom were expected to pay a "moderate sum for tuition and board," while the former were to be educated, boarded, and clothed gratuitously. It was also designed for the benefit of young men who were called to preach, in furnishing them facilities for prosecuting a course of study preparatory to their entering upon the work of the ministry. From the Life of Valentine Cook, written by Dr. Stevenson, and recently published, it appears that this early pioneer of the West and South, whose fervid eloquence startled many a sinner in his career of wickedness, and whose persuasive power brought many a wanderer to the fold, was instructed here. Bishop Asbury was *ex officio* president of the college, and we may claim for him the honour of being the first president of a Methodist college in America, as well as the pioneer bishop of the Church. In regard to the Church, it may be said no man ever lived who projected himself further into the future of all that pertains to her genius, government, and institutions, than did Asbury.

But to return to the college. The course of study embraced the various English branches, the Latin and Greek languages, together with Hebrew, German, and French, a curriculum whose scope is not excelled by any of our institutions of the present day. Founded as it was in religion, and designed to be the *alma mater* of a correct faith as well as sound morals, the most careful provision was made for securing these ends. Hence we find the following in the published plan :

" Our first object shall be to answer the design of Christian education, by forming the minds of the youth, through divine aid, to wisdom and holiness, by instilling into their tender minds the principles of true religion, speculative, experimental, and practical, and training them in the ancient way, that they may be rational, Scriptural Christians. For this purpose we shall expect and enjoin it, not only on the president and tutors, but also upon our elders, deacons, and preachers to embrace every opportunity of instructing the students in the great branches of the Christian religion.

" And this is one principal reason why we do not admit students indiscriminately into our college, for we are persuaded that the promiscuous admission of all sorts of youth into a seminary of learning is pregnant with many bad consequences. Nor are the students likely (suppose they possessed it) to retain much religion in a college where all that offer are admitted, however corrupted already in principle as well as in practice. And what wonder, when (as too frequently it happens) the parents themselves have no more religion than their offspring."

Who has not been struck with the wisdom of the founders of this college in their regulations in regard to the study of the classics, a wisdom which has since been acted upon in furnishing expurgated editions of the classics for our colleges. The whole plan shows conclusively that they were far in advance of the age in which they lived. In regard to this subject the plan says :

" In teaching the languages care shall be taken to read those authors, and those only, who join together the purity, the strength, and the elegance of their several tongues. And the utmost caution shall be used that nothing immodest be found in any of our books.

" But this is not all. We shall take care that our books be not only inoffensive but useful ; that they contain as much strong sense, and as much genuine morality as possible. As far, therefore, as is consistent with the foregoing observations, a choice and universal library shall be provided for the use of the students."

For the recreation of the students they say : " The employments which we have chosen are such as are of the greatest public utility, agriculture and architecture—studies more especially necessary for a new settled country ; and of consequence the instructing of our youth in all the practical branches of those important arts will be an effectual method of rendering them more useful to their country. Agreeably to this idea, the greatest statesman that perhaps ever shone in the annals of history, Peter, the Russian emperor, who was deservedly styled the Great, disdained not to stoop to the employment of a ship carpenter. Nor was it rare, during the purest times of the Roman republic, to see the conquerors of nations and deliverers of their country return with all simplicity and cheerfulness to the exercise of the plough. In conformity to this sentiment, one of the completest poetic pieces of antiquity (the Georgics of Virgil) is written on the subject of husbandry."

The rules for the government of the students in regard to time of rising, hours of study, recreation, and religious services, were of the most wholesome disciplinary character.

The financial business of the college, embracing the raising of funds and their disbursements, as well as the business of the Book Concern, and the raising of funds for the support of western missionaries, all fell upon Asbury. His self-sacrificing devotion to the interests of the Church was of the purest and intensest character. His salary was only sixty-four dollars a year and travelling expenses, about as much as one of our city preachers at the present day would get for delivering a lecture in an adjoining town. Often have the clothes of Asbury been worn threadbare and become shabby in appearance, and he obliged to deprive himself of some of the comforts of life ; but uncomplainingly, unless in behalf of his poor preachers, he went on his way, living not for himself, but consecrating all to God and the Church.

The college was to Asbury a source of constant anxiety, and sometimes gave him trouble. In 1783 the following was entered in his Journal : " I have received heavy tidings from the college ; both our teachers have left, one for incompetency, and the other to pursue riches and honour. Had they cost us nothing, the mistake we made in employing them might be the less regretted."

Cokesbury College had been in existence a period of ten years, and had gained the sympathy and confidence of the Church in all parts of the country. It was watched over by Asbury with the care and solicitude with which a father would watch over an only child. But alas! like many a bright and beautiful object of hope and promise, it was doomed to an early grave. The sad intelligence came to Asbury's ears one morning that the beloved Cokesbury was no more. A heap of smouldering ruins was all that marked the lovely sight where it reared its walls. To none were the tidings of its sad fate more melancholy than to him who was in the most emphatic sense its founder, and the labours of whose head and hands and heart were constantly devoted to its support. The following entry is made in his Journal: "Charleston, South Carolina, Tuesday, January the 5th, 1796. Continued our business in Conference. We have great peace and love, see eye to eye and heart to heart. We have now a second and confirmed account that Cokesbury College is consumed to ashes, a sacrifice of £10,000 in about ten years. If any man should give me £10,000 per year to do and suffer again what I have done for that house, I would not do it. The Lord called not Mr. Whitefield nor the Methodists to build colleges. I wish only for schools—Dr. Coke wanted a college. I feel distressed at the loss of the library." Though Asbury was entirely discouraged, looking upon this calamity as an indication of Providence, that if the Methodists were to engage in the work of collegiate education the present was not the time for embarking in that enterprise, it was not so with Dr. Coke. He immediately agitated the subject of rebuilding, and obtained from the citizens of Abingdon a liberal subscription for that purpose. A number of friends in Baltimore, after consulting together also gave a subscription amounting to between four and five thousand dollars. It was subsequently ascertained that a building every way suited to the purpose could be obtained in Baltimore for the sum of twenty-two thousand dollars, and after due deliberation the purchase was made.

As there was a considerable lot of ground in connection with the building, it was determined to erect a church thereon, which was accordingly done. In due course of time the college was opened under the most favourable auspices. The friends of education in the Methodist Church were greatly encouraged by a prospect of success even more promising than that connected with the commencement of the original Cokesbury.

It was not long, however, that Asbury College was permitted to stand. The fate that attended Cokesbury seemed to hang over it, and like that institution it was consumed by fire. Though these successive cross dispensations suspended for a while the efforts of the Church in the cause of education, it was only a suspension. In Asbury's Journal for 1789 we find the following entry in regard to a Methodist school in Georgia : "The school for the charity boys in Georgia greatly occupies my mind.   Our annual expenditures will amount to one thousand dollars, and the aid we get is but trifling ; the poverty of the people, and the general scarcity of money, is the great source of our difficulties ; the support of our preachers who have families absorbs our collections, so that neither do our elders nor the charity school get much. We have the poor, but they have no money, and the wicked rich we do not choose to ask."   The Conference appointed a committee to procure five hundred acres of land for the establishment of this school.   In 1790, during Asbury's visit to the West, he originated the plan of an academy, which was denominated The Bethel Academy.   A gentleman by the name of Lewis made a donation of one hundred acres of land.   A spacious building was erected, eighty by forty feet, and three stories high.   The design was to accommodate the students in the house with boarding, etc.   The first and second stories were principally finished, and a spacious, hall in the centre.   The building of this house rendered the pecuniary means of the preachers very uncertain, for they were continually employed in begging for Bethel.   The people were very liberal, but they could not do more than they did.   The country was new, and the unsettled state of the people, in consequence of the Indian wars and depredations, kept it in a continual state of agitation.   The Legislature at an early period made a donation of six thousand acres of land to Bethel Academy.   The land was located in Christian county, south of Green River ; it remained a long time unproductive, and proved rather a bill of expense than otherwise.

In the Methodist Magazine for 1819 we find an interesting description of a seminary of learning in New York, under the patronage of the New York Conference.   This institution was divided into male and female departments, and the course of study embraced not only the English branches, but the ancient classics.

Mr. N. Morris was president, and Miss Caroline Matilda Thayer preceptress of the female department.   The Conference visitor reported the institution as in a high state of prosperity.   We cannot trace the history of this seminary, as we have not the necessary items of information.   Since that time seminaries and colleges have sprung up under Methodist patronage in all parts of the land, from Maine to Texas, on the shores of the Pacific, among the Indians, and also in South America and Africa, and, in the language of Edward Everett, there is no Church in the country so successfully engaged in the cause of education as the Methodist Church, nor one that during the last twenty-five years has done more for the advancement of the cause.

CHAPTER IX.

Dismal Swamp—Perilous Journey—Meets Dr. Coke at Charleston—Conference Preaching—Asbury's Travels—Description of Dr. Coke's Sermon at New York—Hempstead Harbour—Preaches in a Paper-Mill—Returns to New York—Trouble in the Church about Congregational Singing—Journey up the Hudson—Description of West Point—Newburgh—Bath—Delivers a Course of Lectures on the Prophecies—Dejection of Mind—First Ordination in the Mississippi Valley—Asbury in gown and bands—Rearranges the Discipline—When First Edition was Printed—New Edition—Questions and Answers omitted—Revised Edition—Fifth Edition—New Sections—Notes on the Discipline—General Conference at Charleston, South Carolina, 1788—Georgia—Crossing the Mountains—Hard Fare—A Stubborn Horse—An Incident—Character of Early Settlers—Letter to a Quaker in Delaware—Tour to the Western Wilderness—Horses stolen by Indians—Perils of the Journey—Conference in Lexington—Return through the Wilderness—Conference at Petersburgh—Bishop's Council—Threatening Letter from O'Kelly—Asbury's Reply—Asbury vindicates himself—Jesse Lee in New England—His Character—First Sermon in Boston—Letter to Asbury—Letter from Poythress.

ON his round in 1787 Asbury was not a little startled and his courage put to the test by being informed by Poythress that the great Dismal Swamp, which lay directly in his path, could not be crossed but with great danger. To travel round it would require a ride of sixty miles. For this he had not time, and he resolved to trust in God and push through, and with a courage which never failed him he entered the dismal waters. He was everywhere surrounded with a wide sweep of waters and deep morasses. "O," exclaimed the pioneer bishop, "what a world of swamps, and rivers, and islands!" After he had passed the swamp he writes: "Three miles on the water and three more on roads under water made our jaunt unpleasant."

Meeting Dr. Coke at Charleston, his spirit was refreshed. On the 25th of March the Conference for the South commenced its session. On Sabbath morning he preached from the text, "I had rather be a doorkeeper in the house of God than to dwell in the tents of wickedness." In the evening he preached from the passage, "For I will rise up against them, saith the Lord of hosts, and cut off from Babylon the name and remnant, and son and nephew, saith the Lord." During the business of Conference all matters pertaining to the temporal and spiritual interests of the Church were fully and freely discussed. On Wednesday Dr. Coke preached a sermon on the qualifications and duties of deacons. On the succeeding day the appointments were announced and the Conference closed.

We find the tireless Asbury frequently riding thirty and forty and sometimes fifty miles a day, and preaching once or twice, often swimming the rivers, and exposed to all kinds of hardships. From Saturday to Saturday he and Dr. Coke rode three hundred miles and preached alternately every day. On his return from the South, taking Baltimore and Philadelphia in his route as usual, he arrived at New York. Of Dr. Coke, Asbury says : "He preached on Friday, Saturday, Sunday, and Monday with great energy and acceptance." On Tuesday he himself preached from the text, "For Zion's sake I will not hold my peace, and for Jerusalem's sake I will not rest until her righteousness go forth as brightness, and the salvation thereof as a lamp that burneth." From New York he crossed over to Long Island, and rode twenty miles to Hempstead Harbour, where he preached in the evening. The next day he preached in the paper-mill from the text, "If any man will do his will, he shall know the doctrine whether it be of God." On Monday he returned to New York, and preached in the evening from, "They shall come from the East, and from the West, and from the North, and from the South, and sit down with Abraham and Isaac and Jacob," etc. His division was as follows : " 1. A Scriptural view of the kingdom of heaven. 2. The subjects or citizens thereof. 3. Sit down with Abraham, famous for faith ; Isaac, for justice, truth, meditation, and walking with God ; and Jacob, mighty in prayer."

This visit was during a time of trouble in the Church, and occasioned a great trial to Asbury, who spent half the night in prayer for patience and resignation. Even at that early day, as we find from Asbury's Journal, the Methodists had trouble about congregational singing. This has been a fruitful theme of difficulty and often of discord in the Church from the beginning, and is likely to remain so until, as with the Germans, singing becomes a part of our education, and all our members learn and love to sing. Until this is the case, all efforts to bring about congregational singing will prove to a great extent abortive.   Tune hymn-books may be multiplied like the leaves of the summer forest, but they will fall as a dead letter without the knowledge and the love of song.

From New York he went up the Hudson, preaching at different points on his route.   Saturday, the 16th of June, 1787, he crossed the mountains, and, to use his own language, "was gratified with the sight of a remarkable recess for the Americans during the last war.   The names of Andre and Arnold, with which misfortune and treachery are so unhappily and intimately blended, will give celebrity to West Point had it been less deserving of notice than its wonderful appearance really makes it.   It is commanded by mountains rising behind, and appears to be impregnable.   On the east are block-houses, and on the west are stores, barracks, and fortifications."   From West Point he crossed what he calls a high mountain, (Storm King,) and went to Newburgh.   Four weeks from this time we find him, after travelling through New Jersey, Pennsylvania, and Virginia, at his favourite retreat, Bath.   He visited the springs at this place for the purpose of availing himself of the medicinal virtue of the waters.   During his stay there he delivered a course of lectures on the prophecies.

Asbury was subject at times to great dejection of mind, and his spirit would often sink within him.   He rarely had much elevation of feeling, and though he frequently preached with ease and comfort to himself, and had occasionally considerable liberty, yet his seasons of gloom, especially after preaching, were sometimes terrific. On one occasion, at Bath, he became completely discouraged at the indifference of the people, and entered the following in his Journal : " I had few to hear me, so I gave them up.   I will return to my own studies.   If the people are determined to go to hell, I am clear of their blood."   Notwithstanding all this, there were occasions when he enjoyed remarkable manifestions.   Once, while preaching at Burton's, in Virginia, from the text, " Behold what manner of love the Father hath bestowed upon us that we should be called the sons of God," he says : " It seems as if I was let into heaven while enlarging upon this passage."

At the annual Conference held in Uniontown, Pennsylvania, in 1788, the first ordination took place in the great valley of the Mississippi.   The solemn and impressive ceremonies connected with the rite of ordination had never been witnessed before in

G

that vast region extending from the Alleghanies to the Father of
Waters. One of the pioneer preachers, then but a mere youth,
thus describes the scene : " Mr. Asbury officiated, not in the costume of the lawn-robed prelate, but as the plain presbyter in gown
and band, assisted by Richard Whatcoat, elder, in the same clerical
habit. The person ordained was Michael Leard, of whom it was
said that he could repeat nearly the whole of the New Testament
from memory, and also large portions of the Old. The scenes of
that day looked well in the eyes of the Church people, for not only
did the preachers appear in sacerdotal robes, but the morning
service was read as abridged by Mr. Wesley. The priestly robes
and prayer-book were, however, soon laid aside at the same time,
for I never saw the one nor heard the other since." The pre-
sumption is, as we have no data from which to form an opinion,
that the period of robes and reading prayers extended from the
time of Asbury's ordination to the episcopacy until the year 1787
or 1788.

About this time Asbury set himself to work to re-arrange the
Discipline, and reduce it to a more systematic form. The first
edition of the Discipline was printed in Philadelphia in 1785, and
is found bound up with the "Sunday Service and the Collection
of Psalms and Hymns," which had been sent over to America in
sheets. In 1786 a new edition of the whole was printed in London.
In this the following questions, contained in the first edition, with
their answers, are omitted :

" *Question* 23. May our ministers or travelling preachers drink
spirituous liquors ?

" *Answer.* By no means, unless it be medicinally.

" *Question* 42. What methods can we take to extirpate slavery ?

" *Answer.* We are deeply conscious of the impropriety of making
new terms of communion for a religious society already established,
excepting on the most pressing occasion, and such we esteem the
practice of holding our fellow-creatures in slavery. We view it
as contrary to the golden law of God, on which hang all the law
and the prophets, and the unalienable rights of mankind, as well as
every principle of the Revolution, to hold in the deepest debase-
ment, in a more abject slavery than is perhaps to be found in any
part of the world except America, so many souls that are all
capable of the image of God.

" We therefore think it our most bounden duty to take immediately some effectual method to extirpate this abomination from
among us, and for that purpose we add the following to the
rules of our society, namely :

" 1. Every member of our society who has slaves in his possession, shall, within twelve months after notice given to him by the assistant (which notice the assistants are required immediately, and without any delay, to give in their respective circuits), legally execute and record an instrument whereby he emancipates and sets free every slave in his possession who is between the ages of forty and forty-five immediately, or at farthest when they arrive at the age of forty-five.

" And every slave who is between the ages of twenty-five and forty immediately, or at farthest at the expiration of five years from the date of the said instrument.

" And every slave who is between the ages of twenty and twenty-five immediately, or at farthest when they arrive at the age of thirty.

" And every slave under the age of twenty, as soon as they arrive at the age of twenty-five at farthest.

" And every infant born in slavery after the above-mentioned rules are complied with, immediately on its birth.

" 2. Every assistant shall keep a journal, in which he shall regularly minute down the names and ages of all the slaves belonging to all the masters in his respective circuit, and also the date of every instrument executed and recorded for the manumission of the slaves, with the name of the court, book, and folio, in which the said instruments respectively shall have been recorded : which journal shall be handed down in each circuit to the succeeding assistants.

" In consideration that these rules form a new term of communion, every person concerned, who will not comply with them, shall have liberty quietly to withdraw himself from our society within the twelve months succeeding the notice given as aforesaid : otherwise the assistant shall exclude him in the society.

" 4. No person so voluntarily withdrawn, or so excluded, shall ever partake of the supper of the Lord with the Methodists, till he complies with the above requisitions.

" 5. No person holding slaves shall, in future, be admitted into society, or to the Lord's Supper, till he previously complies with these rules concerning slavery.

" N. B. These rules are to affect the members of our society no farther than as they are consistent with the laws of the states in which they reside.

" And respecting our brethren in Virginia that are concerned, and after due consideration of their peculiar circumstances, we allow them two years from the notice given, to consider the expediency of compliance or non-compliance with these rules."

Question 63 was also omitted. It reads as follows : " Are there any further directions needful for the preservation of good order among the preachers ?

"*Answer.* In the absence of a superintendent, a travelling preacher or three leaders shall have power to lodge a complaint against any preacher in their circuit, whether elder, assistant, deacon, or helper, before three neighboring assistants ; who shall meet at an appointed time, (proper notice being given to the parties,) hear, and decide the case." And authority is given them to change or suspend a preacher, if they see it necessary, and to appoint another in his place, during the absence of the superintendents.

Also Question 64. " If there happen to be a vacancy in a circuit by the death of a preacher, by his withdrawing himself from the work, or otherwise, in the absence of a superintendent, who are to fill up the vacancy ?

"*Answer.* Three neighboring assistants, called and assembled according to the preceding minute."

This was the last edition of the Discipline containing the Sunday Service with the Psalms and Hymns.

Asbury, assisted by Dickins, in the year 1787, as above-mentioned, made an entire revision of the Discipline, by which he changed its form materially. Up to this time it was made up wholly of question and answer, with very little regard ·to method, but now it was divided into sections under their appropriate headings. This revised edition was submitted to Dr. Coke after his return from Europe, and meeting his approval it was sent to press. Mr. Wesley's name was left out of this edition of the Discipline, and for the first time the term bishop was employed in the place of superintendent. No changes having been made the succeding year a new edition was not necessary, but in the year 1789 the fifth edition appeared. It seems, however, that during the previous year Asbury had been employed in elaborating two new sections, namely, the thirty-first and thirty-second. To the new edition an address by the bishops was prefixed. To it were also added the Articles of Religion and certain doctrinal tracts. These, however, were not embodied, but printed separate and apart from the form of Discipline. It was not until 1796 that Asbury and Coke, in compliance with a resolution of the General Conference, prepared notes on all parts of the Discipline. In these notes everything is proved or illustrated by appropriate passages of Scripture. It must have cost great labor, and the manner in which the work was accomplished evinced a biblical research and a logical acumen rarely surpassed. It may be said with great truth and propriety, that the mind of Asbury was stamped upon the genius and institutions of American Methodism as effectually as was that of Wesley upon English Methodism. From Charleston, South Carolina, where Conference was held in 1788, Asbury proceeded on his tour to Georgia, where another Conference was to be held. It was on this last route that he compiled the two sections of Discipline above alluded to. After attending Conference at the Forks of Broad River, he pursued his way to North Carolina. The hardships he encountered in this journey were great. The reader may form some idea of the bishop's toils from the following : " After getting our horses shod we made a move for Holstein, and entered upon the mountains, the first of which I called Steel, the second Stone, and the third Iron Mountain. They are rough and difficult to climb. We were spoken to on our way by most awful thunder and lightning, accompanied by heavy rain. We crept for shelter into a little dirty house, where the filth might have been taken from the floor with a spade. We felt the want of fire, but could get little wood to make it, and what we did get was wet. At the head of Wautawga we fed, and reached Ward's that night. Coming to the river next day we hired a young man to swim over for the canoe, in which we crossed, while our horses swam to the other shore. The waters being up, we were compelled to travel an old road over the mountains. Night came on. I was ready to faint with a violent headache, the mountain was so steep on both sides. I prayed to the Lord for help. Presently a profuse sweat broke out upon me, and my fever entirely subsided. About nine o'clock we came to Grear's. After taking a little rest here we set out next morning for Cox's, on Holstein River. I had trouble enough. Our route lay through the woods, and my pack-horse would neither follow, lead, nor drive, so fond was he of stopping to feed on the green herbage. I tried the lead and he pulled back. I tied his head up to prevent his grazing and he ran back. As the weather was excessively warm I was much fatigued, and my temper not a little tried. Arriving at the river I was at a loss what to do, but providentially a man came along who conducted me across." This, adds the bishop, " has been an awful journey to me, and this a tiresome day ; and now after riding seventy-five miles I have thirty-five more to travel before I can rest a day."

After this journey he grieved considerably, on reviewing it, that he was not able to pray more on the road. The toils and hardships of Asbury in travelling round the continent can never be fully known. But a short time after the journey above described we find an entry in his Journal of another quite as full of incident. He says : "We had to cross the Alleghany Mountains again at a bad passage. Our course lay over mountains and through valleys, and the mud and mire was such as might scarcely be expected even in December. We came to an old forsaken habitation in Tygart's Valley. Here our horses grazed about while we boiled our meat. Midnight brought us up at Jones's after travelling between forty and fifty miles. The old man—our host—was kind enough to wake us up at four o'clock in the morning. We journied on through devious lonely wilds, where no food might be found except what grew in the woods or was carried with us. We met two women, who were going to see their friends, and to attend the quarterly meeting at Clarksburg. Near midnight we stopped at A——'s, who hissed his dogs at us ; but the women were determined to go to quarterly meeting ; so we journeyed on. Brothers Phoebus and Cook took to the woods ; old —— gave up his bed to the women ; I lay on a few deer skins on the floor. That night our poor horses got no corn, and next morning they had to swim across the Monongahela. After a twenty miles' ride we came to Clarksburg, and man and beast were so outdone that it took us ten hours to accomplish the journey. I lodged with Colonel Jackson. Our meeting was held in a long close room belonging to the Baptists, and our use of the house gave offence. There attended about seven hundred people, to whom I preached with freedom, and I believe the Lord's power reached the hearts of some. After administering the sacrament I was well satisfied to leave. We rode thirty miles to father Haymond's, after three o'clock Sunday afternoon, and made it nearly eleven before we came in. About midnight we went to rest, and rose at five o'clock the next morning. My mind has been severely tried both by the fatigue endured by myself and my horse. O how glad I should be of a plain clean plank to lie on as preferable to the beds ; and where the beds are in a bad state the floors are worse. The gnats are almost as troublesome here as the mosquitoes in the lowlands of the seaboard. The people of this country are many of them of the boldest cast of adventurers, and with some the decencies of civilized life are scarcely regarded, two instances of which I myself witnessed. The great landholders who are industrious will soon show the effects of the aristocracy of wealth by lording it over poor neighbors, and by securing to themselves all the offices of profit and honor. On the one hand savage warfare teaches them to be cruel, and on the other the preaching of Antinomians poisons them with error in doctrine ; good moralists they are not, and good Christians they cannot be unless they are better taught."

While in Virginia he wrote a letter to a Quaker in Delaware, which is so characteristic of the man we insert it.

"NEWTON, VA, *Seventh Month*, 1790.

"MY VERY DEAR FRIEND,—If I have a partiality for any people in the world except the Methodists, it is for the Quakers, so called. Their plainness of dress, their love of justice and truth, their friendship to each other, and the care they take of one another, render them worthy of praise.

"Would it not be of use for that society that make it a point not to come near any others, whether good or bad, to try all means within themselves? Would it not be well, thinkest thou, for them to sit every night and morning, and, if they find liberty, to go to prayer after reading a portion of God's word? As epistles are read from the Friends, would it not be well to introduce the reading of some portion of the Scriptures at public meetings? Would it not be well to have a congregation and a society—an outward and an inward court? In the former, let children and servants, and unawakened people come; in the inward let mourners in Zion come.

"The Presbyterians have reformed; the Episcopalians and the Methodists, why should not the Friends? It was a dark time one hundred and fifty years back. We are near the edge of the wilderness. If this inward court or society were divided into small bands or classes, and to be called together weekly by men and women of the deepest experience, and appointed for that work, and asked about their souls, and the dealings of God with them, and to join in prayer, one or two, or all of them that have freedom, I think the Lord would come upon them.

"I give this advice as the real friend of your souls, as there are hundreds and thousands that never have nor will come near others. These might get more religion if your people were to hear others; they might get properly awakened, and if you had close meetings for speaking they would not leave you. You must not think that G. Fox and R. Barclay were the only men in the world. I am sure there must be a reform, if you could move it in quarterly and yearly meetings for family and society meetings, and adopt rules for these meetings!

"Would it not be well, thinkest thou, to preach against covetousness? God has blessed Friends; they are a temperate, industrious, and frugal people. Tell them to feed the hungry, clothe the naked, visit the sick, and always feel for the spirit of prayer at such times. Would it not be well to deliver a testimony at other places, if Friends felt freedom, and allow others to come into their meetings without forbidding them? Our houses are open to any that come in a Christian spirit.

"I wish Methodists and Friends would bear a stronger testimony against races, fairs, and balls; I wish they would reprove swearing, lying, and foolish talking; watch their young people in their companies; instruct them in the doctrines of Christ; call upon them to feel after the spirit of prayer morning and evening, and strive to bring them to God! If I know my own heart, I write from love to souls; and although it is the general cry, 'You can do nothing with these people,' I wish to lay before you these things, which I think are not contrary to the ancient principles of Friends, and I am sure that we are taught them in the word of God. Think upon them. My soul pities and loves you. You may fight against God in not inculcating these things.

"I am, with real friendship to thee and thy people,

"FRANCIS ASBURY."

As a true pioneer, Asbury had for some time contemplated a tour to what was then denominated the great Western wilderness. Already following the trail of the hunter, and the blazed path of the settler, Asbury's missionaries had penetrated the deep, unbroken forests, and had borne the messages of salvation to the camps and cabins in the canebrakes of Kentucky. Poythress, an heroic pioneer of the cross, wrote to the bishop, entreating him to visit the scattered sheep in the wilderness. Having got all things in readiness, he started with his travelling companions upon his long and perilous journey. After passing over the mountain, they crossed Holstein River, and following its bank down, after a fatiguing journey reached a cabin, where they halted, and turned out their horses to graze. The owner of the house was in quest of horses which had been stolen by the Indians. After waiting at this point for a renewal of their forces before entering fully upon the wilderness, they felt somewhat invigorated for their future journey. While passing through the valley of the Holstein they preached at the different stopping places on their route. At length they crossed Clinch River, passing over a wild rocky road until they came to Moccasin Gap, where the party were joined by Massie and Clark, two noted western hunters, who came to inform them of a Kentucky guard of eight men waiting to escort them through the wilderness. At the valley station the whole number assembled was eighteen men with thirteen guns. Thus armed they moved on, making from thirty-five to fifty miles a day. Crossing Rock Castle River, they stopped at the house of a gentleman whose wife had been taken captive by the Indians. The fatigues connected with the journey over mountains, steep hills, deep rivers, through interminable canebrakes inhabited by nothing but wild beasts and savages, attended with want of sleep and fasting for want of food, wore heavily upon Asbury, but his tireless spirit quailed not. On their route they passed a deserted camp where the Indians had killed twenty-four white men. A woman of the company, wife of one of the victims, made her escape. On the route they were pursued by Indians, but the members of the ᴘompany and their means of defence kept them at bay. Finally, the party reached Lexington, where Asbury preached in a dwelling house. The Conference was held in a private house, and consisted of nine preachers. Among other business transacted was the ordination of Wilson Lee, Thomas Williamson, and Barnabas M'Henry. After visiting several other places in Kentucky, the bishop started on his return track. The company consisted of fifty persons, twenty-five of whom were armed. Articles of agreement for the government of the company were drawn up and signed. The first day's travel brought them to the Hazel Patch ; the next day they discovered signs of Indians, and they judged it best not to encamp, but travel all night ; and the following day they reached the Cumberland Gap, at the foot of which the company separated, Asbury's party proceeding on to Grass Valley.

The next Conference was held in Petersburg, Virginia, where the business was conducted with peace and harmony, until, as Asbury remarks in his Journal, the subject of the bishop's council was introduced, and then "the young men, who appeared to be entirely under the influence of the elders, turned it out of doors." The discussions on this subject were exceedingly vexatious to Asbury, and he remarks : "This business is to be explained to every preacher, and then it must be carried through the Conferences twenty-four times, that is, through all the Conferences for two years." Restless spirits had arisen who looked with envy upon Asbury, and were dissatisfied with his exercise of episcopal prerogative. The bishop had received a letter from O'Kelly, a presiding elder of Brunswick District, who made heavy complaints, and threatened to use his influence against him. In reply to this Asbury says : "There is not a vote given in the Conference in which the presiding elder has not greatly the advantage of me. All the influence I am to gain over a company of young men in a district must be done in three weeks ; the greater part of them perhaps are seen by me only at Conference, while the presiding elder has had them with him all the year, and has the greatest opportunity of gaining influence. This advantage may be abused; let the bishops look to it; but who has power to lay an embargo on me, and to make of none effect the decision of all the Conferences of the Union."

To conciliate the disaffected, at one time Asbury addressed them a letter, saying : " I will take my seat in council as another member, and in that point at least waive the claims of episcopacy ; yea, I will lie down and be trodden upon rather than injure one soul."

If any man could be trusted with power safely it was Asbury. No man exercised it with greater discretion. He had given form and character to American Methodism, and had shown himself from his first landing in the country, by all his acts as assistant, superintendent, and bishop, an American in heart and life, identifying himself with every interest of the Church and the country, resisting stoutly every English prejudice that showed itself among the preachers, and making every sacrifice for the welfare of the Church. He was keenly sensitive to all attacks, and perhaps more careful than necessary to vindicate himself. While suffering from unjust insinuations in relation to his motives and acts, he wrote to Dickins, the book steward, at Philadelphia, as follows :

" MY VERY DEAR BROTHER,—As life with me now is a greater uncertainty than heretofore, I am concerned to communicate these few lines to the public, not doubting but they will give information and satisfaction to the candid and conscientious. It may be thought by those who measure others by themselves, that I have gained much honour, ease, power, and interest in my station in the Church of God. Nay, I have lived upon the providence of God and the charity of a few friends. My method for many years has been to keep an account of what has been given me without solicitation. I have also kept an account of what I have expended annually, charging the connection with my salary of sixty-four dollars per year and my travelling expenses, as another preacher. When I have wanted a horse or carriage my friends have provided for me. My friends in Maryland, Delaware, Philadelphia, Jersey, and New York have chiefly communicated this supply. As to Virginia or the Carolinas, (except in a few extraordinary cases,) as also Georgia, and the Western and Eastern states, I have visited them, taking nothing unless in extreme want on my side, or in the great benevolence of my friends on the other. As to the college, it was all pain and no profit, but some expense and great labour. From the Preachers' Fund the Conferences can witness for me I have taken nothing. Of the book interest you can witness I have received nothing. Of the Chartered Fund I am independent, and wish to keep so. Of money brought to Conference, or collected publicly at times, it has been appropriated with the nicest equality to the wants and deficiencies of the preachers, but not any to me. You have settled my annual accounts and have the book charge. Brother Nelson Reed will do me the justice I demand, he having had the settling of the college books and my accounts. Brothers T. Morrell and Philip Bruce have had a most intimate acquaintance with my temporal affairs, and the inspection of my yearly accounts; yet after all I must die, to prove, by my last will and testament, that I have not made my gain by the Gospel of Christ. And should I die as poor as I have lived, it will be said by suspicious, ungenerous men, that I have made appropriations in my lifetime. I shall call upon the Conferences, John Dickins, Nelson Reed, and Thomas Morrell, as witnesses to the truth of what I have written, as a debt of duty and of love they owe me, who am their brother and companion in the kingdom and patience of Jesus Christ.

"FRANCIS ASBURY."

The following is Dickins's reply to the above:

"As Mr. Asbury is pleased in the above letter to call upon me, as well as a few other persons, to testify to the truth of what he has written, it is with the greatest cheerfulness that I comply with his request. Both from a sense of duty and respect, I now declare in the most solemn manner that Mr. Asbury has never received any money from the book fund, nor ever dropped the most distant hint to my knowledge of desiring or expecting anything either from that fund or from the Charter Fund. And further, I have frequently settled his book and private accounts, in which I have always found that he has charged himself with the donations of his friends, or whatever money he has received, and credited himself with nothing but twenty-four pounds a year and his travelling expenses, and at the close of the year the balance has been carried to the proper side of a new account for another year. And when he left this city last he had not money enough to bear his expenses for one month. I shall conclude with adding, that from my long and intimate acquaintance with him I think I never knew so disinterested a man as Mr. Asbury."

To those acquainted with Asbury all this was entirely super-
fluous; and yet, to put to silence the clamours of envy and suspicion, it perhaps was proper that he should give such an expose
in detail of his private affairs. Asbury had nothing 'to conceal,
for though apparently secretive and unapproachable, he was transparent as the calm, quiet lake that reveals all that lies within its
depths.

In the year 1789 Jesse Lee introduced Methodism into the land
of the pilgrims. It is said by one of his cotemporaries that he
possessed uncommon conversational powers, and a pleasing, fasci-
nating address, which at once prepossessed all with whom he met
most favourably. His wit and readiness at repartee were not excelled by any, and so skillfully did he use this two-edged instrument that he often taught those disposed to be witty at the expense of a Methodist preacher that this dangerous weapon was all
potent in his hands. He possessed the elements essential to make
up a pioneer itinerant in an eminent degree. To great moral
courage was united a well tempered zeal, which nerved him, and
impelled him onward through the most forbidding obstacles and
the most trying labours. There was a naturalness and consequent
ease and grace about his preaching that rendered him one of the
most efficient ministers of his day. He opened his mission in the
land of the Puritans first at Norwalk. From thence he visited
New Haven and Boston, the very seat and citadel of the Puritan
faith. He had been in all parts of the country, and had preached
the Gospel in the far South among the earliest pioneers. Not
being able to obtain a house to preach in, he went out to Boston
Common, and beneath the wide-spreading branches of a venerable
elm which stands to this day, and with a melody for which the
preachers of that day were famous, sang together a large congregation. One who was present on the occasion thus describes the
scene which followed : "I thought the prayer was the best I ever
heard. He then read his text, and began in a sententious manner
to address his remarks to the understanding and consciences of the
people, and I thought all who were present must be constrained to
say, 'It is good for us to be here.' All the while the people were
gathering he continued this mode of address, and presented us with
such a variety of beautiful images that I thought he must have
been at infinite pains to crowd so many pretty things into his
memory. But when he entered upon the subject-matter of his
text, it was with such an easy, natural flow of expression, and in
such a tone of voice, that I could not refrain from weeping, and
many others were affected in the same way. When he had done

and we had an opportunity of expressing our views to each other, it was agreed that such a man had not visited New England since the days of Whitefield. I heard him again, and thought I could follow him to the ends of the earth." But this was not the first Methodist sermon that was preached in Boston. More than a half century before Charles Wesley had preached several times, being driven into Boston harbour by a crazy craft commanded by a drunken captain. One of the churches in which he preached at that time stands to this day.

From the time that the fearless and indefatigable Lee opened his mission on that memorable spot until the present, his name has been a household word in the family of New England Methodism. We do not intend by this to be understood as designing to convey the impression that his labours were of a sectional character, much less that his memory is not equally cherished among all the branches of the Methodist family in this country. The preachers of those days, like their bishop, were general itinerants, circulating, like the life-blood of the human system, from the centre to all the extremities of the land. One year among the Puritans of the North, and the next with the cavaliers of the South, the very system of itinerancy forbade the indulgence of any sectional views or prejudices. With them the whole human family was one, but more particularly the people composing the confederacy where they laboured. The name of Jesse Lee was dear to every Methodist, and with those of his brave and honoured associates will go down to posterity garnered with the most precious things of Methodist history. The following letter from Lee to Asbury, written from New Haven in 1790, was published recently by the Baltimore Historical Society. It is full of interest, especially as it relates to his labours in New England.

" MY DEAR BROTHER,—I received your letter from Petersburgh. I was glad to hear from you that you are safely preserved under all your troubles and from all your enemies. I have enjoyed good health of late, and have reason to bless God that I have not wickedly departed from him. Though I live to but little purpose, I must own that my poor heart is engaged in the work of the Lord ; and I still desire to devote my whole soul and body to his service ; and in the midst of all my troubles I can say, ' The Lord is my portion.'

" I expect you will be glad to hear of the work of the Lord, and the opening prospect we have in New England. We have formed three circuits ; one is a four weeks' and the others two weeks. circuits, but the latter may be enlarged as soon as preachers can be procured. We have seven or eight societies in one of them, and one in the next circuit. In the last one which we formed we have no society yet, but there are several persons who intend to cast their lot among us. In these circuits we have large congregations and many real friends. Many people fall in with our doctrines about election and reprobation as soon as they hear them; but they do not agree with us about the perseverance of the saints. Nevertheless they suppose the doctrine, as we preach it, is innocent. In most places they desire to hear our preachers.

"I have lately taken a tour as far as Portsmouth, the metropolis of New Hampshire. I preached in most of the large sea-ports and cities to large congregations, and in the most of them I was solicited to return. I cannot tell what you may think of the liberty I took of going so far, but I felt so much of the power and presence of God in preaching to the people that I believe I shall never repent that I went. When I got to Boston I could get no house to preach in; but believing God had sent me, I told the people that I would preach on the Common at six o'clock on Sunday evening, at which time I suppose I had one thousand serious hearers. The next week I went further east, preached twice in Marblehead, three times in Salem, once in Danvers, twice in Newburyport, where I saw the remains of Mr. G. Whitefield, and once in Portsmouth. This week I rode one hundred and thirty miles, made my own appointments, preached nine times, returned to Boston, and preached on Sunday afternoon on the Common to three thousand hearers. The next week I spent in Boston. I preached in a Baptist meetinghouse once, three times in private houses, and on the Sabbath on the Common to five thousand hearers.

"I feel attached to the Bostonians. I found several who once belonged to our society. A number pressed me to return, if possible, before our next Conference, when they hope and pray that a preacher may be sent to them. Boston is a large place; the people are much divided in their religions sentiments, and I have no doubt but that in three months I could have a steady congregation. To-morrow I expect to set out for that town again, and to spend eight or nine days in it before I return. I shall do all I can for the reception of a preacher, and do hope that you will send an acceptable one from the Maryland Conference. If possible, get a volunteer who loves the cause of God. If he comes willingly, he will bear his cross with greater courage. If a preacher can be fixed there now, the way will soon be opened in the country around there. They have seventeen houses for public worship in town and eight or ten more in sight of it."

Jesse Lee was the first historian of the Methodist Church, and was eminently fitted for the work of a pioneer. Such were his influence and standing in the country that for several years he served as chaplain to Congress, commanding the respect of men of Revolutionary times, and sustaining throughout the dignity of his vocation and office.

This year Asbury received the following letter from Poythress, presiding elder of the Kentucky District, in relation to the work in that region :—

" MY VERY DEAR BROTHER,—I have heard many souls crying out for mercy, and many have entered into life ; I suppose not less than two hundred at our common meetings. There is a general revival through my district. At our last quarterly meeting we had, it was supposed, seven hundred souls. I believe Methodism will take root in the western country. Upwards of twenty professed to emerge out of darkness into the marvellous light of the Gospel, and many more cried aloud to God for mercy. It is remarkable that this savage land has become a land of praise to God.

" A very remarkable circumstance happened in Lexington circuit, namely : On the 28th of June Brother W. Lee preached at Coleman's chapel ; there was a great appearance of the power of God. One of S.'s daughters was struck under conviction. It was thought in a few days that God delivered her from her burden of sin. As she was her father's favourite daughter, it was thought that he would not be willing that she should join the Methodist society. She went with her sister to sweep out the chapel. As soon as she went in, her sister says she went out, and a little time after returned and went up to the pulpit, stood before it, appeared very awful, and dropped down dead, which was exactly four weeks from the day that she was first awakened, and it was in the same house that she gave her soul to God. He took her from the evil to come, and we have no doubt but that she is now praising him in paradise.

" O my dear father, I think that I am as willing to suffer for my dear Master as you are. I believe that you feel much for the rising generation in America. May God bless you with a long and useful life, and success in all your labours !

" The Indians are still doing mischief. Not far from the first house you came to after you passed through the wilderness, they killed seven men and wounded one. They went to a house near Bourbon court-house, ripped open the beds, and plundered the house. The women and children happily made their escape. O when will the Lord Christianize the savage tribes ! May he hasten the happy moment !"

Poythress was among the noble band of Western pioneers who planted the Gospel in the Western wilderness. His name and memory will be cherished as long as Methodism is known. He and his associates in the ministry stamped their character upon the wild and widely-scattered population of the West, and through their toils it was made to "bud and blossom like the rose."

CHAPTER X.

Doctrine of Celibacy—Apostolic Injunction—Asbury's Reasons for Celibacy— Other Reasons—His Opinion of Dr. Coke's Marriage—Singular Remark about the Women and the Devil—Dialogue on Marriage—Asbury and the Young Lady—Devotion to his Mother—Beautiful Tribute to her Memory.

THE doctrine of the celibacy of the clergy finds no countenance in the inspired word. The priests of the Jewish Church were not only not forbidden to marry but had wives and children. The solitary instance of Paul, who was careful to say that he spoke without Divine authority on the subject, and was only prompted to speak as he did on account of the necessities of the case, furnishes no warrant to the Christian Church to prohibit its ministers from marrying. The injunction of the apostle to the ministers of the New Testament, sanctioned by his own example, to form no matrimonial alliances, was specific in its nature, and grew out of, and was adapted to the exigency of the times. It was considered, on account of "the present distress," not expedient for those whose duty it was to "preach the Gospel to every creature," and who were constantly exposed to privation, persecution, and death, to enter into the married state. The reasons which governed Asbury in the course he pursued in this respect are best stated by himself.

"If I should die in celibacy, which I think quite probable, I give the following reasons for what can scarcely be called my choice. I was called to preach in my fourteenth year. I began my public exercises between sixteen and seventeen. At twenty-one I entered the travelling connection. At twenty-six I came to America.

Thus far I had reasons enough for a single life. It had been my intention to return to Europe, but the war continued, and it was ten years before we had settled, lasting peace. This was no time to marry or be given in marriage. At forty-nine I was ordained Superintendent or Bishop in America. Among the duties imposed upon me by my office was that of travelling extensively, and I could hardly expect to find a woman with grace enough to enable her to live but one week out of the fifty-two with her husband ; besides, what right has any man to take advantage of the affections of a woman, make her his wife, and by voluntary absence subvert the whole order and economy of the marriage state by separating those whom neither God, nature, or the requirements of civil society permit long to be *put asunder*. It is neither just nor generous. I may add to this that I had but little money, and with this little I administered to the necessities of a beloved mother till I was fifty-seven. If I have done wrong I hope God and the sex will forgive me. It is my duty now to bestow the pittance I have to spare upon the widows and fatherless girls and poor married men."

But there were other reasons. In addition to the support of an aged mother out of his pittance of salary, amounting to sixty-four dollars, he had the Book Concern on his shoulders, and all he could raise for the publication fund was sent to Dickins, the book agent at Philadelphia, to enable him to enlarge the Concern and increase the number of Methodist books. His interest in this establishment was lasting as life, and in his last hours he bore it in affectionate remembrance. Some of his friends having bequeathed to him two thousand dollars, he made it all over to the Book Concern in his last will and testament. Besides, he had to look after poor preachers and the missionaries he had sent out to the frontier settlements in the West. He often impoverished himself to relieve their wants. At one time we find him with only two dollars in the world, and his poor preachers ragged and destitute. First his little purse was drained, and then followed his cloak, and watch, and shirt. Under such circumstances it is perfectly obvious that neither he nor any of his travelling companions in the ministry had any need for wives. Had they taken them they would have been "worse than infidels," because they would have placed themselves in a position where it would have been impossible to provide for them." Those who did marry while they were in the travelling connection did so with the full conviction that they would not receive a support from the Church, and hence they almost invariably located after getting married. Many talented and useful ministers were thus lost to

H

the Church, at least their influence and usefulness were greatly
contracted.   On receiving a letter from Dr. Coke, communicating
the intelligence of his marriage and the probability of his not returning to this country only on certain conditions, Asbury said :
" Marriage is honourable in all, but to me it is a ceremony awful
as death.   Well may it be so, when I calculate we have lost the
travelling labours of two hundred of the best men in America or
the world by marriage and consequent location."

In a work recently published, containing " Sketches of Early
Times in Middle Tennessee," we find the following :

" In Virginia there was a circuit where the preachers sent among
the people almost always obtained wives during their service.   The
bishop, supposing the women should be blamed for this state of
things, thought to forestal them by sending to the circuit two
decrepit old men, in the belief that no one would try to allure them
into the bonds of wedlock.   But, to his suprise, both of them
married during the year, and upon hearing the result of his
experiment he remarked, ' I am afraid the women and the devil
will get all my preachers.' "

The following dialogue occurred between Asbury and one of his
preachers stationed in Baltimore.   The preacher, in accordance
with the instructions of the Discipline requiring him to consult
his brethren before taking such a step, sought an interview with
the bishop :

" How old are you ?" said Asbury.

" Twenty-eight years."

" That is the proper age for a Methodist preacher to take that
important step.   How long have you been in the work ?"

" Four years."

" Then you have elder's orders ?"

" Yes, sir."

" All this is proper.   When men enter their probation they have
ministerial characters to form, and ministerial talents to exhibit, to
the satisfaction of the Church.   Prudence says that they ought to
form that character, and exhibit those talents, before they take that
important step.   But few novices have ministerial weight sufficient
to justify them in bringing the expense of a wife and family on the
Church.   The people will feel, and they will make the men feel ;
and the dear sister of sixteen will feel too.   Besides, in green age,
men do not always select such women as the apostle says the wives
of deacons and elders must be, such as may be wholesome examples
for the flock of Christ.   Well, how now ? locate ?"

" No, sir ; that is not my intention."

"Very well ; I should suppose your call was not out. Some men marry fortunes, and go to take care of them ; some men marry wives, and go to make fortunes for them ; and thus, when, for the time, we should have age and experience in the ministry, we have youth and inexperience ; and such have charge ; this, not of choice, but necessity. We must do the best we can."

On one of his continental tours, while stopping at a place in the West, Asbury had an appointment some miles distant in a portion of the country where he had never been before, and there was danger of his missing his way and getting lost in the woods. One of the daughters of the gentlemen at whose house he stopped proposed to accompany him, and pioneer him through the wilderness. He did not positively decline the offer of the fair guide, though it would have suited his notions better to have gone alone if he even had missed his way. The luxury of a carriage at that time, at least in that section, was not known ; indeed if they had possessed them they would have been of no use, as there were no roads, nothing but blind or blazed paths. The only modes of travel were on foot or on horseback.

The horses were soon in readiness for the travellers. The bishop was in his saddle, and with a celerity for which the Western girls were famous in early times, Mary sprang to the back of her spirited steed and was at once by his side. Soon they entered the forest and were lost to sight in its deep thickets. Mary knew the route and led the way. When about half the distance had been passed over the travellers came to a deep but narrow ravine, whose rugged, precipitous banks seemed to forbid a passage. The bishop at beholding it felt relieved, as he thought he had arrived at a Rubicon which his fair companion could not pass. Spurring his noble horse, whose strength and speed had never failed him, he cleared the ravine at a bound. Turning on his horse he congratulated himself that he was now rid of what he felt rather an incumbrance,as he had considerable qualms of conscience about going to the appointment, where he was a stranger, in company with a young lady. He was about bidding her good-by, with the exclamation, "Mary, you can't do that," a most unhappy suggestion for him to make to a proud, spirited, fearless Western girl. Her quick and familiar response was, "I'll try, Frank," and suiting the action to the word, horse and rider were in a moment at his side. Faithful to her task, she accompanied the bishop to the end of his journey, and after the preaching was over returned with him to her father's house. We never heard of any scandal resulting from this excursion.

Asbury, as we have seen, did not, like Loyola and his followers, take the vow of celibacy, though he lived and died an unmarried man. His deep devotion to his affectionate mother, who depended upon him for a support, and for whose sake alone he adopted a prudence in secreting himself at Judge White's in time of the war, which, under other circumstances, would have led him to brave a martyr's fate, perhaps prompted him to repress all those natural desires which would have led him to seek a companion and help proper for him. Beyond his dear venerated mother he had nothing in this world to love or live for but the Church. To be sure he loved the latter more, as for its sake he left father, and mother, and home, and friends, and country, to come to a land of strangers to preach the everlasting Gospel. His beautiful and touching tribute to the memory of his mother shows that he had a heart full of sympathy and affection :

"For fifty years her hands, her house, and her heart were open to receive the people of God and the ministers of Christ, and thus a lamp was lighted up in a dark place. She was an afflicted yet most active woman, of quick bodily powers and masculine understanding nevertheless, so kindly all the elements mixed in her. Her strong mind quickly felt the subduing influences of that Christian sympathy which ' weeps with those who weep,' and ' rejoices with those who rejoice.' As a woman and a wife she was refined, modest, and blameless ; as a mother—above all the women in the world would I claim her for my own—ardently affectionate. As a mother in Israel few of her sex have done more by personal labour to support the Gospel and to wash the saints' feet. As a friend, she was generous, true, and constant."

CHAPTER XI.

Previous Reference to Institutions of Learning—Asbury lays the Foundation of the Book Concern—Founder of the Methodist Missions to Frontier Settlements—Founder of the Chartered Fund—Founder of American Sabbath Schools—Benevolent Institutions the Outgrowth of the Church—Asbury a Bible Distributer—The Sunday School System incorporated with the Discipline—Asbury's Comments—Preached on the Subject of Education—Name of Francis Asbury given to Children—Remembered in his Will—Affectionate Regard for the Young—Organization of District Schools—His Plan—Its Importance—An interesting Sketch.

WE have already seen the relation sustained by Asbury to Methodist institutions of learning ; how he originated them, raised funds by personal application and effort all over the country for their foundation and endowment, acting as founder and agent, and superintending their management, while at the same time he was constantly engaged in travelling annually around the continent, preaching at all times and in all places. Following in the footsteps of Wesley, who early devised a literature for the Methodist people, we find this indefatigable man laying the foundation of a Book Concern, and raising funds for its establishment and support.

In 1787 Asbury made the following reference to the Book Concern : "The last section in the Discipline reads as follows : As it has been frequently recommended by the preachers and people that such books as are wanted be printed in this country, we therefore propose : 1. That the advice of the Conference shall be desired concerning any valuable impression, and their consent be obtained before any steps be taken for the printing thereof ; 2. That the profit of the books, after all the necessary expenses have been paid, shall be applied, according to the discretion of the Conference, toward the college, the Preachers' Fund, the deficiencies of the preachers, the distant missions, or the debts on our churches."

At that time the principal part of the printing business was carried on in Philadelphia. In 1804 it was removed to New York. It was first located in John-street, and then successively in Pearl-street, Church-street, Catharine-street, and Crosby-street, and finally, in 1830, it was removed to Mulberry-street, the site it now occupies.

Asbury was also the father of missions in the Methodist Church, sending out preachers into destitute settlements, and soliciting here and there, all over the country, funds for their support. In addition to this, a plan for a fund for the relief of the preachers was devised by him and carried out, which resulted in a Chartered Fund that exists to this day.

In an early day Bishop Asbury established a fund which was called afterward "The Asbury Mite Fund," and carried with him in his pocket a small subscription-book, in which was inserted the names of subscribers. This fund was afterward denominated the 'Preachers' Fund," and several hundred dollars were obtained. Rev. John Dickins succeeded in having this fund increased, and such was the result that in 1797 the Legislature of Pennsylvania granted a charter under the style and title of "The Trustees of the Fund for the Relief and support of the Itinerant Superannuated Ministers and Preachers of the Methodist Episcopal Church in the United States of America, their Wives and Children, Widows and Orphans." The most of this was subscribed in Philadelphia. Considerable was derived from various other sources, and the amount was subsequently increased by legacies. The whole sum was nearly twenty-five thousand dollars. Loans of money from time to time were made from this fund to enable the Book Concern to carry on its business. Its proceeds are still regularly divided among the Conferences.

Wesley himself never devised and carried into execution so many plans of benevolence in connection with his societies as did Asbury for the Methodist Episcopal Church. Nor was this all. He was the first man on the continent to introduce Sabbath schools. In the year 1786, five years before any other person moved in this matter, he organised a school in Hanover county, Virginia, in the house of Thomas Crenshaw, and, as one of its first fruits, John Charleston was converted to God in that school, and afterward became a useful and successful minister of the Gospel in the Methodist Episcopal Church.

When we consider the vast results accruing to the Church from the far-reaching policy of Asbury, and now, after almost a century of trial, find that the welfare of the Church, in almost everything pertaining to her prosperity, but especially in connection with the institutions founded by him, which have become identified with her progress, is directly traceable to his agency, the profound wisdom of the founder of American Methodism becomes strikingly apparent. He was evidently the man for the times in which he lived; and not only so, but his plans were of such breadth and scope as to be wisely adapted to all times.

Asbury did not wait for the organization of Education, Missionary, Bible, Preachers' Relief, Tract, and Sunday School Societies before entering upon the work connected with these benevolent departments of church action, but combining all these societies in his own person, he originated and carried them into successful operation, and from the fact that these benevolent agencies all stand to this day, constantly increasing in magnitude and power, it is obvious that to this wonderful man belonged a share of wisdom rarely found to exist in man, and such as fitted him in a most eminent degree for the position he occupied as the head of the Methodist Episcopal Church in America.

All these agencies he regarded as the natural outgrowth of the Church, the pulsations of her mighty heart, throbbing with benevolent sympathy for mankind. The Church is in itself a Missionary, Bible, Sunday School, and Mutual Relief Society, and if any of these departments of benevolence are found necessary for their more efficient action to exist in a separate and distinct corporation, they can only be regarded in the light of auxiliaries to the Church for the furtherance of her benevolent design. We have sometimes doubted whether the multiplication of organizations, with the frequently cumbrous and complex machinery of constitutions, managers, officers, and agents, separate and apart from the Church, was as efficient a mode for furthering the objects as it would be if they were brought directly in contact with the Church. When this pioneer missionary started out upon his continental journey, he supplied himself with Bibles and other books, and scattered them abroad as the leaves of the tree of life and knowledge for the healing of the nation. He says in his Journal : " When the bishop was old, and pressed down by many infirmities, when the ' almond-tree was flourishing, and those that look out of the windows were darkened, the grinders ceasing because they were few, and the keepers of the house began to tremble,' his brethren wished him to retire, as God had raised up many strong men ; but the bishop, like the apostolic Wesley, did not wish ' to live to be useless,' and replied, ' No man can do my work.' Forward he would go in his Master's employment ; and though he was not able to preach as formerly, he would place a number of Bibles in his waggon, and distribute them, saying, ' Now I know I am sowing good seed.' "

Having originated Sunday schools, it was not long before Asbury had the subject incorporated in the Discipline of the Church. In 1784, in the section which defined the duties of ministers of the Gospel, we find the following : " What shall be done for the rising generation ? Who will labour for them ?"

" Let him who is zealous for God and the souls of men begin now. 1. Where there are ten children whose parents are in society, meet them at least an hour every week ; 2. Talk with them every time you see any at home ; 3. Pray in earnest for them ; 4. Diligently instruct and vehemently exhort all parents at their own houses ; 5. Preach expressly on education."

Six years subsequently the following appears in the Discipline : " What can be done in order to instruct poor children, white and black, to read ?"

" Let us labour as the heart and soul of one man ·to establish Sunday schools in or near the place of public worship. Let persons be appointed by the bishops, elders, deacons, or preachers, to teach *gratis* all that will attend, and have a capacity to learn, from six o'clock in the morning until ten, and from two o'clock in the afternoon until six, where it does not interfere with public worship. The Council shall compile a proper school-book to teach them learning and piety." After this Sunday schools were established in several places, and the teachers took nothing for their services. The greater part of the scholars were black children, whose parents were reluctant to send them, and but few of them were regular in their attendance, so that in a short time the teachers were discouraged, and seeing little or no prospect of doing good, they gave up the enterprise.

On the subject of this section of the Discipline, Bishop Asbury thus comments : " Alas ! the great difficulty lies in finding men and women of genuine piety as instructors. Let us, however, endeavour to supply these *spiritual* defects. Let us follow the directions of this section, and we shall meet many in the day of judgment who will acknowledge before the great Judge, and an assembled universe, that their first desires after Christ and salvation were received in their younger years by our instrumentality. In towns we may, without difficulty, meet the children weekly, and in the plantations advise and pray with them every time we visit their houses : nay, in the country, if we give notice that at such a time we shall spend an hour or two at such a house with those children who shall attend, many of the neighbours will esteem it a privilege to send their children to us at the time appointed. But we must exercise much patience, as well as zeal, for the successful accomplishment of this work. And if we can, with love and delight, condescend to their ignorance and childishness, and yet endeavour continually to raise up their little minds to the once dying but now exalted Saviour, we shall be made a blessing to thousands of them.

"But let us labour *among the poor* in this respect as well as among the competent. O, if our people in the cities, towns, and villages were but sufficiently sensible of the magnitude of this duty, and its acceptableness to God—if they would establish Sabbath Schools, wherever practicable, for the benefit of the children *of the poor*, and sacrifice a few public ordinances every Lord's day to this charitable and useful exercise, God would be to them instead of all the means they lose : yea, they would find, to their present comfort and the increase of their eternal glory, the truth and sweetness of those words, 'Mercy is better than sacrifice.' Matt. ix, 13 ; xii, 7 ; Hos. vi, 6. But there is so much of the cross in all this ! O when shall we be the true followers of a crucified Saviour !"

The deep interest taken by this devoted man in the subject of the religious education of the children was perfectly apparent in his whole life. His Journal abounds with notices of his having preached on the subject, and shows the earnest solicitude which characterized all his labours in this particular department of Christian effort. Like a true philosopher, he knew that the hope of the country depended upon the proper education of the children, and like a wise master-builder in the erection of the Christian edifice, he was fully impressed with the fact that the hope of the Church as it regarded its symmetry, beauty, and strength, depended upon the rising generations. Now that, after a long life of toil for the salvation of parents and children, he has passed away, his memory is embalmed in the hearts of thousands, who have "risen up and called him blessed." There are perhaps this day more that bear the name of Asbury connected with the Methodist Episcopal Church than that of any other minister. Many of them are in the ministry, and show themselves to be true sons of the immortal father of American Methodism. In his last will and testament he made a provision that all then living who bore his name should have a copy of the Bible, a beautiful edition of which he had procured for the purpose. How far this provision was carried out we know not, but we mention it as an impressive and beautiful incident in the life of that man of "blessed" memory, and at the same time as an exhibition of a trait of character which distinguished him in the relation he bore to the children of the Church. Father Finley, one of the pioneer preachers of the West, relates an incident as bearing upon this point which is truly touching. A youth at a camp-meeting was called by the good bishop, and kindly spoken to on the subject of religion, and the advice he received made such an impression on his mind as ever after remained, and served to mark and mould his destiny, for he afterward became a minister in the Methodist Church, and was instrumental in the conversion of thousands. Asbury never allowed an opportunity to pass where he could speak to the children in the families where he stopped in his itinerant wanderings.

In 1792 Asbury was zealously engaged in organizing what he called district schools. His plan was to establish a school in every presiding elder's district.* This was particularly desirable in the Southern and Western portions of his great field, where there were no common schools ; and was but little less needed in the North, where the academies and seminaries were all monopolized, and under the exclusive control of denominations which had no sympathy for, if indeed they were not hostile to, the Methodists. The writer recollects distinctly when at certain institutions of learning in the country the students were all required by law to study the Westminster Catechism, and on Sabbath were marched rank and file to the Presbyterian church, no matter what their preferences or those of their parents. The same was true of the Episcopal Church institutions. In this movement, however, Asbury found himself, as he did in many other great benevolent enterprises, vastly in advance of his age. Still, he laboured on, drew up an address calling the attention of the people to the subject, and exerted himself in every way to develope and advance the object he had in view. He was not, however, sustained in his laudable efforts, and was obliged to yield to the force of circumstances and abandon the enterprise, however painful to his benevolent heart.

Sixty-five years have passed away since the effort of Asbury to establish preparatory schools for the Church. Time in its ravages has swept away all of this description that then existed in the Church, but from their ashes have sprung up Conference academies and seminaries all over the land, amounting in all, North and South, to one hundred and sixty-two. In the year 1793 a Conference was held at Mount Bethel, South Carolina, at that time the seat of a high school founded by the labours of Asbury. A writer in the "Southern Advocate" furnishes the following interesting sketch of this institution :

"This section of the country was peopled by emigrants from Virginia, among whom we may mention as permanent 'the Finches,' ' the Crenshaws,' 'the Malones,' and others. They had

---

* Each presiding elder's district at this time embraced a whole Annual Conference ; hence the term district in this connection is synonymous with conference.

become Methodists in their native state, and when the subject of a high school was agitated they entered heartily and with liberal subscriptions into the project. Edward Finch gave thirty acres of land as a site for the institution. The buildings had been commenced, but for want of the necessary funds progressed slowly, so that when the Conference aforesaid met they were incomplete, and afforded, as may readily be imagined, but narrow and uncomfortable quarters for thirty preachers. The daily sessions were held ' in an upstairs room of the house of Esquire Finch, twelve feet square.' During the year 1794 the building was completed, and was formally dedicated by Bishop Asbury ' on his next annual visit, on the 20th of March, 1795, with a sermon from 1 Thess. v, 16, and was named Mount Bethel.' On the succeeding Sabbath Asbury preached again and held a 'love-feast,' which proved to be a blessed season of spiritual refreshing. The school was for six years under the rectorship of the Rev. Mark Moore, a man eminently qualified for the post, assisted by two other teachers, Messrs. Smith and Hammond. At the close of this term of service, Mr. Moore resigned, and took charge of a school in Columbia, where, by his influence and preaching ability, which was of the first order, he materially aided in the permanent establishment of Methodism in that city. On the retirement of Mr. Moore, Mr. Hammond, father of ex-Governor Hammond, took charge of the school and taught it with signal ability for many years. For a number of years Mount Bethel and Willington Academy (in Abbeville District, under the control of the celebrated Dr. Waddell) were the only schools of high grade in the interior of the state, and did much in the educational training of the young men of South Carolina. Mount Bethel was largely patronized, and had, from time to time, students from Georgia and North Carolina. A number of the leading men in our own state, in subsequent years, were prepared for college at Mount Bethel, among whom were Hon. John Caldwell, and Chancellor James J. Caldwell, of Newberry District, Judge Earl, the first ex-Governor Manning, of South Carolina, William and Wesley Harper, sons of Rev. John Harper. The first and second classes who graduated in the South Carolina College, received their preparatory training here also. Wesley Harper graduated in the second class of the college, and died soon after. William Harper graduated in the third class in 1808, and subsequently became, as is well known, one of the first jurists in the country.

" The main building of this institution was twenty by forty feet, divided by a partition, with chimneys at each end, constructed of rough, unhewn stone. The upstairs was used as the lodgings of the students.　Several comfortable cabins were also built, and served as residences of the teachers and as boarding houses.　About a hundred yards distant, at the foot of a hill, ran a bold spring of pure cold water of sufficient volume to supply all the wants of the resident population.　Of this monument of Asbury's zeal in the cause of education, nothing scarcely remains.　All the buildings have been pulled down and the location much altered in its appearance, and the traveller who might now visit it would hardly conceive its former glory and usefulness.　Nothing now remains to mark the spot except the three chimneys of 'Father Finch's' house, which yet stand as solitary sentinels over .this classic ground.　Near by is a large grave-yard, in which many of the original settlers and some of the students quietly sleep the sleep of death.　Here, too, lie in modest seclusion the last mortal remains of Rev. John Harper.　A rude stone, some six or eight inches above ground, bearing the letters 'J. H.,' marks his grave.　Mr. Harper was an Irishman, and came to New London, Conn., in company with Rev. Mr. Kingston, missionary from the West Indies.　They were present at the first Conference held in New London, and from which Mr. Harper took a station in Boston.

Bishop Asbury continued annually to visit Mount Bethel school until the year 1815, when old age and increasing infirmities curtailed the field of his labours.　After years of prosperity and usefulness it began to decline, and finally ceased to exist about the year 1820, and was, we believe, superseded by 'Mount Ariel Academy,' in Abbeville District, and that in turn by 'Cokesbury School.'"

CHAPTER XII.

Asbury's Attachment to America when his Associates in the Ministry fled the Country—Writes a Complimentary Letter to an Advocate of American Principles—Admonition to the Conference in relation to the Employment of an English Preacher—His unbounded Admiration for Washington—Proposition to the New York Conference in 1789—Asbury and his Associates introduced to Washington in his Official Capacity—Address of the Bishop—Washington's Reply—The Methodist Episcopal Church the first to recognize the Government of the United States—With other Churches an Afterthought—No Union of Church and State, but Government Protection—The Government Christian—Obedience to Government an Article of Religion—Reflections—Asbury's Example—Tribute to Washington—Thoughts on Religious Liberty—Connecticut and Massachusetts Priest-ridden—View of the United States—Continental Officers.

WE have already remarked that the moment Asbury adopted this country as his home, he became at once and for ever an American in sentiment and action. When those who had come here before him, and those who were associated with him in the government of the Church, in time of trial left the country and the poor scattered flock in the wilderness and returned to England, he bravely stood his ground, resolving with the indomitable Adams, "live or die, sink or swim, survive or perish," he would remain identified with the country of his adoption, and never forsake the people of his charge. We ever find him on the side of the patriots of the Revolution, and stoutly withstanding to the face every English preacher who showed the least want of respect or loyalty to American principles. At one time we find him writing a complimentary letter to a Presbyterian minister who had made a speech in the constitutional convention in favour of the principles of American liberty ; and at another time, when the Conference was engaged in discussing a resolution looking toward the employment of an English preacher who had left his appointment in the West Indies without permission, we hear him in a voice of thunder exclaiming, " *Take care !* *take care !*" and adding, "I have had more trouble with English preachers than all others put together."

He possessed the most unbounded admiration for Washington. He, the first, the greatest, and the best of men, always commanded his highest sympathy and regard. With Washington he had many personal and friendly interviews, and availed himself of such whenever opportunity presented ; and when that great and good man was chosen by the suffrages of his countrymen to preside over the nation as its chief magistrate, he was among the first to congratulate him upon his elevation to so distinguished a post.

Among the prominent acts of the Conference held in New York in 1789, Asbury offered the following proposition : "Whether it would not be proper for us as a Church to present a congratulatory address to General Washington, who has been lately inaugurated President of the United States, in which should be embodied our approbation of the Constitution, and professing our allegiance to the government." The Conference unanimously acceded to the proposition, and enthusiastically recommended the measure, requesting the bishop to prepare such an address. The same day the address was presented and read to the Conference, and meeting its hearty approval, Dickins and Morrell were appointed a committee to wait on the president, and inform him of the action of the Conference, and request him to appoint a day when he would receive the bishop, who would read the address and receive his answer.

At the appointed time, accompanied by Dickins and Morrell, Asbury was introduced to the President in his official character, and in a clear and impressive manner read the following :

"SIR,—We, the bishops of the Methodist Episcopal Church, humbly beg leave, in the name of our society collectively in these United States, to express to you the warm feelings of our hearts, and our sincere congratulations on your appointment to the presidentship of these States. We are conscious, from the signal proofs you have already given, that you are a friend of mankind ; and under this established idea, place as full confidence in your wisdom and integrity for the preservation of those civil and religious liberties which have been transmitted to us by the providence of God and the glorious Revolution, as we believe ought to be reposed in man.

"We have received the most grateful satisfaction from the humble and entire dependence on the great Governor of the universe which you have repeatedly expressed, acknowledging him the source of every blessing, and particularly of the most excellent Constitution of these States, which is at present the admiration of the world, and may in future become its great exemplar for imitation ; and hence we enjoy a holy expectation that you will always prove a faithful and impartial patron of genuine, vital religion, the grand end of our creation and present probationary existence. And we promise you our fervent prayers to the throne of grace, that God Almighty may endue you with all the graces and gifts of His Holy Spirit, that he may enable you to fill up your important station to His glory, the good of His Church, the happiness and prosperity of the United States, and the welfare of mankind."

After Asbury had concluded, Washington rose and read, in a calm but earnest manner, the following reply :

"GENTLEMEN,—I return to you individually, and through you to your society collectively in the United States, my thanks for the demonstrations of affection, and the expressions of joy offered in their behalf, on my late appointment. It shall be my endeavour to manifest the purity of my inclinations for promoting the happiness of mankind, as well as the sincerity of my desires to contribute whatever may be in my power toward the civil and religious liberties of the American people. In pursuing this line of conduct, I hope, by the assistance of Divine Providence, not altogether to disappoint the confidence which you have been pleased to repose in me.

"It always affords me satisfaction when I find a concurrence of sentiment and practice between all conscientious men, in acknowledgment of homage to the great Governor of the universe, and in professions of support to a just civil government. After mentioning that I trust the people of every denomination, who demean themselves as good citizens, will have occasion to be convinced that I shall always strive to prove a faithful and impartial patron of genuine, vital religion, I must assure you in particular, that I take in the kindest part the promise you make of presenting your prayers at the throne of grace for me, and that I likewise implore the Divine benediction on yourselves and your religious community."

The address to Washington was signed by Bishops Coke and Asbury in behalf of the Methodist Episcopal Church in the United States of America, and that of Washington was addressed " To the Bishops of the Methodist Episcopal Church of the United States of America." Thus the Methodist Episcopal Church was the very first, in an ecclesiastical capacity, to recognise the government of the United States ; and its chief magistrate, in a public and formal manner ; and its independent organisation was in turn recognized by the highest authority in the Union. With the Presbyterian and other Churches it was an afterthought to present similar addresses, but nevertheless it was none the less right and appropriate, and deserving of commendation, on that account. Though the government of the United States recognizes no legal union with the Church, or any branch of it, and has in consequence been denounced by our enemies as godless and antichristian, it has nevertheless from the beginning thrown its protecting ægis over the Church, and as sacredly guards the rights of conscience as it does the freedom of political opinion. Our government is as thoroughly Christian, both in its federal and state capacity, as any ecclesiastico-political establishment in the world, and is the only government under heaven where religious liberty exists.

Among the Articles of Religion of the Methodist Church we find the following :—

"XXIII. *Of the Rulers of the United States of America.* The president, the congress, the general assemblies, the governors, and the councils of state as *the delegates of the people,* are the rulers of the United States of America, according to the division of power made to them by the general Act of Confederation and by the Constitution of their respective States. And the said States ought not to be subject to any foreign jurisdiction." Subsequently the following note was added : " As far as it respects civil affairs, we believe it is the duty of Christians, and especially all Christian ministers, to be subject to the supreme authority of the country where they may reside, and to use all laudable means to enjoin obedience to the *powers that be*, and therefore it is expected that all our preachers and people who may be under the British government, or any other government, will behave themselves as peaceable and orderly subjects."

These declarations embrace the doctrine of the Church in regard to civil government, and whoever is not governed by this doctrine, and is not loyal to the government where he resides, cannot be a Methodist of the American stamp. Asbury, the father and founder of American Methodism, has set a noble example to all his sons in the ministry in his attachment to the government, and the respect he paid to its chief rulers. It is readily admitted that the chair of state has not always been occupied by such pure and noble men as Washington, but whoever shall in the providence of God be called or permitted to fill that place, if the man cannot command our love, the office itself should command our respect.

We shall close this chapter by a quotation from Asbury's Journal, referring to the death of Washington. It is a noble tribute, worthy of its author.

"Washington, the calm, intrepid chief, the disinterested friend, first father, and temporal saviour of his country, under divine protection and direction. A universal cloud sat upon the faces of the citizens of Charleston ; the pulpits clothed in black, the bells muffled, the paraded soldiery, the public oration decreed to be delivered on Friday, the 14th of this month, a marble statue to be placed in some proper situation—these were the expressions of sorrow, and these the marks of respect paid by his fellow-citizens to this great man. I am disposed to lose sight of all but Washington. Matchless man ! At all times he acknowledged the providence of God, and never was he ashamed of his Redeemer. We believe he died not fearing death. In his will he ordered the manumission of his slaves—a true son of liberty in all points."

While at Ellington, Connecticut, in 1794, Asbury preached in a school-house, and felt great dejection of spirit at the iron walls of prejudice which existed, and indulged in the following reflections on the subject of religious liberty : "Out of the fifteen United States thirteen are free, but two are fettered with ecclesiastical chains, taxed to support ministers who are chosen by a small committee and settled for life. My simple prophecy is that this must come to an end with the present century. The Rhode Islanders began in time and are free. Hail, sons of liberty ! Who first began the war ? Was it not Connecticut and Massachusetts ? and priests are now saddled upon them. O what a happy people would th'ese be if they were not thus priest-ridden! I heard a most severe letter from a citizen of Vermont to the clergy and Christians of Connecticut, striking at the foundation and principle of the hierarchy. It was the expression of the Vermonters to continue free from ecclesiastical fetters, to follow the Bible, and give equal liberty to all denominations of professing Christians."

In 1796 he read Winterbotham's View of the United States, and remarked that " he had compared the great talk about President Washington formerly with what some say and write of him now. According to some he then did nothing wrong ; it is now said that he was always partial to aristocrats and continental officers. As to the latter I ask, Who bought the liberty of the states? Did not the continental officers, and should they not reap a little of the sweets of rest and peace. These were not chimney-corner whigs. But favours to many of the officers would now come too late. A great number of them are gone to eternity, their constitutions broken with hard fare and labour during the war. As to myself, the longer I live and the more I investigate, the more I am convinced of, and the more I applaud and approve of, the uniform conduct of President Washington in all the important stations which he has filled."

CHAPTER XIII.

WHILE Asbury and Coke were at Port Royal, Virginia, in the spring of 1791, they received the sad intelligence of the death of

I

Wesley. We find in Asbury's Journal the following tribute of respect for that great man : "The solemn news reached our ears that the public papers had announced the death of that dear man of God, John Wesley. He died in his own house in London in the eighty-eighth year of his age, after preaching the Gospel sixty-four years. When we consider his plain and nervous writings, his uncommon talent for sermonising and journalising, that he had such a steady flow of animal spirits, so much of the spirit of government in him, his knowledge as an observer, his attainments as a scholar, his experience as a Christian, I conclude his equal is not to be found among all the sons he hath brought up, nor his superior among all the sons of Adam he may have left behind. Brother Coke was sunk in spirit, and wished to start home immediately. For myself, notwithstanding my long absence from Mr. Wesley, and a few unpleasant expressions in some of the letters the dear old man has written to me, occasioned by the misrepresentation of others, I feel the stroke most sensibly, and I expect I shall never read his works without reflecting on the loss which the Church of God and the world has sustained by his death."

Dr. Coke soon left for Baltimore, for the purpose of taking the first passage that should offer for England. Having arrived in Baltimore, he preached on the occasion of the death of Wesley to a large congregation. It was a solemn and interesting occasion, and was most appropriately improved. Conference was held soon after in that city, and Asbury was present and preached on the succeeding Sabbath. From hence he went to Duck Creek, where he held Conference, and from thence to the Trenton Conference. After attending to the business of the Conference he proceeded to New York. The members of the Conference, which consisted of about thirty preachers, and the members of the two Churches, the old and the new, united in requesting Asbury to preach on the occasion of Wesley's death, which he consented to, preaching in the morning in the John-street, and in the afternoon in the Forsyth-street church, from the text, "But thou hast fully known my doctrine, manner of life, purpose, faith, long-suffering, charity, patience, persecutions, afflictions, which came unto me at Antioch, at Iconium, at Lystra ; what persecutions I endured; but out of them all the Lord delivered me." It was said by those who heard these discourses that they were worthy of their author and the occasion which called them forth.

After the close of this Conference the bishop went to New Haven, Connecticut. At this appointment he had the president of Yale College, some of the professors and students, and quite a number of citizens, as hearers. He gives the division of his subject on that occasion : " 1. What we must be saved from ; 2. What has been esteemed by the men of the world as the wisdom of preaching ; 3. What is meant by the foolishness of preaching." We presume from the division that the text was, " It pleased God by the foolishness of preaching to save them that believe." After he had finished his discourse no one came forward to speak to him. He availed himself of the opportunity of visiting the college chapel during the hour of prayer, and had a desire to visit the different departments of the college and inspect the arrangements, but whether they noticed him or not in the chapel, neither president nor professors deigned to pay any attention to him whatever. If this was designed, which we are rather inclined to think was the case, as such want of courtesy has occurred before where Methodist preachers were concerned, it was unpardonable. True wisdom as well as true religion, to say nothing of politeness, puts not on such supercilious airs as characterised some of the divines of that day.

From New Haven he went to Providence and preached, and from thence to Boston, where he also preached ; but being totally disgusted with the place and its want of hospitality, he exclaimed : " I am done with Boston until we can find a lodging-house to preach in, and some to join us." From Boston he rode to Lynn, a place which he called "the perfection of beauty," situated on a plain under a ridge of craggy hills and open to the sea. Here he found a promising society and an exceedingly well-behaved congregation. " Here," said Asbury, "we shall make a firm stand, and from this central point shall the light of truth and Methodism radiate through the state." How clearly and fully this prophecy has been fulfilled, the present state of the Church in Lynn, the declarations of Parsons Cook to the contrary notwithstanding, abundantly show. While here he wrote the following interesting letter to Daniel Fidler, a young minister who had been sent to Halifax :

" MY VERY DEAR BROTHER,—I called at your father's house, and spent a night there on my way from Old Town Conference. We hope the dear old people will make their way to glory. They will long greatly to see you after two years. You will return to the continent, or at least to the grand American Union, when your way is clear. We have a general growth and increase of souls. I hope that not less than three thousand will be made subjects of grace this year. A pretty general harmony reigns through the body as to travelling preachers. J. O'K***y is nearly left alone. His next move will be among the local line and the membership. Notwithstanding our trouble the work goes on westward, yet the savages are restless. I expect that in a very few years we shall be through New Hampshire, Maine, and Vermont states, and so become near neighbours to Nova Scotia.

" I fear I do not see as much simplicity in our young brethren now as in years past. The love of shining in dress and talents appears to be too prevalent. O my dear child, keep humble, watchful, simple, and walk with God, that you may live as well as preach the very spirit and practice of the Gospel. My heart is toward you in the love of Jesus. If I should see you again, O may you be full of grace and God ! Thine as ever."

After visiting and preaching at Salem, Marblehead, Manchester, Waltham, and Hartford, he returned to New York. Remaining here for a short time, attending to the interests of the Church in its various departments he took up the line of his journey again to the West. After passing through Pennsylvania, Virginia, North and South Carolina, he arrived at Tennessee. Here the bishop heard accounts of the depredations by Indians, which had produced a good deal of consternation in the country. He started from hence again to the wilderness, with a guard to protect him from the savages. After resting on Sabbath at Crabb's, where he preached, the company entered the wilderness. Some were on foot, carrying their packs on their shoulders. Among the number, strange to say, there were some women with their children, who had consented to brave the dangers of the wilderness, and seek a better home in the rich and fertile plains of the West. Kentucky had been described by the pioneer hunter, Boone, and his daring companions, who penetrated its desert wilds years before, as a very paradise for the poor man. And such it was, abounding in every variety of game, and having the richest and most luxuriant soil. With such inducements many were prompted to leave their poor inheritances in North Carolina and other parts, and to seek a better home in the fertile valley beyond the Cumberland. The company at length reached Laurel River, which they were compelled to swim. When they reached Rock Castle station, Asbury remarked that " he found such a set of sinners as made that place next door to hell itself." The next day they were obliged to re-swim the river twice in their journey. Asbury's horse was well nigh worn out, as was himself, being thoroughly wet all day. After a hard day's ride they reached the Crab Orchard late in the evening, wet and weary. In his Journal the bishop says : " How much I have suffered in this journey is only known to God and myself. What added much to its disagreeableness is the extreme filthiness of the houses." While here he wrote an address in behalf of the Bethel Academy, and made arrangements for improvements in the style of the building, which was ill adapted to the purposes for which it was erected.

On Wednesday, April 25th, 1792, the Conference commenced at Bethel. Vast crowds of people attended the ministry. After presiding and making out the appointments of the preachers, he made preparations for a return trip across the wilderness. An alarm was spreading of a depredation committed by the Indians on the east and west frontier of the settlement. It was reported that many men and women were killed. The consequence of such intelligence was that great excitement prevailed throughout that region. The party, however, started on their journey, determined at all hazards to brave the dangers. When the bishop reached Rock Castle he was well nigh worn out with fatigue. With a violent fever and pain in his head he stretched himself exhausted on the cold ground, and borrowing clothes to keep himself warm, he was enabled to sleep four or five hours. At the next stopping-place he could have slept more comfortably, but was deterred from closing his eyes on account of the proximity of the Indians. Seeing the drowsiness of the company he could not be persuaded to lie down, but walked the encampment and watched the sentries during the entire night. The company consisted of thirty-six. At length he reached Virginia and proceeded to Half-acres, and from thence went to Holstein, where the Conference for this region was held.

Passing through a valley where there were fifty miles without a house, he came to Uniontown. We find in his Journal but the merest sketch of his rides and stopping-places, but as landmarks we are enabled by them to trace his journeys round the continent from year to year. Again he is in Pennsylvania and Maryland, New Jersey, New York, Connecticut, and Massachusetts, everywhere preaching the word. As the Angel of the Apocalypse flying in mid-heaven with the everlasting Gospel to preach to all nations, so this pioneer bishop literally flew from state to state, and from territory to territory, with the messages of salvation.

The Conference for the Eastern division of the work was held this year at Lynn, where Asbury met eight preachers and transacted the business of the Church. A church edifice had been commenced, and was partly finished, in which there was preaching every night during the session of the Conference by one of its members selected for the occasion. The ordination sermon

preached by the bishop on this occasion was from the text, "Not
that we are sufficient of ourselves to think anything as of ourselves ;
but our sufficiency is of God ; who also hath made us able ministers
of the New Testament ; not of the letter, but of the spirit ; for the
letter killeth, but the spirit giveth life." From hence Asbury went
to Pittsfield, which he describes as "a pleasant plain reaching
from mountain to mountain, with a population of two thousand
souls. There was a grand meeting-house and steeple, both of
which were as white and glistening as Solomon's temple. The
minister was on the new divinity plan." Asbury enjoyed here the
privilege of "retiring alone to the cool sylvan shade in frequent
converse with his best Friend." "We held," says the bishop,
"our meeting in a noble house built for Baptists, Separatists, or
somebody, and is now occupied by the Methodists. A large and
attentive congregation was present. The eastern people are not to
be moved it is true ; they are too accustomed to hear systematical
preaching to be moved by a systematical sermon even by a Methodist ; but they have their feelings, and touch but the right string
and they will be moved."

He thus describes Lebanon, in the State of New York : "The
medicinal waters here are soft, pure, and light, with no small
quantity of fixed air. I found a poor bath-house. Here the
devil's tents are set up, and, as is common at these encampments,
his children are doing his drudgery." From hence he went to
Albany, and met twenty-one preachers in Conference. The occasion was one of great peace and harmony. Two deacons and four
elders were elected and ordained. Each preacher was called upon
to relate his experience, and the incidents connected with his itinerancy since the last session. These conversations not only embraced personal experience, but a review of doctrines and modes
of preaching. At this Conference Jonathan Newman was appointed
missionary to the whites and Indians on the frontier. Another
was sent to Cataraqui. The questions of theology discussed were
the following : "1. How are we to deal with sinners ? 2. How
should we treat with mourners ? 3. In what manner should
hypocrites be addressed ? 4. How should we deal with backsliders ?
5. What is the best kind of preaching for believers ?" A discussion of these questions we think might be profitable at the present
day. They are certainly vastly more relevant, and more in accordance with the peculiar vocation of a preacher of the Gospel, than
many other subjects which not only seem to engross councils, assemblies, and Conferences, but the pulpit itself, and which in many
instances engender strifes and hinder the progress of religion.

Preaching was held in the market-house, and the meetings were lively and interesting. About two hundred conversions had occurred in the district since the former session of the Conference. From hence Asbury rode to Hudson and Rhinebeck, and dined on his way to New Rochelle at Governor Van Cortlandt's. At New Rochelle he held quarterly meeting, and preached to large congregations with great liberty.

September 27th, Conference opened in New York, twenty-eight preachers being present. Most of the afternoon of the first day was spent in prayer and the relation of ministerial experience. The occasion was one of unusual interest. A Conference lovefeast was held on Friday. We will let Asbury, in his own quaint, nervous, laconic style, describe the thoughts which occupied his mind at this Conference : " My mind has been so bent to the business of, the Conference that I have slept but little this week. Connecticut is supplied much to my mind, several very promising young men having been admitted into this Conference. The societies are in harmony, but not as lively as they should be. I went to hear Dr. L., but was greatly disappointed ; he had such a rumbling voice that I could understand but little in that great house. How elegant the building ! How small the appearance of religion ! Lord have mercy upon the Reformed Churches. O ye dry bones, hear the word of the Lord. I was much obliged to my friend for renewing my clothing and giving me a little pocket-money ; this is better than £500 per annum. I told some of our preachers who were very poor how happy they were, and that probably had they more their wants would proportionally increase."

It is somewhat remarkable that New York supplied, or mostly supplied, Asbury with clothing and outfits for his journey. At least, if he obtained help from other places, with the exception of Baltimore, of this description, he did not make it so frequently a matter of record. In numerous instances he notices the hospitality and benevolence of friends in New York.

On Sabbath the bishop preached a sermon, preparatory to the sacrament of the Lord's supper, from the text, " Purge out therefore the old leaven, that ye may be a new lump, as ye are unleavened. For even Christ our passover is sacrificed for us : therefore let us keep the feast, not with old leaven, neither with the leaven of malice and wickedness ; but with the unleavened bread of sincerity and truth." His object was to show the points of similitude between the passover and the supper of the Lord, in which he noticed the simplicity and purity of bread instead of the flesh of an animal, and wine instead of the blood of a creature ; wine, the blood of Christ, and grace, the life of our souls. He showed that true penitents and real believers were proper communicants ; and also described the manner in which the sacrament was to be taken, not with unleavened bread, but with sincerity and truth.

On his route from New York he stopped at his old friend Judge White's, in Delaware, which we believe is the only place in all his Journal, with the exception of Sherwood's, that he calls "*home.*"

In reading Dr. Langdon on Revelation, he remarks: "I find little new or very spiritual. He is like the Newtons, and all historical interpreters ; one thing is wanting. And might not an interpreter show the present time foretold by these signs, which plainly point to the *why* and the *wherefore* it is that some are Christian bishops and Christian dissertators on prophecy ? A bishopric with one, or two, or three thousand sterling a year as an appendage might determine the most hesitating in their choice. I see no reason why a heathen philosopher, who had enough of this world's wisdom to see the advantages of wealth and honours, should not say, 'Give me a bishopric and I will be a Christian.' In the eastern states also there are very *good and sufficient* reasons for the faith of the favoured ministry. Ease, honour, interest ; what follows ? Idolatry, superstition, death."

After remaining at Judge White's for a few days he proceeded to Milford, where he preached and held a Conference with the local preachers. From thence he travelled on from one quarterly meeting to another, holding local preachers' Conferences, and preaching until he came round again to White's. While here this time he read Jefferson's Notes on Virginia, a book full of romantic incidents of border-life ; and it was at this place he made the remark that he "thought it safer for him to be occasionally among the people of the world than wholly confined to the indulgent people of God. He who sometimes suffers from a famine will better know how to relish a feast."

The following interesting incident in connection with his visits to this place is given by the Hon. Isaac Davis :

"During the time when Governor Bassett was a practising lawyer in the town of Dover, Delaware, previously to his election to the post of chief magistrate of the state, it was his custom, in the business of his profession, to attend the sittings of the court in Denton, Md., and he often, when on his way to and from Denton, would spend a night with his friend Judge White, where Bishop

Asbury enjoyed the comforts of a home when in the State, and where he found a secure retreat for two or three years during the Revolutionary struggle.

" On one of these periodical visits, Judge White being absent, his amiable wife received and entertained their guest. It was not long, however, before Mr. Bassett observed other gentlemen present besides himself, when he sought Mrs. White, and inquired with evident perturbation :

" ' Madam, who are these gentlemen dressed in black ?'

" Mrs. White, knowing that Methodist preachers were not in very high repute, answered evasively, ' They are gentlemen here on very important business.'

" This indefinite reply not being satisfactory to Mr. Bassett, he insisted further :

" ' Madam, I should like to know who these gentlemen are.'

" When Mrs. White replied, ' They are Mr. Asbury and his preachers.'

" This information was no sooner received than Mr. Bassett determined to leave, and said to his hostess, ' I must have my horse.'

" Mrs. White, understanding the case perfectly, replied, ' You cannot leave to-night, sir.'

" Mr. Bassett still demanded, ' I must have my horse, I must be gone.'

" But Mrs. White more positively declared he must not leave, when he resigned himself to his fate, and submitted to the infliction of an evening with the bishop and his co-labourers ; after which he was constrained to admit they were not the most uninteresting in the world, and, as an act of courtesy, he invited Mr. Asbury to visit him the next time he should come into Dover. When Mr. Bassett returned home he told his wife of his adventure, and concluded by saying, ' I have invited the Methodist bishop to visit us. And what will we do, my dear, should he come ?'

" ' Do the best we can,' was the only reply.

" Shortly after Mr. Bassett was busily engaged in his office. Happening to raise his eyes, and looking out on the green, he saw a venerable form on horse-back, riding leisurely toward his door, whom he soon recognized to be none other than the veritable Methodist bishop he had met at Judge White's ; he quickly informed his wife of the arrival, who ran up stairs in a fright. Mr. Bassett cast about in his mind how he should entertain his rather unwelcome guest ; his plan was decided upon ; invitations were sent to the most distinguished gentlemen in the neighbourhood ; the lawyers, doctors, and clergymen were all called in ; Mr. Bassett thought to overwhelm the poor Methodist bishop with an array of intellect ; but Mr. Asbury seemed perfectly composed and at home among gentlemen. After supper the conversation took a more decidedly literary character, and among other things a recent publication came up, upon which several criticisms were passed, Mr. Asbury's being the clearest, most comprehensive, and intelligent. The company conceded to him his proper place. They became listeners, and he the delight of every person present ; and from that evening party must be reckoned the beginning of Mr. Asbury's popularity in Dover.

"The best of the story remains to be told. By request, Mr. Asbury preached the next evening to a large and intelligent audience. Mrs. Bassett gave him a hearing from her piazza, fearing to venture nearer ; next night from the door of the house in which the bishop preached ; the third night she mingled in the congregation, and soon after was converted, and proved the first-fruits of Bishop Asbury's labours in Dover. Who can fail to note the hand of Providence in this whole affair, from the beginning to the ending ?' "

The bishop paid the following merited tribute to the memory of Judge White. As this was his home during a portion of the dark troublous times of the Revolutionary war, when the preachers fled from the country, and others were fined and imprisoned for their adherence to the British government, and he found in this family a safe retreat, he could not but feel, as he expresses himself on hearing of the death of the judge, most sadly :

"Thursday, May 21, 1795. This day I heard of the death of one among my best friends in America, Judge White, of Kent county, in the state of Delaware. This news was attended with an awful shock to me. I have met with nothing like it in the death of any friend on the continent. Lord help us all to live out our short day to thy glory ! I have lived days, weeks, and months in his house. O that his removal may be sanctified to my good and the good of the family ! He was about sixty-five years of age. He was a friend to the poor and oppressed ; he had been a professed Churchman, and was united to the Methodist connection about seventeen or eighteen years. His house and heart were always open, and he was a faithful friend to liberty in spirit and practice ; he was a most indulgent husband, a tender father, and an affectionate friend. He professed perfect love and great peace, living and dying."

CHAPTER XIV.

COKE having returned from England, whither he had gone soon after receiving intelligence of Wesley's death, the two bishops again met in Baltimore just on the eve of the General Conference. An important crisis had now arrived in the history of the Methodist Episcopal Church. Under the superintendency of Asbury the difficulties which in other days had threatened its peace and unity had all been happily adjusted. A separate and distinct organization, effected through the advice and by the authority of Wesley at the general convention of the preachers in Baltimore in 1784, while it removed all the obstacles out of the way of the exercise of full ministerial functions by the ministers, at the same time invested the Church with every right and prerogative to adopt whatever articles of religion it deemed wise and proper, as well as to make all the laws and regulations necessary for its government. Under this state of things the Church continued to prosper, and in 1792 the membership had increased to sixty-five thousand nine hundred and eighty, and the ministry to two hundred and sixty-six. The Church had also enlarged the area of her territory, and extended it from Massachusetts to Georgia. Twenty Conferences instead of three were now held annually, and the number was increasing yearly, so wonderfully did the work of the

Lord spread and prevail. While these eight years had wrought changes in the external appearance of Methodism, and everywhere there appeared the most evident signs of prosperity, there were nevertheless, to the eye of the ever watchful Asbury, signs of discontent. The vast and efficient machinery put so successfully in operation was not without its friction. It was thought by some that the power of the episcopacy was brought to bear too strongly upon the preachers; or, in other words, that the prerogative of the bishop to appoint preachers at his pleasure required some restriction. One of the presiding elders had indulged to a considerable extent in remarks against the exercise of this power, and had to the extent of his influence created quite a sentiment in opposition. It was this, with other matters of moment connected with the interests of the Church, that led the Council, which constituted the highest judiciary in the Church at that time, to suggest the propriety of calling a General Conference, to be composed of all the preachers in full connection.

Before proceeding to describe the deliberations and acts of this General Conference, we deem it proper to bring to view more specifically the causes which led to its formation. In 1789 considerable discussion was had on the subject of a General Conference. To obviate the necessity of such a general convocation, the bishops presented to the Conferences the plan of a *Council*. It was introduced by the following preamble : " Whereas the holding of General Conferences on this extensive continent would be attended with a variety of difficulties and many inconvenencies to the work of God; and whereas we judge it expedient that a Council should be formed of chosen men out of the several districts as representatives of the whole connection, to meet at stated times, Therefore," etc.

To the questions, " In what manner shall this council be formed? what shall be its powers? and what the regulations concerning it ?" the following answer was given :

" 1. Our bishops and presiding elders shall be the members of this Council, provided that the members who form it shall never be less than nine. If any unavoidable circumstance prevent the attendance of a presiding elder at the Council, he shall have authority to send another elder out of his own district to represent him ; but the elder so sent shall not take his seat in the Council without the consent of the bishop, or bishops, and presiding elders present. And if, after the above-mentioned provisions are complied with, any unavoidable circumstance or contingency arise so as to reduce the number to less than nine, the bishop shall immediately summon such elders as do not preside to complete the number.

" 2. The Council shall have authority to mature everything they shall judge expedient, (1.) To preserve the general union. (2.) To render and preserve the external form of worship similar in all our societies throughout the continent. (3.) To preserve the essentials of Methodist doctrine and discipline pure and uncorrupted. (4.) To correct all abuses and disorders. (5.) To mature everything they may see necessary for the good of the Church, and for the promotion and improvement of our colleges and plan of education.

" 3. Provided, nevertheless, that nothing shall be received as the resolution of the Council unless it be assented to unanimously by the Council, and nothing so assented to by the Council shall be binding in any district (Conference) till it has been agreed upon by a majority of the Conference which is held for that district.

" 4. The bishops shall have authority to summon the Council to meet at such times and places as they shall judge expedient."

Though considerable opposition was manifested to this plan, and it was regarded as a dangerous innovation, yet, after due deliberation, it was adopted by a majority, and became a part of the Discipline of the Church. As it may be interesting to the reader, merely as a matter of history, we copy from Lee's History of Methodism the minutes of the first Council, which was held in Baltimore, December 1, 1789. The following members were present : Francis Asbury, bishop ; Richard Ivy, Reuben Ellis, Edward Morris, James O'Kelly, Philip Bruce, Lemuel Green, Nelson Reed, Joseph Everitt, John Dickins, James O. Cromwell, Freeborn Garrettson, elders." When the Council was constituted, an hour was spent in prayer to Almighty God for his direction and blessing. " They then unanimously agreed that a General Conference of the bishop, ministers, and preachers of the Methodist Episcopal Church on the continent of America would be attended with a variety of difficulties, with great expense and loss of time, as well as many inconveniences to the work of God."

The Council then proceeded to form the following constitution, embracing its several duties :

" 1. To render the time and form of public worship as similar as possible in all the congregations.

" 2. To preserve the general union of the ministers, preachers, and people in the Methodist doctrine and Discipline.

" 3. To direct and manage all the printing which may be done from time to time for the use and benefit of the Methodist Church in America.

" 4. To conduct the plan of education, and manage all matters

which may from time to time pertain to any college or house built
or about to be built as the property of the Methodist connection.

" 5. To remove, or receive and appoint the salary of any tutors
from time to time employed in any seminary of learning belonging
to the said connection.

" 6. In the interval of the Council the bishop shall have power
to act in all contingent occurrences relative to the printing business
or the education and economy of the college.

"7. Nine members, and no less, shall be competent to form a
Council, which may proceed to business.

" 8. No resolution shall be formed in such a Council without
the consent of the bishop and two-thirds of the members present."

After adopting the above constitution, the Council then passed
unanimously the following resolutions :

" 1. Every resolution of the Council shall be put to vote in each
Conference, and shall not be adopted unless it obtains a majority
of the different Conferences. But every resolution which is received
by a majority of the several Conferences shall be received by every
member of each Conference.

" 2. Public worship shall commence at ten o'clock on the Lord's
day in all places where we have societies and regular preaching, if
it be practicable, and if not, at eleven o'clock.

" 3. The exercises of public worship on the Lord's day shall be
singing, prayer, and reading the Holy Scriptures, with exhortation
or reading a sermon in the absence of a preacher, and the official-
ing person shall be appointed by the elder, deacon, or travelling
preacher for the time being.

" 4. For the future no more houses shall be built for public
worship without the consent and direction of the Conference and
presiding elder of the district, unless a house shall be built under
the direction of the presiding elder and travelling preachers on
the circuit, and finished without the least debt remaining on it.

" 5. It is required that all the parents and guardians of independent scholars in Cokesbury College may punctually pay for the
students' tuition and board on or before the first of December in
every year, as none will be continued there more than a year on
credit, but will be immediately sent home in case of non-payment.
And for the future, at least one-fourth of the price of twelve
months' board and tuition must be sent with every scholar who
comes from the adjacent states, and half the said price with every
scholar who comes from any distant state.

" 6. Every minister, preacher, and private member shall be
permitted, and is hereby earnestly requested, to devise some means,

and either bring or send his proposals to the next Council,
for the purpose of laying some scheme for relieving our dear
brethren who labour in the extremities of the work, and do not
receive more than six, eight, ten, twelve, or fifteen pounds per
annum.

" 7. Every deacon shall be three years in a state of probation
before he can be elected to the eldership.

" 8. Considering the weight of the connection, the concerns of
the college, and the printing business, it is resolved that another
Council shall be held on the first of December, 1790."

The second Council, which had by this last resolution been provided for, was held in pursuance therewith in the city of Baltimore. Bishop Asbury, F. Garrettson, F. Poythress, N. Reed, J.
Dickins, P. Bruce, J. Smith, T. Bowen, J. O. Cromwell, J. Everitt,
and C. Conoway were present. The first business done was to
settle the question relating to the power with which the electors
had invested the Council, and this they did by declaring unanimously that they were invested with *full* power to act *decisively* in
all *temporal* matters, and that it was their prerogative to recommend to the several Conferences any new canons, or alterations to
be made in any old ones. Various other matters were disposed of,
and the Council adjourned to meet again the next year. O'Kelly,
who had attended the first Council, refused to be present ; and such
was his opposition, and that of Lee and others, to what they regarded as an unwarranted assumption of power, that no Council
was ever afterward held, and it became obvious that nothing would
meet the wants of the preachers and the people generally but a
General Conference. This was agreed to, and accordingly on the
1st day of November, 1792, the preachers in the regular work
collected together from the country and took their seats in General
Conference assembled in the city of Baltimore.

Bishops Coke and Asbury being, *ex officio*, the presiding officers,
the Conference was duly organized by the election of the secretaries
and the appointment of the appropriate committees. The first
thing brought before the Conference for deliberation and action
was the Discipline of the Church. Before any action, however,
was taken upon any subject introduced to the Conference, certain
bye-laws were adopted for its government, among which was a rule
requiring a two-third's vote of all the members of the Conference
to adopt any new rule or abolish any old one, though a bare
majority might suffice to modify or amend any rule. As the subject of discipline came under review of the Conference, those parts
especially which had been the subject of discussion, and regarding

the propriety of which there was a difference of opinion, were the first to elicit attention.   James O'Kelly, the presiding elder (above alluded to) over a district in Virginia, one of the largest in the connection, in an early part of the session brought forward the subject of episcopal power as relating to the appointment of the preachers.   The question was embraced in the following resolution : "Resolved, that after the bishop appoints the preachers at the Conference to their several circuits, if any one think himself injured by the appointment, he shall have liberty to appeal to the Conference and state his objections ; and if the Conference approve his objections, the bishop shall appoint him to another circuit." This resolution brought the whole subject of the episcopacy, and its powers and prerogatives, before the Conference.   As the discussion would necessarily bring the whole administration, involving particularly the episcopal acts of Bishop Asbury, before the Conference, with characteristic liberality, lest any should be deterred from speaking out fully his sentiments on the subject, the bishop withdrew from the Conference-room and forwarded the following letter :

"My Dear Brethren,—Let my absence give you no pain ; Dr. Coke presides.   I am happily excused from making laws by which I am myself to be governed.   I have only to obey and execute.   I am happy in the consideration that I never stationed a preacher through enmity or as a punishment.   I have acted for the glory of God and the good of the people, and to promote the usefulness of the preachers.   Are you sure that, if you please yourselves, the people will be as fully satisfied ?   They often say : ' Let us have such a preacher ;' and sometimes, 'We will not have such a preacher ; we would sooner pay him to stay at home.' Perhaps I must say, ' His appeal forced him upon you.'   I am one, ye are many.   I am as willing to serve you as ever.   I want not to sit in any man's way.   I scorn to solicit votes.   I am a very trembling, poor creature, to hear praise or dispraise.   Speak your minds freely, but remember you are only making laws for the present time.   It may be that, as in some other things, so in this, a future day may give you further light."

The discussion of the question lasted for several days, and was quite animated on both sides.   At length, when the period arrived to take the vote, it was ascertained that a large majority were in favour of continuing with the episcopacy the power given to it at the Conference in 1784.   It may not be improper to remark here, that this question was revived in what was denominated the "Radical Controversy " in 1827, and with that of lay delegation, and some other matters of Church government, it led finally to a secession, the result of which was the organization of the Methodist Protestant Church, now a large and influential body of Christians. Several of the ablest and most distinguished ministers were lost to the Church in this controversy ; a calamity which we pray may never befall the Church again.

In Lee's History of Methodism, published in 1810, we find the following in relation to the controversy in the General Conference on the subject of the appointing power, as elicited by the resolution offered by O'Kelly : " This motion brought on a long debate ; the arguments for and against the proposal were weighty, and handled in a masterly manner. There never had been a subject before us that so fully called forth all the strength of the preachers. A large majority of them appeared at first to be in favour of the motion, but at last Mr. John Dickins moved to divide the question thus : First, shall the bishop appoint the preachers to the circuits ? And secondly, Shall a preacher be allowed an appeal ? After some debate the motion to divide the question prevailed. The first question being then put, it was carried without a dissenting voice ; but when we came to the second question, namely, Shall a preacher be allowed an appeal ? there was a difficulty started, which was, whether this was to be considered a new rule, or only an amendment of an old one. If it was to be regarded as a new rule, it would require a two-third's vote to carry it. After considerable debate it was decided by vote that it was only an amendment of an old rule. Of course, after all the lengthy debates, we were just where we began, and had to take up the question as it was originally proposed. One rule for our debates was, that each person, if he choose, shall have liberty to speak three times on each motion. By dividing the question, and then coming back to where we were at first, we were kept on the subject called the *Appeal* for two or three days. On Monday we began the debate afresh and continued it through the day, and at night we went to Mr. Otterbein's church and continued it till near bed time, when the vote was taken, and the motion was lost by a large majority."

Having disposed of this difficult subject, the Conference proceeded to the discussion of the questions pertaining to the appointment, ordination, and trial of a bishop. The Church being, as we have seen, disconnected from the Wesleyan connection, and existing as a separate and independent organization, the power to appoint a bishop could no longer come from without, and the General Conference was hence made the source of episcopal power, the exercise of which was placed exclusively under its control, holding original jurisdiction over all its bishops.

K

The question relating to presiding elders was fully discussed at this Conference. By the authority of the bishop alone a number of circuits had been formed into districts, and from the organization of the Church, in 1784, they had been placed under the charge of a presiding elder. We say this was done by the authority of the bishop, as the Conference had made no rules or regulations on the subject. As considerable objection had been urged against this usage, and several expressed doubts as to the authority of the bishop in appointing the presiding elders, the Conference, under the head of episcopal duties, made it the duty of the bishop to appoint the presiding elders, and gave him the power to change them at pleasure, provided that he should not allow an elder to preside over the same district for more than four consecutive years. The duties of presiding elders were also more specifically defined. Until this Conference no provision whatever was made for the support of the wives of travelling preachers. If a preacher married, his salary of sixty-four dollars remained the same as before, the design being evidently to keep up the celibacy of the clergy, an example of which was so strongly and perseveringly maintained by the bishop. The Conference, however, after a thorough investigation of this matter, in all its present and prospective bearings, adopted a rule allowing the wife an equal claim with her husband. The sum total of the allowance or salary for a Methodist preacher and his family was thus increased to the amount of one hundred and twenty-eight dollars. Such was the allowance, but it did not follow by any means that this amount was received. In numerous instances the half of it was not obtained, and the preachers and their wives were obliged to live in the most abject poverty, or on the most cringing dependence.

At this Conference John Dickins was reappointed agent of the Book Concern in Philadelphia, and for his services was allowed a house and book-room, and six hundred and sixty-six dollars thirty-three cents per annum, which was to be paid out of the profits arising from the sale of books. The Conference also appropriated out of the proceeds of the Book Concern four thousand dollars, to be paid in four annual instalments. Six hundred and sixty-six dollars were also appropriated out of the same fund for the benefit of distressed preachers, and also the bishop was allowed to draw annually on the Book Concern the sum of sixty-four dollars for the support of district schools. The profits of the Book Concern at that time amounted annually to about two thousand five hundred dollars.

Previous to this Conference it was not only contrary to usage, but contrary to the law of the Church for any preacher to take a fee for performing the marriage ceremony. This, like the other ordinances of the Church, was not to be purchased with money, and there were some who thought it a species of simony to take anything for celebrating the rites of matrimony. The General Conferences, however, came in their deliberations to a different conclusion, and allowed those who should be called upon to perform this ceremony to receive whatever might be given on the occasion. But though the Conference allowed preachers to take a fee for performing the rites of matrimony, yet the money thus received was not to be regarded as their own. The amount was placed in the hands of the stewards of the respective circuits, and equally divided between the travelling preachers of the circuit who had not received their full disciplinary allowance. Where such necessity for its appropriation did not exist, it went into the hands of the District or Annual Conference, to be appropriated accordingly to its discretion; in no case, however, was it the property of the preacher who performed the ceremony.

With a view of bringing all the preachers upon a level, as it regarded salary, and thereby prevent any unpleasant feeling that might arise, a rule was adopted requiring all the preachers to present an exact account of all and singular the presents they might have received, either in money or other articles, and until this was done no money could be appropriated to him from any fund or collections to make up deficiencies.

The Conference, also, with a view to prevent any imposition upon the societies from unworthy members, or those who were impostors outright, adopted a rule requiring all members, on their removal to another society, to take a certificate of good standing, and this rule remains in force to this day. The rules, however, relating to salaries, marriage fees, and presents, have long since become obsolete, and have passed away from the discipline. Though the salary nominally allowed a preacher is one hundred dollars, and his wife the same, with a small sum for each of his children under a certain age, together with his travelling, fuel, and table expenses, yet under these heads, especially the latter, our ministers at the present day can receive in salary, table expenses, presents, and marriage fees, any amount. Some we know of who receive annually on these accounts from two to three thousand dollars. As a whole, however, the Methodist ministry are poorly paid, many of them on the poorer circuits not receiving more than two or three hundred dollars, and some even less.

An important rule on the subject of arbitration was adopted at this Conference. This rule had special reference to the settlement of disputes arising between brethren in regard to debts. It has been modified from time to time, and has proved of great service in preventing litigation, and keeping "brother from going to law with brother." The chapter relating to the manner of conducting public worship was inserted in the Discipline at this Conference, and with slight modifications from time to time still remains.

Asbury in his journal, alluding to this Conference, and the opposition manifested against the appointing power, says : " Perhaps a new bishop, new Conference, and new laws, would have better pleased some. I have been much grieved for others, and distressed with the burden I bear, and must hereafter bear. Oh, my soul, enter into rest ! Some of the preachers having their jealousies about my influence in the Conference, I gave the matter wholly up to them and to Dr. Coke, who presided. I am not fond of altercations ; we cannot please everybody, and sometimes not ourselves. Mr. O'Kelly, being disappointed in not getting an appeal from any station made by me, withdrew from the connection and went off. For himself, the Conference well knew that he could not complain of the regulation. He had been located in the Southern District of Virginia for about ten successive years, and upon his plan might have located himself and any preacher, or set of preachers, to the district, whether the people wished to have them or not. The General Conference went through the Discipline, Articles of Faith, Forms of Baptism, Matrimony, and the Burial of the Dead, as also the Offices and Ordination. The Conference ended in peace, after providing for another General Conference, to be held four years afterward. By desire of the brethren, I preached once on 1 Peter, iii. 8. My mind was kept in peace, and my soul enjoyed rest in the stronghold."

CHAPTER XV.

Second Decade of Methodism passed—Results of Twenty-six Years—Position
of the Church—Southern Tour—Whitefield's Orphan House in Georgia—
Melancholy Reflections—Asbury crosses the Wilderness—Sick—Continental
Tour—Great sickness in New York—Few Preachers at Conference—Yellow
Fever in Philadelphia —Day of Fasting, Humiliation, and Prayer—Pestilence
in Maryland—Pass from a Health Officer— Preaches in Baltimore—Takes up
Winter Quarters at Charleston—Midnight Journey—Father Harper's Plan-
tation—Asbury at Baltimore, June, 1724— Portrait taken at request of
Preachers—Original Picture in possession of Baltimore Methodist Historical
Society—Travels to Boston—Remarks—New York Conference—Preaching
—Yellow Fever at Baltimore—Whisky insurrection in the West—Charleston
—Rough Treatment—Leaves the South—Trip Northward—At New York,
Fourth of July—Rev. Mr. Ogden's Work on Revealed Religion—New
England—Grave of Embury at Ashgrove—Residence of Garrettson—Go-
vernor Van Cortlandt—At the Mansion of his friend Wells in Charleston—
His Slaves—Asbury's Labours in Charleston—"Ben," the Half-blood Indian
Warrior—Thrilling Account of Mrs. Dickenson—Constitution for a Relief
Fund—Asbury in New York—Explains the Discipline to the Leaders—His
Definition of Schism—New England Conference—Rumours of Yellow Fever
—Crossing the Bay in a Storm—Conference in Philadelphia —Short Sketch
of Benjamin Abbott.

THE second decade of Methodism in America had passed, and the
middle of the third had been reached at the session of the First
General Conference. What mighty results had been achieved
through the instrumentality of the pioneer missionaries during the
period of twenty-six years! In considerably less than one generation, the Methodist Church in America had risen from the
smallest and feeblest beginnings to a large denomination, embracing the whole country, from Maine to Georgia, in the field of its
operations, besides including portions of the province of Canada.
From a small society, composed, as we have seen, of six persons,
who met to listen to the instructions of a carpenter in his rude
shop on Barrack-street, New York, the number had increased to
sixty-five thousand; and instead of one local preacher, there were
two hundred and sixty-six engaged in the regular work, besides
hundreds who, like Embury, laboured with their hands for a support during the week, and on Sabbaths visited destitute localities,
preaching the gospel without fee or reward. From a feeble and
unorganised society, without the ordinances and without a "regularly authorised ministry," Methodism had risen up to take its
position with an ordained ministry, and the full possession of all the

ordinances as a separate and distinct organisation among the Churches of the land.

After the session of the General Conference Asbury started out on his Southern tour, and travelled as far as Georgia. While at Savannah he visited the ruins of Whitefield's Orphan House. He gazed with melancholy interest upon the blackened walls, and recognised among the ruins the copper-plate inscription which had been inserted in the main building. While Whitefield was eating his last dinner at this house, it is said he remarked as follows : " This house was built for God, and cursed be the man that puts it to any other use." Asbury was led to the following reflections in regard to this enterprise : " I reflect upon the present ruin of the Orphan House, and taking a view of the money expended, the persons employed, the preachers sent over, I was led to inquire, where are they ? The earth, the army, the Baptists, the Episcopal Church, the Independents, have swallowed them all up at this *windmill of the continent.* A wretched country this ; but there are souls, precious souls, worth worlds."

From Georgia he passed through the country aud returned by way of Kentucky, crossing the wilderness to Virginia, and thus on through New Jersey to New York. From hence he passed through Connecticut and Massachusetts and returned to New York. In all this tour he was in labours more abundant, preaching at every point, and superintending the various business connected with the Conferences. Though he had been sick four months of the time, yet he had travelled three thousand miles since General Conference. When he returned to the city of New York he found great sickness prevailing. But few preachers attended the Conference, on account of the pestilence. While here he received intelligence of the prevalence of yellow fever in Philadelphia, and was dissuaded from going to that place, as it would be attended with great danger. But duty called, and he felt that in following the behests of duty he was safe, ay, even immortal till his work was done. The following, which we find in his Journal of Friday, 6th of September, will show the state of the city at that time : "Ah, how the ways mourn ! how low spirited are the people while making their escape! I found it awful indeed. I judge the people die from fifty to one hundred in a day ; some of our friends are dying, others flying. Sabbath I preached on the text, ' Cry aloud, spare not ; lift up thy voice like a trumpet, and show my people their transgressions, and the house of Jacob their sins.' The people of this city are alarmed, and well they may be. I went down to Ebenezer Church, but my strength was gone ; however, I endeavoured to open and apply Micah vi. 9 : " The Lord's voice crieth unto the city, and the man of wisdom shall see thy name : hear ye the rod, and who hath appointed it.' The streets are now depopulated, and the city wears a gloomy aspect. Poor Philadelphia ! ' The lofty city, He layeth it low ' " The preachers, in view of the calmity, appointed a day of fasting and humiliation, and after Sabbath left the city ; but Asbury remained.

The pestilence also prevailed in Maryland, and on his route he stopped at a quarterly meeting at the Cross Roads, where he preached from the text, "Yea, in the way of thy judgments have we waited for thee." In this discourse he showed that God sent pestilence, famine, blasting, and mildew, and that only the Church, and the people of God know and believe his judgments ; that God's people waited for him in the way of his judgments, and that they improved and profited by them. Having been in the infected region, he could not travel without a pass from the health officer, and hence, when he was en route for Baltimore, he found a guard stationed one hundred miles from the place. At Baltimore he preached from the words, "Give glory to God before he cause darkness, and before your feet stumble upon the dark mountains, and while ye look for light he turn it into the shadow of death, and make it gross darkness." Having delivered his testimony, he proceeded to Annapolis, and then returned to meet the Conference in Baltimore. From hence he started out on his southern tour. This year he declined going to the West, and gave the following as his reasons : "The American Alps, the deep snows and great rains, swimming the creeks and rivers, riding in the night, sleeping on earthen floors, more or less of which I must experience if I go to the western country, might cost me my life. I have only been able to preach four times in three weeks." He accordingly proceeded south, and took up his winter-quarters at Charleston, which he describe as "the seat of Satan, dissipation, and folly."

The following description of a midnight journey in North Carolina at this time will serve as a specimen of many of Asbury's adventures in travelling: "At length we came to Howe's Ford, on the Catawba River, where we could get neither canoe nor guide. We entered the river at the wrong place, and were soon among the rocks and in the whirlpools. My head swam and my horse was affrighted ; the water was to my knees, and it was with difficulty we retreated to the same shore. My horse being afraid to take to the water a second time, my companion crossed over, and sent me his horse, the guide which had been procured from the other side taking mine across. We passed on ; but our troubles were not at an end. It was very dark, and rained heavily, accompanied with tremendous lightning and thunder. We lost our path and wandered in the wilderness past midnight until we struck one, which we followed. This path fortunately led us to dear old father Harper's plantation. We made for the house, and called. He answering, but wondering who it could be, inquired whence we came. I told him we would tell him when he let us in, for it was raining so powerfully we had no time to talk. When I came dripping into the house he cried, 'God bless your soul, is it Brother Asbury? Wife, get up.' "

In June, 1794, he arrived at Baltimore, and worn and weary sought a little rest. While here he had his portrait taken at the request of the preachers. In regard to this he says : " It seems they will want a copy ; if they wait longer perhaps they will miss it. Those who have gone from us in Virginia (alluding to the O'Kelly secession) have drawn a picture of me which is *not taken from the life*." The original portrait of the venerable bishop is in possession of the Baltimore Methodist Historical Society. From Baltimore the bishop started out on his northern tour, passing through Pennsylvania, New Jersey, New York, and Connecticut to Massachusetts. In Boston he writes : " Like our Lord, we had to preach in an upper room, but we shall yet have a work in Boston." On his return he held a Conference at New York. While here he preached on Sabbath in John-street in the morning, and in Forsyth-street in the afternoon. The next Sabbath he preached in the new church in Brooklyn. Intelligence came to him of the raging of the yellow fever at Baltimore, and the insurrection in the West on account of the excise law relative to the manufacture of whisky.

Again he started south, and meeting with the usual incidents on the way, of swimming rivers, wading swamps, riding all day in the rain, and nearly all night in the dark, preaching as he went " in weariness and painfulness," and often " in perils in the wilderness," he at length reached Charleston, his southern home. To save himself, if possible, he concluded to spend a portion of the winter in this place. The mild climate was favourable to his health, though the city was very offensive to his moral feelings. He was frequently insulted in the streets, and while engaged in prayer with a few persons, those outside would shout at him in derision.

While here at this time he was unusually dejected. He says in his Journal : "I have been lately more subject to melancholy than for many years past, and how can I help it ; the white and the worldly people are intolerably ignorant of God ; playing, dancing, swearing, racing, these are their common practices and pursuits.

Our few male members do not attend preaching, and I fear there is hardly one who walks with God; the women and Africans attend our meetings, and some strangers also. Perhaps it may be necessary for me to know how wicked the world is that I may do more as a president minister. There is some similarity between my stay here and at Bath." Further on he says : "The people have high work below stairs, laid off for each day this week. The western regiment parades to-day, the eastern to-morrow. Wed-. nesday is the president's birthday ; Thursday, Friday, and Saturday, come on the races. I intend to keep close to my room, except when attending meetings in the evenings ; I am in a furnace, may I come out purified like gold." When the period arrived for his leaving he preached a parting discourse. The congregation was very large, and he remarked that if the people were prudent, and the preachers faithful, there would be a work of the Lord even in that "seat of wickedness."

When spring returned to melt the frozen fetters of the North, he left the sunny South and entered upon his itinerant career. After attending Conference at Holstein, he crossed the mountains and proceeded along the valley between the Blue Ridge and the Alleghanies, to the heads waters of the Shenandoah, which he followed to its mouth, crossing the Potomac near Harper's Ferry, and proceeding to Baltimore. In seven days he rode two hundred and twenty-seven miles. From thence he bent his course for New York, where he arrived on the 4th of July, amid the ringing of bells, the firing of cannon, and the shouts of liberty. The Rev. Mr. Ogden, of New York, presented him on this visit with a copy of his work on Revealed Religion, being an answer to Paine's Age of Reason. He took from hence his tour through New England on the old route, and on his return for the first time visited Vermont. During this visit he had an opportunity of seeing the grave of Embury at Ashgrove. He visited the residence of Garrettson at Rhinebeck, one of the first native American Methodist preachers, a faithful, devoted, and talented minister of the Gospel, cheerfully submitting to all privations, shrinking from no toils or hardships, bearing all persecutions for the sake of his Master, and among the first to bear the glad tidings of salvation to Western New York. He also visited Governor Van Cortlandt at Croton, whose princely mansion was always open for Methodist preachers, and who afterward dedicated a magnificent grove near his residence as a place for holding the yearly camp-meeting. Asbury could appreciate and enjoy hospitality, and though he never courted, yet when Providence opened his way he never shunned the society of the wealthy. After having toiled through the wilderness, sleeping in cabins or in the woods, and living on the coarsest fare, he would enjoy the rest and comfort afforded at the mansions of Mr. Van Pelt on Staten Island, Judge White in Delaware, General Russell in Holstein, Mr. Wells in Charleston, General Lippett, in Cranston, R. I., Mr. Phelps in Virginia, Mr. Johnson in Massachusetts, Govenors Worthington and Tiffin in Ohio, and several others in different sections of the country.

On his southern tour we find him again at the mansion of his old friend Wells in Charleston. An incident occurred here which shows how deeply Asbury sympathized with the coloured people. He says : " I was happy last evening with the poor slaves in Brother Well's kitchen, while our white brother (the stationed preacher) held a sacramental love-feast in the front parlour up stairs." During his stay in the city this time, which was about two months, he attended the business of the Conference, preached eighteen sermons, met fifteen classes, wrote eighty letters, besides more than three hundred pages on subjects interesting to the Church, read several books, and visited thirty families again and again, and yet in the review of all this he asks : " What have I done ? who are made the subjects of grace ?" We doubt if there are any regular pastors without any other duties who can present an exhibit of labour in their charges superior to this.

On his return trip, in crossing the ridge which runs through Russell county, Virginia, he says of the people : " They have lived in peace ever since the death of Ben, the half-blood Indian warrior, who was shot through the head while carrying off two women. He was a dreadfully wicked wretch, and had been the agent of death to nearly one hundred people in the wilderness and on Russell." While in this section of the country he inserts the following in his Journal : " This day in the evening Brother Kobler was called upon to perform the funeral services of Mrs. F. Dickenson, who has been as great a female sufferer as I ever heard of. She was married to a Mr. Scott, and lived in Powell's Valley ; at which time the Indians were very troublesome, often killing and plundering the inhabitants. On a certain evening, her husband and children being in bed, eight or nine Indians rushed into the house ; her husband being alarmed, started up, when all that had guns fired at him. Although he was badly wounded, he broke through them all, and got out of the house. Several of them closely pursued him, and put an end to his life. They then murdered and scalped all her children before her eyes, plundered her house, and took her prisoner. The remainder of the night they spent around a fire in the woods, drinking, shouting, and dancing. The next day they divided the plunder with great equality; among the rest of the goods was one of Mr. Wesley's hymn-books; she asked them for it, and they gave it to her; but when they saw her often reading therein they were displeased, called her a conjurer, and took it from her. After this they travelled several days' journey toward the Indian towns; but, said she, my grief was so great I could hardly believe my situation was a reality, but thought I dreamed. To aggravate my grief one of the Indians hung my husband's and my children's scalps to his back, and would walk the next before me. In walking up and down the hills and mountains, I was worn out with fatigue and sorrow; they would often laugh when they saw me almost spent, and mimic my panting for breath. There was one Indian who was more humane than the rest. He would get me water, and make the others stop when I wanted to rest. Thus they carried me on eleven days' journey, until they were all greatly distressed with hunger. They then committed me to the care of an old Indian at the camp, while they went off hunting.

"While the old man was busily employed in dressing a deer skin, I walked backward and forward through the woods, until I observed he took no notice of me. I then slipped off, and ran a considerable distance and came to a cane-brake, where I hid myself very securely. Through most of the night I heard the Indians searching for me, and answering each other with a voice like that of an owl. Thus was I left alone in the savage wilderness, far from any inhabitants, without a morsel of food, or any friend to help, but the common Saviour and friend of all; to him I poured out my complaint in fervent prayer that he would not forsake me in this distressing circumstance. I then set out the course that I thought Kentucky lay, though with very little expectation of seeing a human face again, except that of the savages, whom I looked upon as so many fiends from the bottomless pit; and my greatest dread was that of meeting some of them while wandering in the wilderness.

"One day as I was travelling, I heard a loud human voice, and a prodigious noise, like horses running. I ran into a safe place and hid myself, and saw a company of Indians pass by, furiously driving a gang of horses which they had stolen from the white people. I had nothing to subsist upon but roots, young grape vines, and sweet cane, and such like produce of the woods. I accidentally came where a bear was eating a deer, and drew near in hopes of getting some; but he growled and looked angry, so I left him, and quickly passed on. At night, when I lay down to rest, I never slept but I dreamed of eating. In my lonesome travels I came to a very large shelving rock, under which was a fine bed of leaves. I crept in among them, and determined there to end my days of sorrow. I lay there several hours, until my bones ached in so distressing a manner that I was obliged to stir out again. I then thought of, and wished for home; and travelled on several days, till I came where Cumberland River breaks through the mountain.

"I went down the cliffs a considerable distance until I was affrighted, and made an attempt to go back, but found the place down which I had gone was so steep that I could not return. I then saw but one way that I could go, which was a considerable perpendicular distance down to the bank of the river. I took hold of the top of a little bush, and for half an hour prayed fervently to God for assistance. I then let myself down by the little bush until it broke, and I went with great violence down to the bottom. This was early in the morning, and I lay there a considerable time with a determination to go no further. About ten o'clock I grew so thirsty that I concluded to crawl to the water and drink, after which I found I could walk. The place I came through, as I have been since informed, is only two miles, and I was four days in getting through it. I travelled on until I came to a little path, one end of which led to the inhabitants, and the other to the wilderness. I knew not which end of the path to take. After standing and praying to the Lord for direction, I turned to take the end that led to the wilderness. Immediately there came a little bird of a dove colour near to my feet, and fluttered along the path that led to the inhabitants. I did not observe this much at first, until it did it a second or third time. I then understood this as a direction of Providence, and took the path which led me to the inhabitants.

"Immediately after her safe arrival she embraced religion, and lived and died a humble follower of Christ."

From this point Asbury pursued his journey until he arrived in Baltimore, where he made a review of his southern travels since leaving that place, as follows:—"From the best judgment I can form, the distance is as follows : from Baltimore to Charleston, S. C., one thousand miles; thence up the state of South Carolina, two hundred miles; from the centre to the west of Georgia, two hundred miles; through North Carolina, one hundred miles; through the state of Tennessee, one hundred miles; through the west of Virginia, three hundred miles; through Pennsylvania and the west of Maryland, and down to Baltimore, four hundred miles. It will be seen that this tour of two thousand three hundred miles did not embrace the wilderness of Kentucky and Ohio, the most dangerous and difficult portion included in his annual round.

While in Philadelphia, on his northern tour, he drew up a constitution for a general fund, designed for the support of the travelling ministry, and to be applied, first, to the single men that suffer and are in want ; second, to the married travelling preachers; third, to the worn-out preachers ; fourth, to the widows and orphans of those who have died in the work ; fifth, to enable the annual conferences to employ more married men ; and lastly, to supply the wants of all the travelling preachers, under certain regulations and restrictions, as the state of the fund would admit.

New York seems to have been one of the fields of his greatest labours. Frequently we find him preaching three times and visiting six classes on one Sabbath, an amount of labour that none of his successors of the present day would think of performing. On one occasion, after preaching twice on the Sabbath to sixteen hundred hearers each time, he said : " The preachers had pity on me, and desired me only to preach twice." While in this city, in 1796, he found it necessary to call a meeting of the leaders of the different classes for the purpose of explaining the Discipline in regard to the right of the preacher in charge to expel members when tried before them, or a select number of them, and found guilty of a breach of the law of God and the rules of the Church. He also explained the nature of an appeal. On the subject of schism he made the following remark : "Schism is not dividing hypocrites from hypocrites, formal professors from people of their own caste. It is not dividing nominal Episcopalians from each other, nominal Methodists from nominal Methodists, or nominal Quakers from nominal Quakers ; but schism is the dividing real Christians from each other, and breaking the unity of the Spirit." This is the true apostolic definition of schism, which consists in "rending the body of Christ," and not in any disruption of a false Church.

From New York, Asbury passed on through New England. preaching everywhere, "in labours more abundant," and looking with a fatherly anxiety over all the interests of the Church. Returning to New York, he made preparations for the approaching Conference. When the period arrived, several preachers were detained at home on account of rumours of yellow fever in the city. Enough, however, arrived to attend to the business of the Conference, and a peaceful, profitable session was held. After preaching in John-street and in the new church, Asbury ordained eight deacons and seven elders, the services connected with which required him to be on his feet six hours in the course of the day. On Monday, not being able to find a passage at Powles Hook, on account of the stormy weather, two of the preachers went to Whitehall, where they found a boat which, in the language of Asbury, "would sail, sink, or swim for Van Deezen's Landing on Staten

Island." He felt rather reluctant about entering the craft and braving the dangers, but finally embarked. He says : " We passed the bay, ten miles over, in the space of an hour. When we were within one mile of the dock the wind shifted and blew powerfully ; the people on shore were alarmed, and had the skiff ready to take us up, expecting we should fill and sink, or be beaten off and strike the rocks. After a time we secured the boat and landed the men, but left the landing of the horses for better weather."

At Philadelphia he preached in the Ebenezer and St. George's Churches, to large and attentive congregations. At the Conference there were present between forty and fifty preachers, and the session was characterised by great harmony and prosperity. For the first time since Asbury had been on the continent, it was announced that sufficient money had been raised to pay the salaries of all the preachers, and besides there was a surplus of two hundred dollars, which was appropriated to relieve the preachers from embarrassment and pay their debts. From hence the bishop directed his course toward Baltimore, where the General Conference was to be held in November.

One of the remarkable men in the itinerancy of the times about which we are now writing, was Benjamin Abbott. He was a man of great simplicity of manner and good native talents, though entirely uncultivated. His success as a preacher was of the most wonderful character. Wherever he went crowds were attracted to hear him, and he rarely preached a sermon that was not attended with immediate results in the conversion of souls. Beyond his Bible and Hymn Book he did not extend his studies, but seemed to have been shut up to them entirely. He had deep experience in spiritual things, and his labours were characterised with great faith and zeal. Having strong faith, all his movements partook of its nature, and he as confidently expected souls would be converted as that the Gospel was preached. It was this element in his character that gave him such power in preaching, and made him one of the most successful ministers of his day. He travelled, like most of the preachers of that day, over a wide extent of country, and precious fruits of his ministry were gathered in all parts of the land. Of the graces of oratory or elocution he knew nothing ; a child of nature, he obeyed her impulses alone, and with a heart full of love to God and love to man, he was like a minister from Pentecost, with a heart of fire and a tongue of flame. Hence his word was with power, and none could resist the eloquence or gainsay the wisdom with which he spoke. His last labours were on the eastern shore of Maryland, and a fire was kindled throughout the length and breadth of the peninsula which burns even to this day. Like the holy lamp of the sanctuary, he was a flame ever burning : but in serving others he consumed himself, and thus literally burned out his life, a living sacrifice to the holy cause in which he was engaged. Thus lived and thus died this wonderful man.

CHAPTER XVI.

In the fourth decade of Methodism in this country, we shall embrace the General Conference held in Baltimore on the 19th of November, 1796. About one hundred preachers were present at this Conference, and the session began under the most favourable auspices. It was an occasion of great interest to see those hardy sons of itinerent toil assembled together from the extremes of the continent in that cradle of southern Methodism, the Light-street Church. The first thing they did was to receive the fraternal quadrennial greetings of their brethren in England. Though Wesley and the first class of itinerants associated with him had closed their career and entered into rest, their successors still retained an ardent attachment to all the members of the wide-spread family of Methodism. In their address the British Conference say : " We see an absolute necessity of strictly adhering to our first principles, by firmly sustaining our original doctrines, and that plan and discipline which we have so long proved to be the very sinews of our body. Herein we doubt not you are likeminded with us. We consider you a branch of the same root from which we sprung, and of which we can never think but with inexpressible gratitude. We congratulate you on the honour which our blessed Lord has put upon you in crowning your endeavours with such amazing success, and blessing you with the enjoyment of civil and religious liberty, for which we also have great cause to be thankful."

Up to this period in the history of the Church the bishops exercised discretionary power in appointing as many Annual Conferences as they judged expedient for the convenience of the preachers and people ; but as the General Conference possessed the legislative power to make rules and regulations, it was deemed best at this session to settle definitely the question in regard to their number, and also to define the respective boundaries of each. Accordingly the number of Conferences agreed upon was six, with the proviso that should it be considered essential to the demands of the work in New England, the bishop might organize an additional one in the province of Maine. The following were the Conferences authorized to be holden :—

1st. *The New England* Conference, embracing the States included under that name, and so much of the State of New York as lay east of Hudson River.

2nd. *The Philadelphia* Conference, embracing the remainder of the State of New York, New Jersey, all that part of Pennsylvania lying east of Susquehanna River, the State of Delaware, and the remainder of the peninsula.

3rd. *The Baltimore* Conference, including the remainder of Pennsylvania and Maryland, and the Northern Neck of Virginia.

4th. *The Virginia* Conference, embracing all that part of the State lying south of Rappahannock River, and all that part of North Carolina lying on the north side of Cape Fear River, including also the circuits on the branches of the Yadkin.

5th. *The South Carolina* Conference, embracing South Carolina, Georgia, and the remainder of North Carolina.

6th. *The Western* Conference, embracing the States of Kentucky and Tennessee.

Among the reasons given by the General Conference for its

action in the establishment of these Conferences, we find the following : "For several years the annual Conferences were very small, consisting only of the preachers of a single district, or of two or three very small ones. This was attended with many inconveniences. There were but few of the senior preachers whose years and experience had matured their judgments who could be present at any one Conference ; and, besides, the Conferences wanted that dignity which every religious synod should possess, and which always accompanies a large assembly of Gospel ministers. The itinerant plan was exceedingly cramped from the difficulty of removing preachers from one district to another. To all which it may be added that the active, zealous, unmarried preachers may move on a larger scale, and preach the ever blessed Gospel far more extensively through the sixteen states and other parts of the continent ; while the married preachers, whose circumstances require them in many instances to be more local in their sphere of labour than the single men, will have a considerable field of action opened to them, and also the bishops will be able to attend the Conferences with greater ease and without injury to their health."

For the purpose of securing the church edifices which had been built for the Methodist Episcopal Church, a plan of a deed of settlement was adopted by the Conference. The qualifications necessary for such as were candidates for elder's orders were also agreed upon and defined. Certain arrangements were made in regard to the publication of books, and also in relation to the management of the press, which were deemed important. The Conference decided upon establishing a monthly magazine. They also adopted a system of rules for the regulation of all the seminaries of learning under the patronage and control of the Church, which are alluded to elsewhere. A Chartered Fund, to be sustained by voluntary contributions, the principal stock of which was to be funded under the direction of trustees, and the interest accruing applied by order of the General Conference, was also established. The stock of the Preachers' Fund was merged into that of the Chartered Fund, and the annual profits of the Book Concern were appropriated to increase the stock. It was agreed that the money subscribed for the fund might be lodged on proper security in the states respectively where it had been subscribed, provided the securities were such as the trustees in Philadelphia approved. The sole design in the establishment of this fund was to secure to the Church the services of those ministers who otherwise, from sheer necessity, would have been obliged to retire from the work and engage in some secular employment for the support of their families.

L

Regulations were made at this Conference in regard to the subject of marriage of such a nature as to prohibit a member of the Church from marrying one who was not a member, or at least an awakened person, and requiring all who had the charge of circuits to enforce the discipline in all such cases, and exclude them from the Church. The Conference also gave directions in regard to the use and sale of ardent spirits ; and while it protested against any design whatever to trench upon the civil or religious liberty of any members of the Church, yet it considered the use of ardent spirits, unless in cases of necessity, and their sale, unless for mechanical, chemical, or medicinal purposes, such a crying evil that it was called upon, under the circumstances, to legislate against them. The subject of African slavery, which had more or less excited the attention of the Conferences from time to time, was also brought before this General Conference, and became a matter of serious and deliberate investigation. The members believed it their duty to seek in all proper legitimate ways the extirpation of the evil. The following were the regulations adopted :

" We declare that we are more than ever convinced of the great evil of African slavery, which still exists in these United States, and do most earnestly recommend to the yearly Conferences, quarterly meetings, and to those who have the oversight of districts and circuits, to be exceedingly cautious what persons they admit to official stations in our Church ; and in the case of future admission to official stations, to require such security of those who hold slaves, for the emancipation of them immediately or gradually, as the laws of the states respectively and the circumstances of the case will admit. And we do fully authorize all the yearly Conferences to make whatever regulations they judge proper in the present case respecting the admission of persons to official stations in our Church. No slaveholder shall be received into the society till the preacher who has the oversight of the circuit has spoken to him freely and faithfully on the subject of slavery. Every member of the society who sells a slave shall, immediately after full proof, be excluded the society ; and if any member of our society purchase a slave, the ensuing quarterly meeting shall determine on the number of years in which the slave so purchased would work out the price of his purchase. And the person so purchasing shall immediately after such determination, execute a legal instrument for the manumission of such slave at the expiration of the term determined by the Quarterly Conference ; and in default of his executing such instrument of manumission, or on his refusal to submit this case to the judgment of the quarterly meeting, such member shall be excluded the society. Provided, also, that in the case of a female slave it shall be inserted in the aforesaid instrument of manumission that all her children which shall be born during the year of her servitude shall be free at the following times, namely, every female child at the age of twenty-one, and every male child at the age of twenty-five. Nevertheless, if the members of our society executing the said instrument of manumission judge it proper, he may fix the times of manumission of the children of the female slaves before mentioned at an earlier age than that which is prescribed above. The preachers and other members of our society are requested to consider the subject of negro slavery with deep attention till the ensuing General Conference, and that they impart to the General Conference, through the medium of the yearly Conferences or otherwise, any important thoughts upon the subject, that the Conference may have full light in order to take further steps toward the eradicating this enormous evil from that part of the Church of God to which they are united."

An address was drawn up by a committee appointed for that purpose to the British Conference. Among other items contained in this address, we find the following :

" We candidly confess that we were very fearful, when the Lord took that eminent man, Rev. John Wesley, to his reward, that division would take place among you from the delicate circumstances in which you were placed. Among you he superintended for half a century to the admiration we had almost said of the entire civilized world. But our God is infinitely kind to us all. He has preserved both you and us in a wonderful manner. We rejoice in your union, and can bless God that we were never more united than at present. A few, indeed, who were as great enemies to the civil government under which they lived as to our Discipline, have left us, and we have now not a jarring string among us. At present you have the largest field of action in respect to the number of souls; but we are humbly endeavouring to sow those seeds of grace which may grow up and spread in this immense country, which in ages to come will probably be the habitation of hundreds of millions."

At the close of this Conference Asbury started out upon his Southern tour. His constitution, though naturally robust, had been undermined and shattered by disease. Exposure in all weathers, connected with excessive labours, brought on long attacks of inflammatory fever. He rode during this tour six hundred miles with a fever on him. Having Coke and Whatcoat as travelling companions, he was saved however from preaching as much as usual. While in Virginia he was amazed to hear that one of his oldest and most valued friends had been converted to the views of O'Kelly by being told by that reformer that he (Asbury) had offended Wesley, and for fear of being called to an account had cast him off altogether. To this he replies : "Query, Did not J. O'Kelly set aside the appointment of Richard What-coat ? and did not the Conference in Baltimore strike that *minute* out of our Discipline which was called *a rejecting of Mr. Wesley ?* and now, does J. O'Kelly lay all the blame on me ? It is true, I never approved of that binding minute. I did not think it practical expediency to obey Mr. Wesley, at three thousand miles distance, in all matters relative to Church government, neither did Brother Whatcoat, nor several others. At the first General Conference I was mute and modest when it passed, and I was mute when it was expunged. For this Mr. Wesley blamed me, and was displeased that I did not rather reject the whole connection or leave them if they did not comply. But I could not give up the connection so easily after labouring and suffering so many years with and for them." Thus it will be seen that it was not that Asbury loved Wesley the less, but that he loved the infant American Methodism more.

The sad intelligence came to him while in South Carolina that the Light-street Church and Cokesbury College, in Baltimore, in connection with Mr. Hawkins's elegant house, were consumed by fire. In this calamity the Methodists in Baltimore had the sympathy of the Episcopal, and the English and German Presbyterian Churches, which were kindly tendered for their occupancy. At Charleston he found his old friend, Mr. Wells, in a very dangerous sickness. After preaching on Sabbath he went to hear Dr. Coke in the evening. On Monday the preachers who had been attending the Conference left, and after accompanying Dr. Coke to Clement's Ferry, he returned to Mr. Wells's house, where 'he instructed his slaves in the kitchen, and then prayed with their master for the last time. On Tuesday he returned and found him dead, and "the widow in prayers and tears, and also the dear children and servants." The following testimony of regard for his friend we find in his Journal : "It is twelve long years next March since he received Henry Willis, Jesse Lee, and myself into his house. In a few days he was brought under great distress for sin, and soon after professed faith in Christ, since which he has been a diligent member of the society. About fourteen months ago, when there was a revival of religion in the society and in his own family, it came home to his own soul ; he was quickened and remarkably blessed, and continued so until his death. The last words he said were that he knew where he was ; that his wife was with him, and that God was with him. He was one much for the feeling part of religion ; a gentleman of spirit, and sentiment, and fine feelings ; a faithful friend to the poor, and warmly attached to the ministers of the Gospel." Dr. Coke pronounced an oration over his grave, and the succeeding Sabbath Asbury preached a funeral discourse on the text, " Be thou faithful unto death and I will give thee a crown of life."

While here he was quite ill with intermittent fever, but occupied his time with Dr. Coke in writing the Notes to the Discipline, which was continued until the latter sailed for Ireland, which he did on Friday, the 10th of February, 1797. When he parted with the doctor he felt unusually sad. About this time his spirits were more depressed than ever before. He says : " My depression of spirits at times is awful, especially when afflicted. That which is deeply constitutional will never die but with my body." When he left the city this time he felt like one escaped from prison. The balmy breath of spring revived his spirits, and as he rode along through the country he exclaimed : " Hail, ye solitary pines ! the jessamine, the red bud, and dog-wood ! How charming in full bloom ; the former most fragrant." Before him was a journey of two thousand miles, and his outfit consisted of but three dollars ; yet in courage and confidence he was resolved to prosecute it, and be found in the way of duty however discouraging the circumstances. His route lay through North Carolina and Tennessee on to Maryland, and thence to New York. Some of the most magnificent scenes are presented to the eye of the traveller in the route yearly taken by the bishop in passing through the borders of North Carolina and crossing what is called the Gap in the mountain. The ascent is gradual until the summit of the Blue Ridge is gained. From this point the scene is the most enchanting that can be imagined. Spread out in beauty, such only as nature can produce, as far as the eye can reach, beautiful plains and flowery woodlands, presenting, as it were, a continuous but ever-varying panorama, nothing can be more inspiring.

While at the Widow Sherwood's, in New York state, a family he frequently visited, and which was much loved by him, he says : " It is now eight weeks since I have preached—awfully dumb Sabbaths ! I have been most severely tried from various quarters. My fevers, my feet, and Satan would set in with my gloomy and nervous affections. Sometimes subject to the greatest effeminacy, to distress at the thought of a useless, idle life ; but what brought the heavy pang into my heart, and caused the big tear to roll, was the thought of leaving the connection without some proper men of their own election to go in and out before them in my place, and to keep that order which I have been seeking these many years to establish." While in New York he received a letter from Dr. Coke, who had gone from Ireland to England. He makes the following comments on this letter : " The three grand divisions of the Wesleyan connection are alarming. It is a doubt if the doctor comes to America until spring, if at all until the General Conference. I am more than ever convinced of the propriety of the attempts I have made to bring forward episcopal men : first, From the uncertain state of my health ; secondly, From a regard to the good order and union of the American body and the state of the European connection. I am sensibly assured that the Americans ought to act as if they expected to lose me every day and had no dependence upon Dr. Coke, taking prudent care not to place themselves at all under the controlling influence of British Methodists."

On his return to Baltimore he was called upon to open the new Light-street Church. His text for the occasion was : " Now therefore ye are no more strangers and foreigners, but fellow-citizens with the saints and of the household of God, and are built upon the foundation of the apostles and prophets, Jesus Christ himself being the chief corner-stone." From hence he went to Virginia, where he held a Conference, and then, believing that a journey to Charleston would be fatal, he concluded to take up winter-quarters at Mr. Drumgold's. His health was such that he could not preach, and his time was occupied in study and writing letters. When he could neither read nor write, he had such a horror of being idle that he occupied his time in winding cotton. While here he received a letter from Charleston Conference, representing all things in a peaceful and prosperous condition. He was prompted to review in this connection the labours of Methodist preachers. He says : " I make no doubt but others have *laboured;* but in England, Scotland, and Ireland, and those kingdoms that have been civilized and improved one thousand years, and which are under such improvements, no minister could have *suffered* in those days and in those countries as in America, the most ancient parts of which have not been settled two hundred years, some parts not forty, others not thirty, twenty, nor ten, and some not five years. I have frequently skimmed along the frontiers for four and five hundred miles, from Kentucky to Green Briar, on the very edge of the wilderness, and thence along Tagert Valley to

Clarksburg on the Ohio. I am only known by name to many of our people and some of our local preachers, and unless the people were all together they could not tell what I had to cope with. I make no doubt the Methodists are and will be a numerous and wealthy people ; and their preachers who follow us will not know our struggles but by comparing the present improved state of the country with what it was in our days, as exhibited in my Journal and other records of that day. Many other Churches go upon the paths already trodden two or three hundred years. We formed our own Church, and claim the power of a reform every four years. We can make more extensive observations, because our preachers in six or seven years can go through the whole continent and see the state of other Churches in all parts of this new world."

From his retreat he went out to Maryland, and passed through Delaware, Pennsylvania, New Jersey, and on to New York. While here he preached in John-street and at the Bowery Church, and rode out to Kingsbridge, where he also preached. On his return he preached in Brooklyn. A letter from England informed him of the death of his father, and he entered the following reflections in his Journal : "I now feel myself an orphan with respect to my father. Wounded memory recalls to mind what took place when I parted with him nearly twenty-seven years ago. He was a man that I seldom, if ever, saw weep ; but when I came to America, overwhelmed with grief and tears, he cried out, ' I shall never see him again !' For about thirty-nine years my father has had the Gospel preached in his house."

The indomitable Jesse Lee having penetrated the distant province of Maine, and organised societies and circuits, the time had now arrived for holding a Conference in that region. Asbury had a great desire to visit the noble and heroic band of Methodist preachers in Conference assembled. He had met Hall, Mudge, Merritt, Broadhead, and others associated with Lee in the New York Conference, but he wished to hold communion with them on the field of their toil and conflict. He accordingly, on the first month of the summer of 1798, left New York, and proceeded through Connecticut, Rhode Island, and Massachusetts, passing through Boston, Lynn, Salem, and Newburyport, to Portsmouth New Hampshire. Crossing the Piscataqua River, he stepped for the first time upon the soil of Maine. Proceeding along the sea shore, through Old York, the parish of the eccentric "Father Moodie," who never received anything for his salary but the prayers of the people ; through Wells, with its lovely bay and beautiful beach, over the pine plains of Kennebunk, and around the saline marshes of Scarborough, he arrived at Portland, where he found himself among strangers. Proceeding on to the Presumpscot River, he preached in a barn. At Gray he preached in a school-house, and at New Gloucester in the house of a widow. Making his way through the woods to the Androscoggin, he crossed near Lewiston Falls, and went on to Monmouth, where he preached in an unfinished church, the second erected in the state of Maine. At Winthrop an appointment had been made for him at the Congregational Church, but he was unable to fulfil it. From thence he beat his way through the woods, which he describes as being " as bad as the Alleghany Mountains and the Dismal Swamp, or the shades of death," until he reached Readfield, where the Conference was to be held.

After Conference he returned to Portland, and preached in a small back room to about twenty-five persons. He visited Boston, and from thence returned to New York, and rested a little at Widow Sherwood's. The intelligence he received of the prevalence of the yellow fever in New York and Philadelphia, was truly alarming. Crossing the ferry six miles above New York, he went on to Crosswicks, in New Jersey, where he heard of the death of John Dickins, who fell a victim to the pestilence. Of Dickins he says : " For piety, probity, profitable preaching, holy living, the Christian education of his children, secret closet prayer, I doubt whether his superior is to be found either in Europe or America." From Baltimore he took his usual Southern trip, attending the Conferences and preaching on the way, and returned in the spring. While in Delaware a consultation of physicians, consisting of Doctors Cook, Anderson, Ridgley, and Neadham, was had in his case, in which they advised him to desist from preaching entirely, as he was threatened with a consumption, which would speedily end his days. From the Cross Roads he went to Philadelphia, where he held a Conference, retiring every night to the Eagle Works, on the Schuylkill, to the residence of Mr. Henry Foxall. After Conference he went to New York, where Conference was opened. Notwithstanding the advice of his physicians, he preached and exhorted during the session. We give the following interesting description of this Conference from the unpublished autobiography of Rev. William Thacher :

" As the Conference of 1799 was the first in which I was ever honoured with a place and a seat, I may give a brief account of my adventure on the occasion. About a dozen of us, Methodist preachers, passengers from the East, landed at New York, and made our way to the old head-quarters in John-street, bearing on our arms our saddle-bags; we were horseback men, and did not use trunks for travelling; we were all plain men, plain enough. We were welcomed at the little old parsonage by the Revs. Thomas Morrell and Joshua Wells, ministers in the station. Brother W. took us as he found us, bag and baggage, formed us in rank and file, and placed himself as captain at the head of the company. We were in Methodist preacher's uniform, in military style. Our walk, especially through Chatham-street, seemed to attract attention. We were soon disposed of at different places. Conference was held in the old hive of Methodists, John-street Church. What a congregation of Methodist preachers! What greetings, what love beaming in every eye, what gratulation, what rejoicing, what solemnity! The clock strikes nine. We are in the old sanctuary, in Conference, assembled around the altar, within which sits the venerable Asbury, Bible in hand. A chapter read, a hymn sung, we kneel. How solemn, how awful, how devout the prayer! What amens are responded, what a Divine effusion! Inspiration seemed to pervade the whole. Prayer ended, the secretary calls the roll, and we proceed to business. Six hours are spent each day for the transaction of business, from nine to twelve and from three to six, each session opening by reading the Scriptures, singing, and prayer, and closing by prayer. At length the Conference draws to a close; the bishop looks solemnly around upon us, the doomsday document trembling in his hand; he reads intuitively each countenance, tracing the suspense and solicitude of his anxious sons, all trembling to fly to their work, yet fearing as to the place where they shall be sent. Although the suspense was painful, the slow, solemn, concluding address of the bishop gradually rolls along, occasionally stopping in its progress until its close. Then taking the Hymn-book he reads:

> ' The vineyard of the Lord
> Before his labourers lies,
> And lo ! we see the vast reward
> Which waits us in the skies.'

We sing, we kneel, and O what a prayer! What unction from heaven! We arise, and then the hidden, sealed instrument is all a revelation, the benediction is pronounced and we separate."

From New York he bent his course southward, and, accompanied by Lee, visited many of the quarterly meetings and all the Conferences as far as Georgia. On his return he held a Conference in Charleston. While there intelligence was received of the death of Washington, and on the Sabbath Asbury delivered a discourse on the occasion. No one entertained a higher regard for Washington than did Asbury and his coadjutors. After the Conference closed Lee was requested by the bishop to visit, as his assistant, several places in Georgia, he being unable to go in consequence of illness. Here he remained preaching, when he was able, until Lee returned, when, accompanied by him and Snethen, he set out for the North. The latter of these travelling companions was as great a favourite with the bishop as Lee, and in alluding to a certain sermon which he preached in Virginia during this journey, he says : N. Snethen preached a great discourse on 2 Cor. xiii. 5-7." In the route they were joined by M'Kendree and other preachers, who were making their way to the General Conference, which was to be held in Baltimore. From the 10th of February to the 27th of April, Asbury had travelled eleven hundred miles.

CHAPTER XVII.

General Conference in Baltimore in 1800—Address of the British Conference—Explanation of Dr. Coke—Address of Asbury to the British Conference—His Determination to resign his Office—Resolution of the Conference—Election of Richard Whatcoat to the Episcopacy—Asbury and Whatcoat at Perry Hall—Abingdon—Ruins of the College—New York Conference—Revival in the Bowery Church—Widow Sherwood's—Boston—Bishops preach in the Tabernacle—Mother Livingston—Her Conversion—Hospitality—Garrettson's—Crossing the Wilderness—Conference at Bethel—Preachers present—Nashville—Origin of Camp Meetings—Asbury confined at Philadelphia—Western Conference in Tennessee—Poythress—Recrosses the Mountains—Spends the Winter in South Carolina — Baltimore —Maine — A charming Spot—His Mother's Death—Tribute to her Memory—Death of Rev. Devereux Jarratt—Memorial—Funeral Sermon—New York Conference—Fredericktown—Natural Bridge—Revival at Holstein—Conference—At Station Camp—Night Encampment—Mountain Dew—No Tent—Opinion of Southern Planters—Baltimore—Compliment to — Perry Hall—Miss De Peyster's Legacy—Sermon in John-street—Ordains Joshua Soule—Ashgrove—Pittsburgh—Zane's Trace—Lancaster—Western Conference in Kentucky—Visit to Dr. Hinde—Interesting Incident — Illness—Depression—Legacy—Tennessee—Virginia.

On the 6th of May, 1800, one hundred and sixteen itinerant preachers had congregated from all parts of the United States in Baltimore, for the purpose of holding another General Conference. After the Conference was opened, Dr. Coke, who had returned from Europe, read the address of the British Conference, and at considerable length explained those portions of it which related to himself in regard to his return to Europe. He remarked in conclusion that the address was not his own, and that he was not consulted in relation to it, and he left the decision of the case entirely at the disposal of the General Conference. At the previous General Conference he had pledged himself to his American brethren after the following manner : "I offer myself to my American brethren entirely to their service, all I am and have, with my talents and labours in every respect, without any mental reservation whatever, to labour among them and to assist Bishop Asbury ; not to station the preachers at any time when he is present, but to exercise all the episcopal duties when I hold a Conference in his absence, and by his consent, and to visit the West Indies and France, when there is an opening and I can be spared."

As no official action could be had in relation to the desire of the British Conference, which had previously been made known to the Conference in Virginia in 1797, Bishop Asbury addressed that body as follows :

"RESPECTED FATHERS AND BRETHREN,—You, in your brotherly kindness, were pleased to address a letter to us, your brethren and friends in America, expressing your difficulties and desires concerning our beloved brother Dr. Coke, that he might return to Europe to heal the breach which designing men have been making among you, or prevent its threatened overflow. We have but one grand responsive body, which is our General Conference, and it was in and to this body the doctor entered his obligations to serve his brethren in America. No yearly Conference, no official character dare assume to answer for that grand federal body.

" By the advice of the yearly Conference now sitting in Virginia, and the respect I bear to you, I write to inform you that in our persons and order we consent to his return and *partial* continuance with you, and earnestly pray that you may have much peace, union, and happiness together. May you find that your divisions end in a greater union, order, and harmony of the body, so that the threatened cloud may blow over, and your divisive party may be of as little consequence to you as ours is to us.

"With respect to the doctor's returning to us, I leave your enlarged understandings and good sense to judge. You will see the number of souls upon our Annual Minutes, and as men of reading you may judge over what a vast continent these societies are scattered. I refer you to a large letter I wrote our beloved Brother Bradburn on the subject.

" By a probable guess, we have, perhaps, from one thousand to one thousand two hundred travelling and local preachers. Local preachers are daily rising up and coming forward, with proper recommendations from their respective societies, to receive ordination, besides the regulation aud ordinations of the yearly Conferences. From Charleston, South Carolina, where the Conference was held, to the Province of Maine, where another Conference is to be held, there is a space of about one thousand and three hundred miles; and we have only one worn-out superintendent, who was this day advised by the yearly Conference to desist from preaching till next spring, on account of his debilitated state of body. But the situation of our affairs requires that he should travel about five thousand miles a year, through many parts unsettled, and other thinly peopled countries. I have now with me an assistant, who does everything for me he constitutionally can ; but the ordaining and stationing the preachers can only be performed by myself in the doctor's absence.

"We have to lament that our superintendency is so weak, and that it cannot constitutionally be strengthened till the ensuing General Conference. How I have felt and must feel, under such critical and important circumstances, I leave you to judge.

"To write much on the subject would be imposing on my own weakness and your good understanding. I speak as unto wise men ; judge what I say.

"Wishing you great peace and spiritual prosperity, I remain your brother, your friend, your servant for Christ's sake."

In conformity with the permission given in this letter for his absence from America for a short season only, after remaining for a while and assisting Bishop Asbury, Dr. Coke returned to Europe, and was usefully employed in visiting the societies in various parts of the United Kingdom, particularly in Ireland, during a rebellion which broke out in 1798, in which he was successful in his attempts to shield the Methodist preachers from all blame, until the session of this General Conference, when he appeared to fulfil his engagements with his American brethren, or be honourably released. After deliberating for some time upon the request of the British Conference for Dr. Coke's return, the following resolution was concurred in by the General Conference :

"That, in compliance with the address of the British Conference to let Dr. Coke return to Europe, this General Conference consent to his return upon condition that he come back to America as soon as his business will allow, but certainly by the next General Conference."

In accordance with the spirit of this resolution, the Conference addressed their British brethren as follows :

"We have considered, with the greatest attention, the request you have made for the doctor's return to Europe ; and after revolving the subject deeply in our minds, and spending part of two days in debating thereon, we still feel an ardent desire for his continuance in America. This arises from the critical state of Bishop Asbury's health, the extension of our work, our affection for and approbation of the doctor, and his probable usefulness, provided he continue with us. We wish to detain him, as we greatly need his services. But the statement you have laid before us in your address, of the success of the West India missions under his superintendence, the arduous attempt to carry the Gospel among the native Irish requiring his influence and support, and the earnest request you have added to this representation, 'believing it to be for the glory of God,' had turned the scale at present in your favour. We have, therefore, in compliance with your request, *lent* the doctor to you for a season, to return to us as soon as he conveniently can, but at farthest by the meeting of our next General Conference."

Asbury's health having declined more rapidly within a few years past, and finding it difficult to travel and superintend the work generally, he had come to the conclusion to resign his office as bishop. Being unable to perform its duties, he could not consent to remain in a relation for which he was evidently unfitted, and which Providence indicated should be dissolved. He was keenly alive to the responsibility of his position, and having been able during the last quadrennial period to render only partial service, he feared that there was a dissatisfaction existing in the minds of the preachers on that account. To disabuse his mind the Conference unanimously passed the following :

"*Resolved,* That this General Conference consider themselves under many and great obligations to Mr. Asbury for the many and great services he has rendered to the connection, and that they earnestly entreat a continuance of his services as one of the General Superintendents of the Methodist Episcopal Church, as far as his strength will permit."

In view of the inability of Bishop Asbury to do effectively the work of an itinerant general superintendent, the Conference subsequently resolved to go into an election of an additional bishop, and as the result of such election Richard Whatcoat was chosen. He was shortly after duly ordained to the office, and became the episcopal colleague of Asbury.

After the transaction of the ordinary business pertaining to the Conference it adjourned, and the preachers started out again to their different and distant fields of itinerant toil.

In company with the newly ordained bishop, Asbury left Baltimore and went out to "Perry Hall." · The family of Mr. Gough,
like the family visited by the Saviour at Bethany, manifested the
most enlarged and open-hearted hospitality, and the visits of Asbury were hailed with delight.   From this place they went to
Abingdon, the site of the late Cokesbury College, whose charred
and blackened walls presented a sad and melancholy appearance.
Passing through Delaware and New Jersey, they came on to New
York, where the Conference was held.   During the session there
was quite a revival in the Bowery Church.   From this place they
went out to the Widow Sherwood's for the purpose of enjoying
quiet and rest.   While here Asbury preached at Sherwood's
Chapel.   From thence the bishops pursued their eastern route
through Connecticut and Rhode Island on to Boston, where they
both preached in the Tabernacle.   On their return they fell in
company with Garrettson, who had been attending the funeral of
the venerable Mother Livingston, who died suddenly at the age of
seventy-eight.   In regard to this lady Asbury says : "About
thirty-four years ago this godly woman was awakened, under the
first sermon the Rev. Dr. Sadley preached in the Reformed Low
Dutch Church in New York ; as she told me, not she alone, but
six or eight other respectable women.   Madame Livingstone was
one who gave invitation to the Methodist preachers to come to
Rhinebeck, and received them into her house, and would have
given them more countenance had she been under no other influence than that of the spirit of God and her own feelings.   I
visited her one year before her death, and spent a night at her
mansion.   She was sensible, conversable, and hospitable."   After
leaving Rhinebeck, where they stopped and enjoyed the hospitalities of Garrettson's pleasant home, and at the "elegant mansion"
of Dr Tillotson, commanding a charming view of the Hudson, they
started out upon their route and came to Poughkeepsie, concerning
which Asbury remarked, "This is no place for Methodism."   Again
in New York, after recruiting a little, they started out on their
Southern tour, passing through the intervening states, preaching
at Baltimore and other places, until they arrived at Virginia,
where they made preparations for their "grand route to Kentucky."
After crossing the Wilderness, they reached the seat of the Western
Conference on the 3rd of October.   The place selected was Bethel,
on the Kentucky River, about forty miles above Frankfort.   We
give the names of the preachers present on that occasion : William
M'Kendree, William Burke, John Sale, Hezekiah Harriman, Benjamin Lakin.   At this Conference Lewis Hunt, Thomas Allen,
and Jeremiah Lawson were readmitted.   Two were admitted on

trial. After spending two weeks in that section of the country, Asbury, Whatcoat, and M'Kendree started for Nashville. He thus describes his visit to this city : " This is a place long heard of, but never seen by me until now. Some thought the congregation would be small, but I believed it would be large. Not less than one thousand people were in and out of the stone church, which if floored, ceiled, and glazed, would be a grand house. We had three hours' public exercises. Mr. M'Kendree preached upon ' The wages of sin is death ;' myself upon Romans x. 14, 15, and Brother What-coat on ' When Christ, who is our life, shall appear, then shall we also appear with him in glory.' " While in Tennessee they attended a meeting which had been in progress four days. It was one of those remarkable meetings called sacramental occasions, held by Presbyterian ministers, and which, on account of the great numbers that attended them, gave rise to camp-meetings. At this meeting Asbury, Whatcoat, and M'Kendree were invited to participate, and it was continued several days longer. The follow-ing graphic description of this meeting we find in his Journal : " The stand was in the open air, embosomed in a wood of lofty trees. The ministers of God, Methodists and Presbyterians, united their labours, and mingled with the childlike simplicity of primitive times. Fires blazing here and there dispelled the darkness ; and the shouts of the redeemed captives, mingling with the cries of precious souls struggling into life, broke the silence of midnight. The weather was delightful, as if heaven smiled, while mercy flowed in abundant streams of salvation to perishing sinners."

By means of these meetings great revivals prevailed throughout the South and West, and extended to the Middle and Eastern States. So great were the multitudes, collected far and near from the surrounding country, that from ten to fifteen thousand persons have been estimated to be present at a single encampment. The congregations being so immense it was impossible for the voice of one preacher to reach them, and stands were erected at different points, where ministers of different denominations, but all in the same spirit, and actuated by the same motives, held forth to the listening thousands the words of life. So great was the excitement which pervaded the encampment at times, that hundreds if not thousands might have been seen prostrate upon the earth at once in the greatest distress, or wild with joy, on their feet, shouting the praises of God. So many descriptions have been written of this remarkable revival, and the wonderful exercises accompanying it, that we do not deem it necessary to occupy space in repeating them, and shall refer the reader who may not have seen them, or

who desires a further account, to Finley's Sketches, or the Autobiography of the Rev. Jacob Young, both of whom were present
at the meetings.

From the South Asbury returned to Philadelphia, where he was
confined by lameness for two months, and in August, 1801, he
again commenced his continental journey. An arrangement had
been made that he should go West, taking with him as a travelling
companion Nicholas Snethen, while Whatcoat was to attend the
Southern Conference. Proceeding through Delaware, Maryland,
and Virginia, to Holstein River, he met the Western Conference
at Ebenezer, Tennessee.

We have before us a copy of the Journal of the Western Conference from the beginning, and, to show the preachers of the
present day the manner in which the Journals were then kept, we
will make an extract or two. In the minutes for 1801 we find the
following: "John A. Granade came recommended for admission
on trial. It is the judgment of the Conference that he has a
certain hardness and stubbornness in his temper which has produced some improper conclusions ; but as he has given some hopeful assurance that in future he will be more teachable, and as his
piety and zeal are not doubted, the Conference is of opinion that
he may be admitted after receiving a special counsel from the
bishop." Granade was a man of remarkable eccentricity of character,
and would often express his thoughts in poetic verse. He proved
an efficient itinerant; but his zeal carrying him beyond his
strength, and being exposed to the hardships of the wilderness, his
health failed, and after a few years he was obliged to retire from
the work. At this Conference the health of Poythress was such
that he was obliged to give up the itinerancy. In giving the
reasons for the selection of Cumberland as the seat of the next
Conference, the Journal records the following : "1st. The union
and friendly state of affairs between the Methodist and Presbyterians ; and, 2d, There never was a Conference held there,"
reasons which proved conclusive.

From this Conference they recrossed the mountains, and spent
the winter travelling and preaching in South Carolina and Georgia.
In the spring he returned to Baltimore, and after attending the
Middle Conferences he accompanied Whatcoat to Maine. Returning, he stopped at Waltham, and found a quiet retreat in the
hospitable mansion of his old friend, Mr. Abraham Bemis. This
delightful place, surrounded by beautiful scenery, and adorned with
all the elegancies of wealth and refinement, was a favorite resort of
Asbury. The contrast between such a place of rest and refresh-

ment, and one where there was but one room and fire-place, and a half-dozen inmates, where "he had to preach, read, write, pray, sing, talk, eat, drink, and sleep," was doubtless very great. In many of his rides through the western wilderness the pioneer bishop sometimes had not even as good accommodations as we have just described. Often he had to sleep in the woods, if sleep he could for the wild beasts which infested them.

During this year the following remarks occur in his Journal: "I find reasons enough in my own mind to justify myself against the low murmurs of *partiality* in which some have indulged. I am impartial. I spend as much time in the extremities, and know no Maryland or Delaware, *after the flesh*, more than Kentucky, Cumberland, Georgia, or the Carolinas. It is our duty to save the health of the preachers where we can, to make particular appointments for some important charges, and it is our duty to embrace all parts of the continent and Union after the example of primitive times, and the first and faithful preachers in America."

While at the session of the Baltimore Conference this year, the sad intelligence of the death of his mother reached him. We find in his Journal the following touching and beautiful tribute to her memory : -

"Her paternal descent was Welsh, from a family ancient and respectable of the name of Rogers. She lived a woman of the world till the death of her only daughter, Sarah Asbury. How would the bereaved mother weep and tell of the beauties and excellencies of her lost and lovely child, pondering on the past in the silent suffering of hopeless grief! This afflictive providence graciously terminated in the mother's conversion. When she saw herself a lost and wretched sinner she sought religious people. But 'in the times of this ignorance' few were 'sound in the faith,' or 'faithful to the grace given.' Many were the days she spent alone, chiefly in reading and prayer. At length she found justifying grace and pardoning mercy."

The parents of Asbury were not by any means in affluent circumstances. He was constantly remitting to them all the money he could possibly spare from America. Some of his letters to them are preserved, and they exhibit a beautiful specimen of filial love. "I have had," says he, in a letter to his father and mother in 1793, "considerable pain of mind from information received that the money was not paid. I last evening made arrangement for a remittance to you. It will come into your hands in the space of three or four months. My salary is sixty-four dollars. I have sold my watch and library, and would sell

M

my shirts before you should want. I have made a reserve for you. I spend very little on my own account. My friends find me some clothing. The contents of a small pair of saddle-bags will do for me, and one coat a year. Your son Francis is a man of honour and conscience. As my father and my mother never disgraced me by an act of dishonesty, I hope to echo back the same sound of an honest, upright man. I am well satisfied that the Lord saw fit you should be my parents rather than the king and queen, or any of the great. I sometimes think you will outlive me. I have made my will, and left my all to you, and that is soon done. While I live and do well, I shall remember you every year. O that your last days may be your best, and that you may not only live long, but live well and die well!'"

By the following extract it would seem he was seriously thinking of returning to England to provide for his parents, or of their removing to America, so as to be near him : " I have received several letters expressive of your paternal love and gratitude toward me. I have often revolved the serious thought of my return to you. I have frequently asked myself if I could retire to a single circuit, step down and act as lay preacher. This, if I know my own heart, is not my difficulty. With humility I may say one hundred thousand respectable citizens of the new world, three hundred travelling, and six hundred local preachers, would advise me not to go. I hope the voice of the people is the voice of God. At present we have more work than faithful workmen. I am like Joseph. I want to have my parents near me. I am not ashamed of your *poverty*, and I hope, after so many years professing religion, you will not be wanting in *piety*. I have considered you have that which is my joy and my glory ; that you have had for forty years open doors for religious exercises when no other would or even dare do it. It is a serious subject whether you think it is your duty still to keep a place for preaching, or if on your removal the Gospel will be taken from the place. Yet when I think you have no child with you, nor friend that careth for you, the distress of the land, and the high prices of provisions, I wish to see you, and have you near me. It is true, while I live you will live also, if I keep my place and piety. I study daily what I can do without. One horse, and that sometimes borrowed, one coat, one waistcoat— the last coat and waistcoat I used about fourteen months—four or five shirts, and four or five books. I am in doubt, if I should be called away, you will not be provided for so well in England as in America, among those for whom I have faithfully laboured these twenty-four years. It is true, you are not immortal any more than myself, and judging according to the nature of things you may go first, one or both of you. All these things I have weighed in my mind. I wish you to consider the matter, and ask much counsel of God, and of your best and most impartial friends, I wish you, after considering the matter, to send me another letter. Whether I be present or absent, dead or alive, I trust my friends in Baltimore will take care of you by my help. You have spent many pounds upon Christian people, I know, from my childhood. Happy was I when this was done, and I hope it will come home to you in mercy. You must make it matter of much fasting and prayer before you attempt anything. You must not expect to see me more than twice a year."

He afterward concluded, however, that their interest would be best promoted by remaining in England, and wrote as follows : " Perhaps I was constrained, from the high sense of filial duty I had, to invite you here. I now think you are much better where you are. I sincerely wish I could come to see you, but I see no way to do it without sinning against God and the Church. Since I wrote I have travelled nearly two thousand five hundred miles, through Georgia, South and North Carolina, Virginia, Maryland, and Delaware. Hard wear and hard fare ; but I am healthy and lean, gray-headed and dim-sighted."

On making his parents a remittance of money in 1795, he says : " Were it ten thousand per year, if I had it in my possession, you should be welcome, if you had need of it."

After news had arrived of the death of his father, he wrote as follows to his mother: " From the information I have received, I fear my venerable father is no more an inhabitant of this earth. You are a widow, and I am an orphan with respect to my father. I cannot tell how to advise you in this important change. You have made yourself respectable and extensive friends, who, though they cannot give to you, can comfort you. I have been, as you have heard, afflicted by excessive labours of mind and body. I had to neglect writing, reading, and preaching for a time. I had to stop and lie by in some precious families, where parents and children, in some measure, supplied your absence. I lay by in Virginia. When you hear the name you will love it unseen, for you will say : ' That is the place where my Frank was sick.' I am now much mended. I move in a little carriage, being unable to ride on horseback. Were you to see me, and the colour of my hair—nearly that of your own ! My eyes are weak even with glasses. When I was a child, and would pry into the Bible by twinkling firelight, you used to say, ' Frank, you will spoil your eyes.' It is a grief to me that I cannot preach as heretofore. I

am greatly worn out at fifty-five; but it is a good cause. God is
with me; my soul exults in God."

These extracts we have given in order to exhibit the amiable
and filial spirit of this good man, who, though prevented by the
pressing duties of his responsible station from ever visiting his
father and mother in their old age, spared no pains to cheer and aid
them in the decline of life. The high position he occupied in
America did not make him forget the village of his birth, nor,
amid all the thousands in America who admired and loved him,
did he forget the humble Joseph and Elizabeth Asbury. Much
did he desire to see them again; but their faces he saw no more;
father and mother had

> " Gone from a world of grief and sin,
> With God eternally shut in."

When he arrived at Petersburgh, Virginia, he learned that his
old friend, the Rev. Devereux Jarratt, was no more. He was, as
we have already seen, a zealous and devoted minister of the Protestant Episcopal Church, and a most successful preacher. He
had witnessed several revivals of religion in his parish. When he
began his labours there was no other evangelical minister in the
province. He travelled into several counties, and there were very
few parish churches within fifty miles of his own in which he had not
preached, and to which labours of love he added preaching the
word of life on solitary plantations. He was the first who received
the despised Methodist preachers; when strangers and unfriended,
he took them to his house and had societies formed in his parish.
The friends of Mr. Jarratt desired the bishop to preach his funeral
discourse, which he did to an immense congregation from the passage, "Well done, good and faithful servant; thou hast been faithful over a few things, I will make thee ruler over many things:
enter thou into the joy of thy Lord." The following is an outline of the discourse : I. A good servant is only *good* in the relation which his practice and experience bear to the example and
precept of his Divine Master. Hence his goodness is a Christian
goodness, founded altogether on grace. II. A faithful servant is
one who is faithful to his ministerial character, faithful in the discharge of the duties pertaining to his holy calling, (1.) in preaching
the word; (2.) in administering the sacraments and ordinances;
(3) in ruling the Church of God. III. The results of such fidelity.
A glorious entrance to heaven.

At the New York Conference in 1802 Asbury presided, and to
show the estimate placed upon him by the preachers of that day,

we insert the following testimony from one who has recently entered into rest: "The beloved Bishop Asbury, that true son of Wesley, that apostle of American Methodism, sent out from the evangelical school of the purest order and best authority of original Methodists in England, grown up with our growth, a pioneer among our mountains, and vales, and forests, over our rivers and lakes till our Revolutionary war, when he retired for a season, as he was a messenger of peace. He has shown, by the path of love and moderation, the Gospel example amid the roar of cannon, and the din of war, and effusion of human blood, and the shout of liberty, that he was a true son of peace. He awaited for the dove with the olive-branch, when he came from his retirement and emerged from the clouds a star of the first magnitude, whose glory has known no eclipse. He steadily shone in our hemisphere till mortality was swallowed up of life. This is that disciple who steadied our helm and commanded our ship. With the affection of a father he conducted our business and appointed our work. A man, dead to the world, of one work—the salvation of souls. The zeal of the Lord's house consumed him till he wore out in the work and expired at his post. In the intervals of Conference he made out all the stations alone, often dropping on his knees, then rising and writing down appointments according to the wisdom given him."

On his way South, after reaching Fredericktown, Virginia, he remarked: "At last, after more than thirty years' labour, the Methodists have a house of worship here and thirty souls in fellowship" On his way to Tennessee he passed through that portion of Virginia in which the Natural Bridge is found, of which he gives in his Journal an exact description. As he gazed upon the beautiful arch thrown over the chasm one hundred and sixty feet above the surface of the stream below, he was filled with admiration at the scene. When he reached the Holstein, he found a gracious revival in progress. At witnessing this work of the Lord he was led to exclaim: "Fourteen or fifteen times have I toiled over the mighty mountains, and nearly twenty years have we laboured upon Holstein, and lo! the rage of wild and Christian savages is tamed, and God hath glorified himself." After having attended Conference at Station Camp, Tennessee, he started with M'Kendree for West Point. He was greatly afflicted at this time with acute pain in his whole system. On his way he was attacked with a most torturing pain in his knee, attended with a swelling of both his feet. Notwithstanding this, however, he travelled on. After crossing the Cumberland River night overtook them, and

they encamped under what he called a heavy mountain-dew.   He
thus describes the encampment : "Brother M'Kendree made me
a tent of his own and John Watson's blankets, and happily saved
me from taking cold while I slept two hours under my grand mar-
quee.   Brother M'Kendree threw his cloak over the limb of a
tree, and he and his companion took shelter beneath and slept
also.   I will not be rash in my protestations against any country,
but I think I will never more brave the wilderness without a tent.
My dear M'Kendree had to lift me up and down from my horse
like a helpless child.   For my sickness and sufferings I conceive I
am indebted to sleeping uncovered in the wilderness.   I could not
have slept but for the aid of laudanum ; meantime my spirits and
patience were wonderfully preserved in general, although I was
hardly restrained sometimes from crying, Lord, let me die, for
death hath no terrors ! and I could not but reflect upon my escape
from the toils and sufferings of another year." Notwithstanding
all his sufferings, he toiled on over rugged mountains and through
dense forests until he completed his usual journey of six thousand
miles for the year.

While in South Carolina he made the following observation in
regard to the planters : "Whenever our preachers gain the confidence of the lowland planters, so that the masters will give us
all the liberty we ought to have, there will be thousands of the
poor slaves converted to God.   The patient must be perso-
nally visited by the physician before advice and medicine will be
proper, and so it is and must ever be with the sin-sick soul and the
spiritual physician."   And thus it proved ; for notwithstanding
the reiterated declaration of the Church on the subject of slavery,
the confidence of the master has been gained, and masters and
slaves have alike been converted to God, and brought into the
same Christian brotherhood.   Had any other course been adopted
than what Asbury suggested and advised, the two hundred thousand slaves now in the bosom of the Church would have been in a
state of the most wretched spiritual bondage, and more effectually
excluded from the Gospel than their brethren in the wild and
hitherto inaccessible regions of Africa.

On his return from his Southern tour he held Conference in
Baltimore.   Sixty-four effective preachers were now connected
with the Conference.   On Sabbath he preached three times, morning, afternoon, and evening, and gave the following reasons why he
did not preach more during the session : 1. Because there were
many zealous, acceptable preachers present ; 2. Because he desired
to be a man of one business, and to have his mind free : and 3.

Because he had neither bodily nor mental strength to preside in the Conference, and take so great a part in particular duties as its head, to receive the continual application of so many preachers on so many subjects presented at that time.

The bishop paid the following merited compliment to the Baltimore Conference : "In regard to finances they have had a surplus. They have supported wives, widows, and children, and in the present instance have supplied the contingencies of those preachers who have gone to distant parts, besides giving one hundred dollars to the Philadelphia, and as much to the Conferences of New York and Boston." The Baltimore Conference, it must be conceded by all, has raised the proudest monument to American Methodism in the zeal and success which has crowned her labours, and Baltimore, one of the ancient seats of Methodism, deserves to hold the urn that contains the ashes of the sainted Asbury. It is not the least praise of this monumental city that the sons of the devoted Asbury have, with characteristic nobleness of spirit, resolved to erect a monument over his remains.

After the Conference was ended he sought rest in the calm and quiet retreat of Perry Hall. From hence he went to Philadelphia, and so on through New Jersey to New York. While here he signed a memorial for obtaining in court a legal claim to the £400 left by Miss De Peyster to the bishops and clergy of the Methodist Episcopal Church, for the benefit of the same. On Sabbath he preached in the John-street Church from James iii. 17. His sermon was spoken of at the time as one of great interest and power. The following is an outline :

I. The wisdom that cometh from above is revealed and inspired. It is pure, *negatively* : It is not mixed by its Divine Author with that wisdom which is earthly, sensual, and devilish. It is not mixed with the policy, or pleasures, or profits of this world, or of sin, which is of hell. The apostle hath written, "pure religion," and this cannot be when mingled with such qualities, all of which spring from men or devils.

II. The wisdom that cometh from above is pure, *positively* : It is pure in conviction, repentance, faith, regeneration, and sanctification. It is the operative principle of grace in the soul as internally and externally manifested. It is peaceable in relation to God and all mankind, to the Church and the world, and the tranquillity of the soul. It is gentle, amiable in all its ministrations, never stormy, or sour, or haughty and overbearing. Easy to be entreated to do and suffer anything that is right for the glory of God and the good of souls. "Impartiality." This is the Christian dress. Not bound and pinched by countries, names, forms, and opinions. It neither envies the rich on account of their affluence, nor despises or neglects the poor on account of their poverty. "Without hypocrisy." Sincerity is the incontestible evidence to God and man of our possession of the heavenly treasure, of that wisdom that cometh from above. People may go upon fancies, and be ready to die with raptures ; but if they are turbulent, un-governable, self-willed, and false toward their fellow or toward their God, their religion is vain. Whatever it may once have been, it is not the gold of the sanctuary now, but a counterfeit, alloyed by a mixture of the wisdom of this world."

From New York he proceeded on his Eastern tour through Con-necticut to Boston, where he held a Conference. Speaking of New England, he says : " Poor New England, she is the valley of dry bones still ! Come, O breath of the Lord, and breathe upon these slain, that they may live !" At this Conference he ordained Joshua Soule and Nathan Emery Elders, the former of whom is the senior bishop of the Methodist Episcopal Church, South, now ad-vanced in years and quite feeble in health ; the latter a few years past closed his earthly labours in Ohio.

From Boston he directed his course to Ashgrove on the Hudson, where, as we have seen, the father of Methodism in New York had taken up his abode, and where his ashes now rest. Passing through New Hampshire and Vermont, he at length reached Ashgrove, where he held the New York Conference. Nearly seventy preachers were present, and on Sabbath Asbury preached to two thousand hearers. Crossing the Hudson he passed over into New Jersey, and thence, after stopping and preaching at different places on the route, he proceeded on to Philadelphia.

This year (1803) he took a different route to the West. He went by Lancaster, Columbia, and York, to Carlisle, and from thence, through Shippensburg, Strasburg, and Emmetsburg, he proceeded to the Juniata, which he crossed near Bedford. From thence he went to Connelsville, on the Youghiogheny, and thus on to the Monongahela, which he followed down to Pittsburg. He then proceeded down the Ohio to Wheeling, and from thence through the woods to Zanesville, a long and weary ride. Taking Zane's Trace, he started for Chillicothe, stopping on the way at Lancaster. From Chillicothe he struck again for the Ohio, and proceeded to Paris, Kentucky, where he held the Western Con-ference. During this tour he was considerably afflicted, and at times unusually dispirited. He says, however, in the midst of all his toils and hardships : " I felt wholly given up to do and suffer the will of the Lord, to be sick or well, to live or die at any time and in any place, the fields, the woods, the house, or the wilderness. Glory be to God for such resignation! I have little to leave except a journey of five thousand miles a year, care of more than a hundred thousand souls, and the arrangement of four hundred preachers yearly, to which I may add the murmurs and discontents of ministers and people. Who wants this legacy? Those who do are welcome to it for me."

While in Kentucky he paid a visit to his old friend, Dr. Hinde, a physician who resided in Clark county. Here he was received with the greatest cordiality, and treated as a patriarch and the honoured father of Western Methodism. Dr. Hinde was the family physician of the celebrated General Wolfe. He was a native of England, but came to America with General Wolfe in the time of the French war. He had been a professed deist, and a decided enemy to Christianity, but was converted from the error of his way through the example of his wife. His conversion was brought about on this wise. His wife and daughter having joined the Methodist Church, the latter was banished from home and the former put under medical treatment for what the doctor feigned to regard as insanity. His remedy was a blister plaster extending the whole length of the back, which was left on for several days. The fortitude and meekness with which the Christian wife bore her persecutions resulted in the doctor's conviction and subsequent conversion.

Dr. Hinde was now considerably advanced in life, and had not attended to any professional calls for many years. At a late hour in the night a messenger arrived at his house with two horses, in great haste. A neighbour of his in the country had been seriously and suddenly attacked with a disease which baffled the skill of the physician in attendance, and at his suggestion Dr. Hinde was sent for. When the messenger rapped at the door, the doctor hoisted the window, and received from him the request of the attending physician, that if it was possible he would come to his assistance, as the man must have relief soon or die. The doctor was in feeble health, and replied that he did not think he was able to undertake the journey. The night was dark and stormy, and the road through the woods rough and dangerous. Asbury overheard the conversation, and shouted out, "Go, doctor, instantly, and save the man's life." "It seemed," as Dr. Hinde afterward remarked, "that the voice was as it were from heaven," and he could not disobey. He dressed himself as quickly as possible, and was soon in the saddle of the extra horse, following his guide through the dark and tangled thicket of the wood. After riding several miles as fast as they could for the darkness, they at length arrived at the cabin of the sufferer. He found his patient in great agony, and apparently dying. He soon, however, detected the cause of the disease which was working death, and immediately applied a remedy. The man was speedily relieved, and early in the morning the doctor arrived at home. When he met Asbury, the first words that fell upon his ear were, "Well, doctor, how is your patient?" His reply was, "To you, bishop, under the blessing of God, that man owes his life, as he must have died before morning." "As long as you can drag yourself about always be found doing something," said the bishop.

Of this advice Asbury was himself a living example. Neither old age nor sickness, when he could but just sit upon his horse, having frequently to be lifted to and taken from the saddle, deterred him from the work; he was still found in the discharge of duty.

About this time several preachers, who had located and engaged somewhat in land speculation, were handled pretty severely by the bishop in his sermons. Speaking of a certain place where there were a number of this class, he said : "The place is cursed with apostate Methodist preachers, and unless they repent and go back to their work God will curse them." In many instances this, alas! proved true. Some who had engaged in such speculations, and others who had become traders and merchants, failed, and became hopelessly bankrupt in property and character.

When the bishop arrived in Tennessee, he writes: "What a road we have passed! Certainly the worst on the whole continent, even in the best weather; yet bad as it was there were four or five hundred crossing the mountains while we were. I was powerfully struck with the consideration that there were at least as many as a thousand emigrants from East to West annually. We must take care to send preachers after these people. A man who is well mounted will scorn to complain of the roads when he sees men, women, and children, almost naked, paddling barefoot and bare-legged along, or labouring up the rocky ascent, while those who are best off have only one horse for two or three children to ride at once. If these adventurers have little or nothing to eat, it is no extraordinary circumstance, and not uncommon to encamp in the wet woods after night. In the mountains it does not rain, but pours."

From Tennessee he travelled through North and South Carolina and Georgia, visiting the Churches. While in the latter state he took occasion to make a few observations on the ignorance of foolish men who rail against the government of the Church. "The Methodists," he said, "acknowledge no superiority but what is founded on seniority, election, and long and faithful services. For myself, I pity those who cannot distinguish between a Pope of Rome and an old worn man of about sixty years, who has *the power* given him of riding five thousand miles a year, at a salary of eighty dollars, through summer's heat and winter's cold ; travelling in all weathers, preaching in all places, his best covering from rain often a blanket ; the surest sharpener of his wit, hunger, from fasts, voluntary and involuntary ; his best fare for six months in the year, coarse kindness ; and his reward from too many, suspicion, murmurings, and envy all the year round." Well did this faithful servant of the Church need a "testimony in heaven, and a record on high." From Georgia he returned to Virginia and held Conference, and from thence directed his course to Baltimore, where the General Conference was to be held, which ended his continental tour this year.

An incident occurred during this tour of the West in 1803, which we will relate. After attending the Western Conference, near Cynthiana, Kentucky, where he preached to ten thousand people in the woods, he started out, in company with several preachers, on his return tour. In the midst of the wilderness, between the Crab Orchard and Powell's Valley, he halted one night at a rude log cabin tavern, a kind of half-way house in the wilderness. The house was filled with a rough company of wild mountain hunters. They had been drinking and carousing, and when the preachers entered, loud oaths fell upon their ears from a company around a card-table. Low-bred as the landlord was, he had sufficient respect left to invite his newly-arrived guests into another room. One of the bar-room company, an old Englishman, on finding that the persons who had recently come were preachers, immediately sauntered in, and walking up to the bishop, commenced asking him some questions on the subject of religion. The bishop asked him if he had been seeking religion.

"O yes," replied the old man, "for a long time, but I have not found it yet. I have succeeded in one thing ; a Baptist preacher has broken me off from swearing profanely."

"Ah," replied the bishop. "Well, keep on reforming, and you may come out a good man at last."

The bishop evidently had little faith in his sincerity, and was afterward abundantly confirmed in his opinion by hearing him, in a loud voice, cursing and swearing in the other room. At length, opening the door, the bishop said to him : "You told me a certain

Baptist preacher had broken you off from swearing, but I find you can lie and swear both."

At this the Englishman approached him and said, "I beg your pardon, Bishop Asbury."

"Ask pardon of God, whose name you have blasphemed ; repent of your sins, and that right speedily, or iniquity will prove your ruin."

This reproof affected the whole company of rioters, and they soon left the house to quietness and the preachers. After supper the bishop had the whole family called in, read a chapter in the Bible, gave a short lecture, and offered a most fervent prayer.

Early next morning, while preparing for their departure, the landlord came to the bishop with a bottle and a glass, and asked him to take a little whisky. "Nay," said the bishop, "I make no use of the devil's tea."

It was not without some misgivings that the preachers started out upon their journey, as the mountain hunters had among them a class of desperadoes who would frequently stop at these wilderness taverns, and on becoming acquainted with the character of the travellers who stopped for the night, would leave, and laying aside their hunting dress, would paint themselves and put on the garb of Indians, and intercepting the path of the travellers, would fall upon and murder and rob them. Preachers were doubtless often protected from the fact that they had but little that would be an object of plunder except their horses.

CHAPTER XVIII.

THE General Conference of 1804 was held in Baltimore. There were one hundred and eleven members, representatives from seven Conferences, present. Sixty-seven were from the Baltimore and Philadelphia Conferences, constituting more than two-thirds of the entire number. Of the remaining portion, twelve were from the New York, seventeen from the Virginia, four from the Boston, three from the Western, and five from the South Carolina Conference. The Conference was composed of all the preachers who had travelled four years consecutively since their admission on trial in the connection. After adjusting some preliminary matters, such as adopting rules for the government of the body, and settling the question as to who were entitled to seats, the Conference resolved to proceed to a revision of the Discipline. It was agreed that in the revision it should be read chapter by chapter, section by section, and paragraph by paragraph ; that the assent to every paragraph which was not debated should be decided by the members sitting, and the assent to every paragraph which was debated should be decided by the members rising. The assent to every section, except such parts as had been expunged or abolished, was to be decided by rising.

After settling the question of the boundaries of the several Annual Conferences, a long and animated discussion was had on the subject of presiding elders. The discussion was elicited by a motion to abolish the office entirely. The motion, however, was lost. In alluding to the debate on this subject, Asbury remarked: "Attempts were made upon the ruling eldership. We had a great talk. I talked little on the subject, and was kept in peace."

The subject of slavery was introduced by a resolution offered by Freeborn Garrettson, the import of which was, that the bishops be requested to draft a section for the Discipline, embracing such regulations and provisions as would adapt it to the southern as well as northern states. The action of the last Conference on the subject had created no little dissatisfaction, and especially the Address to the Methodist people. The way of the preachers had evidently been hedged up in several places, and it was considered important that the General Conference should modify its action on the subject. Bishop Asbury declining to act with the episcopal committee, the subject was referred to a committee of seven, who, after due deliberation, presented a report which was incorporated in the Discipline and made section nine, entitled, "Of Slavery." The section contained five rules, requiring, 1st. That all who held slaves should give security for their emancipation, immediately or gradually, as the laws of the states respectively and the circumstances of the case would admit; 2nd. When any travelling preacher became an owner of a slave or slaves by any means, he was to forfeit his ministerial standing unless he executed, if practicable, a deed of emancipation conformably to the laws of the State where he lived; 3rd. No slaveholder was to be received into full membership until the preacher in charge had spoken to him fully and faithfully on the subject; 4. No one who sold a slave, except in cases of mercy or humanity, was to be allowed to remain in society, and if any one purchased a slave the quarterly meeting Conference was to determine the number of years the slave should serve as the price of his purchase, at the expiration of which time the master was to set him free. Other regulations were made in regard to female slaves, providing for the manumission of such of their children as might be born during servitude. This and the preceding rules contained the remarkable proviso exempting the states of North Carolina, South Carolina, and Georgia from their operation. The fifth and last rule required the preachers from time to time, as occasion served, to admonish and exhort all slaves to render due respect and obedience to the commands and interests of their respective masters.

The Conference, agreeably to the request of the European Conferences, granted Dr. Coke leave to return to England, with the proviso that at the call of three Annual Conferences, in the interval of the General Conference, he should come back to the United States. In the address of the General Conference to the British and Irish Conferences, the following allusion is made to the doctor : " With respect to our much esteemed friend and beloved brother, Dr. Coke, we would say, he arrived among us last Autumn, and was received by us with sincerest sentiments of respect and affection. Since he came into these States he has travelled about three thousand miles, visiting our principal societies, and preaching to crowded assemblies of our citizens. Your request for his return was taken into our most serious and solemn consideration, and after a full and deliberate examination of the reasons which you assigned in favour of his return, we have concluded that there is a probability of his being more eminently useful at present in the way you point out, than for us to retain him, especially as our beloved brother Asbury now enjoys better health than he did some years ago. We therefore have consented to the doctor's return to Europe on the express condition that he will come back to us at any time when three of our Annual Conferences shall call him, or at farthest that he shall return to our next General Conference."

To that favoured retreat, Perry Hall, after the Conference was ended, Asbury directed his course, where, after a brief rest, he started out on his Eastern tour, holding Conference in Philadelphia and New York. From the latter place he rode to New Haven, where he preached in a small house to a few people. While here he entered the following in his Journal: "My soul has constant peace and joy, notwithstanding my labours, and trials, and reproach, which I heed not, though it comes, as it sometimes does, from the good, when they are not gratified in all their wishes. People unacquainted with the causes and motives of my conduct will always more or less judge of me improperly. Six months ago a man could write to me in the most adulatory terms to tell me of the unshaken confidence reposed in me by preachers and people. Behold, his station is changed, and certain measures are pursued that do not comport with his views and feelings. Then I am menaced with the downfall of Methodism, and my influence, character, and reputation are all to find a grave in its ruins. First, my mountain is made so strong I shall never be moved. Anon, O man, thou hidest thy face and changest thy voice and I must be troubled forsooth. But I am just as secure as ever as to what man can do or say."

Censure is a tax invariably imposed upon all men who rise to eminence in Church or state, and it was not to be expected that Asbury would escape. It will be seen, however, from the above that he bore it with Christian patience and magnanimity. As a Christian bishop and father, he did not lay up anything against those who censured him; at least, he never allowed a remembrance of past injury to weigh a feather in the exercise of his episcopal authority in stationing the preachers. His motto was to overcome evil with good.

From New Haven he went to Middletown, where the members of the Church were about purchasing a lot whereon to build a small house of worship. The Conference had given him Sylvester Hutchinson as a travelling companion, who frequently supplied his place in the pulpit. Passing through Rhode Island and New Hampshire, they came to Buxton, where the Conference was held, and at which fifty souls were converted. Asbury generally considered it a barren time if there was no revival at a Conference.

While journeying through Massachusetts he came to Enfield, near to which was a settlement of the Quakers, concerning whom he said, "Poor souls, they have landed where all other sects have landed. O this love of the world; but the Shakers are near the end of the world: they forbid to marry; they are as the angels in heaven." After passing through a portion of Massachusetts, he directed his course to Rhinebeck, on the Hudson, where he preached on Sabbath in an orchard to about one thousand people. The next two or three days he spent at Widow Sherwood's, and the succeeding Sabbath went to New York, where he preached in John-street, complaining that all the congregations in the city were a valley of dry bones. From New York he took his usual route through New Jersey, Delaware, and Maryland.

At the yearly Conference held in Chestertown, Maryland, an address was sent to the Quarterly Conference of the Delaware District, embracing nearly all the territory now included in the Philadelphia Conference. The address was written and signed by Asbury, and as it is interesting, both from its matter and style, we insert it. It bears date May 5, 1805, and is as follows:

"DEARLY BELOVED IN THE LORD,—Grace be unto you, and peace and love be multiplied. It is scarcely possible for you, in your local situation, to have correct views of what our God hath done for us as a people in the space of thirty-five years. We think it a duty we owe to you to make the following statement. The Gospel, by our ministry, has made a glorious progress through the seventeen United States, the territorial settlements, and Canadian provinces, as may be seen by our Annual Minutes.

Should we compute the distance from St. Mary's in Georgia, to Montreal in Canada, it would be found to be seventeen or eighteen hundred miles ; and from the extremities of the district of Maine to the Natchez, two thousand miles. What but a travelling ministry, and a very rapid one, too, could so extensively propagate the Gospel in the midst of so much opposition. There are now more than one hundred thousand souls in fellowship with us, and perhaps six times that number who look up to us for ministerial services, and to hear the word of life, which you know by happy experience to be the power of God unto salvation, as well as many thousands of happy souls whom we doubt not have already gone to glory. We have upwards of four hundred travelling preachers, besides about two thousand local preachers and exhorters ; a source from whence we can draw supplies to strengthen and replenish our travelling connection.

" We unanimously express our high regard for our *local brethren,* many of whom have long travelled, laboured, and suffered with us in the vineyard of the Lord, and others who would have travelled but for secular affairs. Dear brethren, we acknowledge your great usefulness. You cheerfully labour with us when we are present, preserve the union of the societies, keep up the congregations and prayer-meetings when we are absent, and your influence can and does do much in raising class collections for our support. Our apparent increase (in the Philadelphia Conference) this year is small, owing in part to migrations to new settlements, and the uncommon sickness and mortality of last autumn. But when we bring into view the great wastage among twenty-eight thousand seven hundred and twelve, and the number necessary to repair that wastage, we shall see that the number received must have been very considerable to give us an addition of six hundred and twenty-four.

" Our finances for the present year are better than they were last, owing in part to the Albany district (where the deficiencies were usually great) being attached to the New York Conference, and yet many of the preachers were deficient more than twenty-three per cent., though they received nothing for their children. The circuits which have given liberally will please accept our thanks. We have received eight preachers upon trial, and discontinued —— from their probation, and are exceedingly sorry to add that some of their cases were truly humiliating and distressing ; nevertheless the Lord hath in great mercy blessed us with unusual moderation and peace, through the whole of our critical decisions.

" Dear brethren, we have laboured and suffered with you and

N

for you, and are willing and determined so to do. We have confidence that you will endeavour to walk worthy of your vocation, and unite with us in all laudable endeavours to promote the Redeemer's kingdom. Let us in love continue to watch over and pray for each other, keeping the unity of the spirit and the bond of peace until we are come to the fullness of the measure of the stature of Christ, that we may finally rest with him for ever."

One of the most remarkable camp-meetings ever known was held in the autumn of this year near the town of Suffolk, in Virginia. The meeting commenced on Friday, and was continued with but little intermission until Monday night. From the very beginning the power of God was wonderfully manifested, and during its continuance four hundred persons were converted. The accounts of this meeting which appeared at the time would seem incredible had they not been vouched for by those who were present. Another meeting of the same description was held about ten miles from Wilmington, in North Carolina. The revival commenced on the first day of the meeting, and continued with increasing interest and power until Sabbath. Persons of all descriptions and all ages, from the child nine years of age to the hoary-headed sinner, were subjects. The revival did not close with the meeting, but spread abroad among the surrounding settlements until three hundred were converted. A camp-meeting was also held at a place called Hampton, belonging to General Ridgeley, about ten miles from Baltimore, which lasted four days. There were about thirty preachers present, and a large number of people were made the subjects of converting grace. Meetings of the same description were held at Linville's Creek, Rehoboth, and Big Levels in Virginia, and in the Mississippi territory, some of which lasted more than a week, and at all of which numbers were converted.

Near Uniontown, Pa., Asbury was confined more than a month with sickness, and was obliged to desist from going to Kentucky. It was a great trial to be kept so long from his loved employment; but he bore it with patience. After his recovery he passed slowly through Virginia, accompanied by Bishop Whatcoat, and continued the journey through North and South Carolina. The Conference was held in Charleston. On their return through Virginia they preached at different points. While at Joseph Moody's, Asbury learned of quite a number of members who had left the O'Kelly secession and returned to the Church. Among the number were General Wells and family. Speaking of O'Kelly, the bishop says : " He has come down with great zeal, and preaches three hours at a time upon government, monarchy, and Episcopacy, occasionally varying the subject by abuse of the Methodists, calling them aristocrats and tories, a people who, if they had the power, would force the government at the sword's point. Poor man, the Methodists have but two of their very numerous society members of Congress, and until these democratic times we never had one. I question if in all the legislative bodies in the seventeen states there are more than twenty Methodists. No ; our people are a very independent people, who think for themselves, and so do the preachers, and are as apt to differ in politics and divide at the hustings as those of any other denomination, and surely they are not seekers of the offices of this world's profit or honour ; if they were, what might they not gain in many parts of the United States ! While one rails at us, others, who are always fond of fishing in troubled waters, take those who are already in our net, or, hunting on forbidding ground, pick up our crippled game."

After holding Conference in Virginia Asbury returned in the spring to Baltimore, where Conference was opened on the first of April, 1805.

From hence he and Whatcoat started eastward, preaching at different places in Delaware, New Jersey, and Pennsylvania until they arrived in New York. While here Asbury attended a camp-meeting at Musquito Cove, on Long Island, and preached to a vast multitude on Sabbath. The meeting was attended with a gracious outpouring of the Spirit, and many were converted. On Monday evening he returned to Brooklyn and preached. He and Whatcoat preached also in New York, and then started for White Plains, where they held services on Sunday.

About this time there was a considerable discussion going on in the State on the subject of the regular succession, and the consequent right to administer the ordinances. Asbury's short way of meeting the objections to his authority was presented on this wise : 1. Divine authority ; 2. Seniority in America ; 3. The election of the General Conference ; 4. Ordination by Dr. Coke, Rev. W. P. Otterbein, of the German Reformed Church, and Revs. Richard Whatcoat and Thomas Vasey ; 5. Showing the signs of an apostle. He might have rested his authority in the first consideration, namely, his Divine call to the ministry, for it is not to be presumed that God will call any man to this great work and at the same time not invest him with authority to administer all the ordinances connected therewith. The call is of itself *prima facie* evidence of the authority, and the fact that souls are converted and saved through his instrumentality is proof that the minister is an ambassador for God, invested with plenipotentiary power to transact all the business pertaining to the Divine vocation.

From White Plains they crossed the Peekskill mountains, and after spending the Sabbath at Rhinebeck, they passed through Claverack, Kinderhook, Lansingburgh, and Waterford, on to Stillwater, where a camp-meeting was to be held. At this meeting there were preachers from Canada, Vermont, Massachusetts, Connecticut, New York, and New Jersey. The meeting lasted four days and was very largely attended. From the camp-meeting the bishops proceeded to Ashgrove, where the New York Conference was held. Leaving the banks of the Hudson they crossed the Berkshire mountains by Pittsfield, descended the valley of the Connecticut, and proceeded to Lynn, where they met the New England Conference, and returned by Wilbraham, Hartford, and New Haven to New York. They were not permitted, however, to enter the city, because they had passed through New Haven, where the yellow fever was prevailing. On arriving at Philadelphia they were for the same reason debarred entrance to that city, and they accordingly directed their course westward across the Alleghany Mountains to Pittsburgh. From thence they proceeded down the Ohio to Wheeling, and across the country, by Zanesville, to Chillicothe, where they enjoyed the hospitalities of Hon. Edward Tiffin, then governor of the State of Ohio. Leaving Chillicothe for the Falls of Paint Creek, they lost their path and wandered about in the woods until they brought up at Bullskin, where they were kindly entertained by Michael Haines, who conducted them on their way. From this point they struck for the Little Miami and reached the house of Judge Gatch. Here they held meeting on the Sabbath. While here a messenger came from Cincinnati inviting the bishops to visit that place, and on Monday, the 15th of September, 1805, Asbury for the first time entered what has since become the Queen City of the West. He preached in the house of Mr. William Lines from the text, "Seek ye the Lord while he may be found."

Crossing the Ohio at Cincinnati they went through Kentucky to the Holstein, and from thence over the mountains through North Carolina, South Carolina, and Georgia. Asbury was accompanied in this tour by Joseph Crawford, who did most of the preaching on the way. Having attended the Southern Conferences, he returned and held Conference in Virginia, and proceeded on to Baltimore. Among other business transacted at this Conference was the drawing up of a reply to Dr. Coke's letter, and the passage or a resolution requesting the bishop to lay it before all the annual Conferences for concurrence. The Conference also by resolution recommended all the Annual Conferences to take into consideration the propriety of having the General Conference composed of delegates, for the purpose of securing a more equal representation than had heretofore been had by the Southern, Western, and Eastern Conferences. His next Conference was Philadelphia, which he attended, and where he heard of the dangerous illness of Bishop Whatcoat at Dover. From hence he went to New York, and visited the ground at Philip's Manor, selected for a camp meeting. He rested two days at "Sherwood's Vale," as it was in the vicinity of the camp-ground. The meeting began on Friday. On Sabbath he preached, and had what he called "an open season." At this meeting there were about one thousand Methodists and about six thousand people. As to the result, about two hundred were converted.

On Friday, the 16th of May, 1806, Conference was held in New York. At this Conference a paper was read setting forth the uncertain state of the episcopacy, and proposing the election of seven elders from the seven Conferences to meet in Baltimore on July the 4th, 1807, for the sole purpose of establishing the American episcopacy on a surer foundation. The Conference, by resolution, requested the bishop to pass the paper around among the Conferences for concurrence. During this Conference preaching was held in the "Park" as well as in the Methodist churches, and a day of fasting and prayer was set apart for the health of the city.

After Conference he took his usual Eastern tour, holding the New England Conference in New Hampshire. On his return he passed through New Jersey, Maryland, and Virginia, on to Tennessee, where the Western Conference was held. It was here that the poverty of the preachers was such as to induce him to part with his watch, and coat, and shirt to relieve their necessities. Passing through North and South Carolina, he went down into Georgia, where he was lost in the woods and camped out all night. He held Conference at Sparta. The paper in relation to the delegated General Conference was adopted, and the delegates to the elders' meeting in Baltimore elected. This Conference closed up the labours of the year 1806, and with it the fifth decade of American Methodism.

CHAPTER XIX.

Mountains of Western Virginia—Camp-meeting scenes—Asbury's Visit—Rev.
Henry Boehm—Reese Wolf—Hockhocking—Preaching—Tour through Ohio
—Pioneer Settlers—Log Cabins—Hospitable but hard Fare—Asbury's Lec-
ture — Interesting Incident—Love-feast — One of Asbury's Converts—
Virginia—Hospitality—Social Gathering—Description of Guests—Subjects of
Conversation.

AMONG the mountains of Western Virginia the pioneer Methodist
preacher had formed his circuit, and established preaching places
in the cabins of the settlers. Camp-meetings were generally held
in the valley of the Kanawha during the summer months, where
from various and distant parts of the wilderness the people would
congregate and pitch their tents. Hundreds and thousands would
collect together upon such occasions, and the native forests would
be made vocal with the praises of the assembled throng. Preachers
from adjoining circuits and districts would attend these annual
feasts, and, with a fervency and zeal characteristic of pioneer
preachers they would pour forth strains of burning eloquence that
would find their way to the most impenitent hearts ; and multitudes to whom the Gospel would otherwise perhaps never have
come, were made the happy subjects of converting grace.

On one of Bishop Asbury's Western tours he turned aside from
his direct journey to visit one of these encampments. He was
now in the sixty-fifth year of his age, and though worn down with
the fatigues of long weary rides, and incessant labours, still he was
determined to toil on, unwilling that any part of his vast field
should be neglected. The presiding elder, who was the Rev. James
Quinn, of precious memory, thus describes this visit :

"It was in the month of September, in the West one of the most
bland and beautiful months of the year, that we pitched out tents
in a beautiful sugar-grove on the lands of Richard Lee, two miles
above Parkersburg, on the banks of the Kanawha. It was at the
time of full moon and at night. The camp was well illuminated
with pine lights. The meeting commenced under the most
auspicious circumstances, and from the beginning to the close we
had evidences of the presence and approval of the great Head of
the Church, in the conviction and conversion of many souls, and
the upbuilding of believers in the most holy faith. Having retired
to the preachers' tent for some relaxation and rest, the work still

going on in the camp, about ten o'clock a person came to the tent and informed me that an old man at the gateway wished to see me. I arose and went forthwith, and to my great surprise and joy, who should I see in the clear moonlight, but the venerable Asbury and his travelling companion the Rev. Henry Boehm. I conducted him to the house of Richard Lee, and said to him, Rest and be happy for the night. You are now in the house of the brother of your old friend, Rev. Wilson Lee. At this the good old man appeared to be pleased, nor were Brother and Sister Lee less gratified at having the privilege of entertaining, if not unawares, at least unexpectedly, that angel of the Church below. I returned to the encampment, and witnessed a glorious night of the presence and power of the Most High. The bishop had a good night's rest, which he said was the first he had enjoyed since he left Wheeling, and he came on the ground quite early in fine spirits, expressing himself highly pleased with the arrangements and good order which he saw on the camp ground. He preached twice during the meeting with great life, light, and power. Surely the Lord helped him and great good was done. He also ordained a preacher who had been elected by the Baltimore Conference to the office of an elder.

"Our camp-meeting closed well on Monday morning, and we repaired to Brother Reese Wolf's, the old local preacher who led the way, and invited Methodism on to the Little Kanawha, by the itinerant preachers, in 1799. Here we met a kind reception, and rested till next morning. At three o'clock the bishop preached a plain and powerful sermon in Parkersburgh, which was a small place then. O what awful appeals to the understanding and to the heart! There was no daubing with untempered mortar.

"We crossed over the Ohio into Belpre, and were kindly received and lodged at the house of Esq. B. The lady of the house was an intelligent old lady, from the land of steady habits, who had heard Whitefield preach, and was greatly delighted in seeing and conversing with the Methodist bishop. But O, her regrets on account of the great privations in coming to the West : ' Yonder we had such fine meetinghouses, comfortable pews, organs, and such delightful singing ; and then, O such charming preachers ! O bishop, you can't tell !' etc. 'Yes, yes,' said the bishop, ' Old Connecticut for all the world :

> " A fine house and a high steeple,
> A learned priest and a gay people."

But where shall we look for Gospel simplicity and purity ? Let us go back to the days of the Pilgrim fathers.' 'Well, bishop, who are you going to send to us next year? I hope you will send us a very good preacher.' 'Come, send you a good preacher!' 'Yes, sir; don't you send them just where you please?' It was evident that the bishop was disposed to waive the subject, upon which one present said, 'Madam, I'll tell you how it is; we send him and tell him to send us, and then he must come and see us; for he must travel at large, and oversee the whole work, and must not stop without our leave.' 'Indeed! Well, now I guess I understand it better. Well, well, bishop, where do you live?'

> 'No foot of land do I possess,
> No cottage in this wilderness,
> A poor wayfaring man.'

At this the old lady appeared much surprised, and so the the conversation closed.

"Next morning we started very early, and called at several farmhouses on the way down the river, whose inmates were not Methodists, and the good man prayed with them all. Indeed, I have seldom known him to leave a family without prayer, whether they were professors or not, for he was always intent upon doing good. At three o'clock he preached in a school-house opposite Blennerhasset's Island; and truly it might be said of the sermon, as I once heard him say of Horneck's Great Law of Consideration, 'It was a dagger to the hilt at every stroke.' After preaching we were kindly invited by Col. Putnam, son of Gen. Putnam, of the Revolution, to the house of his son, Major Putnam, where we were treated with every attention. Some six or eight of the principal men, with their ladies, came in to see and spend the evening with the Methodist bishop. Most of these were Revolutionary men. The conversation of the evening was quite of an interesting character, in which the bishop took a lively part. But ever and anon an important religious sentiment was thrown in, or a moral application made, to which the company bowed silent assent, their countenances, in the mean time, showing that the weight was felt. The evening closed with devotional services. The company retired, and we were conducted to our lodgings; and where should we find ourselves but in the splendid ball-room. 'Here,' said the bishop, 'they were wont to worship the devil; but let us worship God.' I was informed that the decree was passed soon after, that no more balls were to be held there. Next morning we set out for Athens. As we were crossing Little Hockhocking, I said: 'Here, Mr. Asbury, in 1800, the man used to set me over ferriage free, saying he never charged ministers or babes; for if they do no good they do no harm.' 'Ah,' said he, 'that is not true of ministers; for the minister who does no good does much harm.' We reached Athens on Friday at noon, and commenced our camp-meeting. It went on well, and closed well on the fourth day, and the bishop left us in good spirits for Chillicothe, having preached two powerful sermons. In making his tour, he had diverged from a straight road at least fifty miles, and added to his journey more than one hundred miles. What love had he for the souls of men, as the purchase of the Redeemer's blood!"

Another interesting reminiscence is given by the same writer, in which he describes a tour with Asbury through Ohio. The sketch thus runs: "I once had the pleasure of accompanying Bishop Asbury ten days on one of his Western tours through the then infant state of Ohio in the days of log-cabins; and they were not such unsightly things, if coon and wild cat-skins were hanging round the walls, and deer horns strewed over the roof, and wild turkeys' wings sticking about in the cracks, for they were, with few exceptions, the best dwellings in the land. Well, in many of these we met a smiling welcome, and were most hospitably entertained, and the good bishop always made himself pleasant and cheerful with the families, so that they soon forgot all embarrassment, and appeared as easy in their feelings as if they had received the bishop into ceiled and carpeted parlours, as some of them had in the old states. Some of them were very neat and clean, fitted up in good taste, which showed that if madam could not play on the pianoforte she had taken lessons from Israel's wise king, and knew well how to look to the affairs of her house, if it was a cabin. It must be confessed, however, that all were not so; for it was our sad lot to fall in with one or two that were miserably filthy and fearfully infested with vermin. This was a heavy tax on the feelings of the poor bishop, for he had as fair, and as clear, and thin a skin as ever came from England, and in him the sense of smelling and tasting were most exquisite. But, dear souls, they were as kind as you please, and the bishop did not hurt their feelings, but prayed for them, and talked good to them. Many of them have got better houses since that time, have made good improvements, and their daughters have come out quite polished. But we got to quarterly meeting, for he was passing my district, and a most blessed season we had: sinners awakened, souls converted, believers quickened, backsliders reclaimed. O the Master of assemblies was with us of a truth! Quarterly meeting Conference came on. 'Well, Mr. Asbury, you will attend with us and preside?' 'No, son,' was the

reply ; 'Let every man stand in his lot and do his part of the
work ; when you shall have got through your business let me know
and I will come and see you.' So we went to business pretty ex-
peditiously, expecting an address from the bishop. We had no
long, tough speeches, and those repeated, but went through, brought
our business to a close in due time, and sent a messenger to inform
him that we were ready to receive him. He came, took the chair,
and after a short pause commenced taking notice of the infancy of
the state, the infancy of the Church, the toils and privations, the
trials and temptations, peculiar to such a state of things, and the
great necessity of watchfulness and prayer, and diligent attendance
on the means of grace, both public and private. He spoke of his
own toils, cares, and anxieties with some emotion ; of the great and
glorious extension and spread of the work of God in the East and
South, also in the West and South-West, both among the Methodists and other Christian People. He spoke with much feeling.
'But the Quarterly Conference, the importance of this branch of
our ecclesiastical economy, " *to hear complaints, to receive and try
appeals,*" and thus guard the rights and privileges of the membership against injury from an incorrect administration ; to try, and
even expel, preachers, deacons, and elders ; to examine, license, and
recommend to office in the local department ; to recommend for
admission into the travelling connection persons as possessing grace,
gifts, and usefulness for the great and important work of the
Gospel ministry ; surely you will see and feel the highly responsible station which you fill as members of this body. We send
you our sons in the Gospel to minister to you the word of life and
watch over your souls as they that must give account. That they
may become men, men of God and even fathers among you, help
them in their great work ; and that you may help them under-
standingly, read, mark, learn, and inwardly digest your excellent
Discipline. It is plain, simple, and Scriptural. It is true, speculative minds may find or make difficulties where there are none. [I
am not ashamed to confess that I learned something during this
lecture that I thought well worth taking care of.] But a few
words about your manner of living at the present. You are now
in your log-cabins, and busily engaged in clearing out your lands.
Well, think nothing of this. I have been a man of cabins for
these many years, and I have been lodged in many a cabin as clean
and sweet as a palace ; and I have slept on many coarse, hard beds,
which have been as clean and as sweet as water and soap could
make them, and not a flea nor a bug to annoy. [Here I had to
hang my head. Dear old gentleman, he had not forgotten the

other night when he got no sleep.] 'Keep,' said the bishop, 'the whisky-bottle out of your cabins, away far from your premises. Never fail in the offering up of the morning and evening sacrifice with your families. Keep your cabins clean for your healths' sake and for your souls' sake, [put this on to your wives and daughters,] for there is no religion in dirt, and filth, and fleas. But,' said he, 'of this no more. If you do not wish the Lord to forsake your cabin, do not forsake his; you will lose nothing, but be gainers, even in temporal things, by going and taking your household with you, even on a week day; you cannot all have Sabbath preaching. It is time we close for evening service.' A few words more in commending us to God and the word of his grace, and then what a prayer! how spiritual, how fervent, how fully adapted to the state of the country and the Church as they then were! Truly it might be said, he was mighty in prayer."

On one of Asbury's Excursions, after travelling hard through a Western wilderness to reach a quarterly meeting which lay on his route to a distant Conference, he was unusually tempted at not having seen, for some time, any direct fruit of his personal labour in the conversion of souls. He felt inclined to the belief that his mission had expired, and he had better retire from the work. With this depression of spirit he entered the love-feast on Sabbath morning, in a rude log chapel in the woods, and took his seat, unknown to any, in the back part of the congregation. After the usual preliminary exercises had been gone through with by the preacher, an opportunity was given for the relation of Christian experience. One after another testified of the saving grace of God, and occasionally a verse of some hymn was sung, full of rich and touching melody. The tide of religious feeling was rising and swelling in all hearts, while a lady rose whose plain but exceedingly neat attire indicated that she was a Methodist. Her voice was full and clear, though slightly tremulous. , She had travelled many miles to the meeting, and her feelings would not allow her to repress her testimony. She remarked that she had not long been a follower of Christ. "Two years ago," said she, "I was attracted to a Methodist meeting in our neighbourhood by being informed that Bishop Asbury was going to preach. I went, and the Spirit sealed the truth he uttered on my heart. I fled to Jesus and found redemption in his blood, even the forgiveness of my sins, and have been happy in his love ever since.

"'Not a cloud doth arise to darken my skies,
Or hide for a moment my Lord from my eyes.' "

She sat down, and ere the responses which her remarks had awakened in all parts of the house had died away, Bishop Asbury was on his feet.   He commenced by remarking that "he was a stranger and pilgrim, halting on his way for rest and refreshment in the house of God, and that he had found both ; and," said he, with uplifted hands, while tears of joy coursed each other freely down his face, "if I can only be instrumental in the conversion of one soul in travelling round the continent, I'll travel round till I die."

The following story was told us by Father Finley: When Asbury was spending a few weeks in one of the cities of the Union, and preaching every day, he was refreshed in spirit by witnessing the conversion of a number of souls.   Among them was a young lady. She had just returned from a fashionable boarding school, having finished the course of study, and having received a diploma setting forth her attainments and accomplishments.   Special attention had been bestowed upon her musical education.   She had a voice of great power and melody, and her performance on the piano exhibited rare attainments in the art.   Her father was a gentleman of wealth, and took great pride in his daughter.   At fashionable parties she was a star of general attraction, and her musical power, as well as prepossessing appearance and manners, made her society extremely desirable.

This gifted and accomplished young lady was induced to go one evening to hear Asbury.   His voice and manner riveted her attention, and ere she was aware, as the man of God presented the claims of religion upon the young, her heart was touched.   She yielded to the persuasive power of the Gospel, and in penitence sought and found the blessings of religion.   Her conversion was as sudden as it was unexpected by her friends, but it was, nevertheless, clear and genuine.   No place to her was now so attractive as the house of God, and thither she wended her steps from evening to evening, enjoying the rapturous bliss

"Of a soul in its earliest love."

Of course, it was not long until the change wrought upon her by the power of the Gospel was known to her parents, who strange to say, felt grieved and indignant at the result.   They were worldly and thoughtless, not only neglecting the claims of religion themselves but wholly careless in regard to their children.   Their only object was to fit them for moving in fashionable circles, and no pains or expense were spared to effect it.

To win her back to the world was now the design of the father.

He was too much of a gentleman, and had too much respect for himself and the proprieties of life, to resort to any coercive measures. He accordingly brought around her the thoughtless and the gay of her companions, and threw her as often as possible into their society. Naturally amiable, and loving her parents with all the devotion of an affectionate child, she yielded to her father's requests to visit different places of mirth and gaiety ; and though she did not put on the morose look of cloistered piety, yet she was serenely quiet and affable in her manners, preserving the true dignity of the Christian. She had a heartfelt joy to which the worldly are strangers, and while she felt sympathy for the pursuers of shadows, she allowed not her anxiety for their spiritual welfare to destroy their brief uncertain joy. She preferred holding up the light of a Christian example in a calm, quiet, unobtrusive manner, rather than resort to any effort to convince them of the error of their way. All the efforts of her father were, however, of no avail to lure her from the purpose she had formed to lead a religious life.

As a last resort he gave a large party, and sent out invitations to the most wordly and fashionable of the city. The evening at length arrived ; the company came together ; all was a scene of gaiety and mirth, for the pleasure-loving throng were there. In the midst of this scene it was arranged that she should be invited to sing and play on the piano one of those fashionable airs to which they had been wont to listen with so much interest previous to her conversion. She made no objection as she was led by her father to the piano. Taking her seat, she commenced in a strain the most touching, because it came from her heart, and sang, with a full clear voice, that beautiful hymn of Charles Wesley :

> " No room for mirth or trifling here,
> For worldly hope or worldly fear,
>   If life so soon is gone ;
> If now the Judge is at the door,
> And all mankind must stand before
>   The inexorable throne.

> " No matter which my thoughts employ—
> A moment's misery or joy ;
>   But O ! when both shall end,
> Where shall I find my destined place ?
> Shall I my everlasting days
>   With fiends or angels spend ?

> " Nothing is worth a thought beneath
> But how I may escape the death
> That never, never dies ;
> How make my own election sure,
> And when I fail on earth secure
> A mansion in the skies.

She had not sung through one verse, before her father, who stood by her side, was seen to drop his head. Every whisper ceased, and the most intense feeling was evidently pervading the entire company. Every word was distinctly heard, and each seemed an arrow from the Spirit's quiver, going directly to the hearts of the hearers. When she ceased her father was gone. His feelings were too great to be suppressed, and he sought another room, where he gave vent to his tears. Mary had conquered, and from that hour she was free from the allurements of the world. For many years she lived to adorn her profession, and then went up to join the song of the redeemed in heaven.

In the summer of 1802 Asbury spent a few days in the vicinity of Stevensburg, Virginia, at the house of his warm-hearted brother, Rev. Elisha Phelps, where he received his friends. The Rev. James Quinn thus describes the interview : "A most interesting company convened at this lovely country residence, where true Virginia hospitality, in old style, stood ready to receive them with smiling welcome. As soon as the company were seated in the not splendid but neatly arranged parlour, in order that all things might be sanctified by the word of God and prayer, the bishop, in his usually laconic and comprehensive style, addressed the throne of grace. Although the prayer was short, it seemed to take in all for which man or minister should pray. O how much unprofitable, not to say vain, repetition do we sometimes hear in the long prayers of some well-disposed persons ! Not so prayed Asbury. The prayer concluded, the company resumed their seats ; and what then ? Light chit-chat, mixed with peals of laughter, in which all persons talk and no one hears ? No, no ; it was 'the feast of reason and the flow of soul.' In a free flow of conversation on a variety of interesting topics, chiefly of a moral and religious character. The state of the Old World, in religion and politics, occupied part of the time. The revolutions in Europe, the shaking of thrones, the fulfilment of prophecy, the overthrow of the beast and the false prophet ; Newton, Faber, Bengelius, and Wesley, on the fulfilment of prophecy ; infidelity in Europe and America ; the spread of the Gospel, the rolling of the stone cut out of the mountains, the glorious 1836, which, according to some, was to usher in the glories of the Millennium; these, together with the state of affairs in our own America, God maintaining his own cause, making bare his arm, pouring out his Spirit gloriously on different branches of his Church, etc., entered largely into the social entertainments of that pleasant day.

"And now, if I could, I would most cheerfully give the reader a minute description of that social band. I fear a failure, but will try. Well, then, here were our host, Rev. E. Phelps, and hostess. He had been a travelling preacher of respectable talents. His heart was still warm in the cause, though he had retired from the work. His open, good-natured countenance told his guests that they were welcome, and that was enough. His deeply-pious lady, somewhat in advance of him in years, was of the olden style, a sensible, well-informed woman, without the tinsel and frippery of modern etiquette. She was a daughter of Colonel Hyte, of Revolutionary fame. Her orderly movements, and countenance beaming with good nature, said to her friends, Feel yourselves welcome.

"Then here was Mr. Asbury, in better health than usual, and in fine spirits; I never saw him in a more cheerful and pleasant mood; for the Lord was then gloriously pouring out his Spirit in many places, and many souls were coming home to God; and this always cheered the heart of the good man.

"That tall, swarthy southerner, of ministerial garb and mien, who was that? That was Rev. Philip Bruce, a bachelor. He brought good news from the south of Virginia. His district was all in a flame.

"Well, that somewhat robust, fine-looking gentleman, with black band, with Virginia cotton homespun, and that sickly-looking lady near him, who are they? That was Rev. Samuel Mitchell, of Bottetourt, Va. He was a whole-souled Virginian, who, by word and deed, carried out the first principles of the doctrine contained in the Declaration of American Independence. His heart was all on fire. The news of the great work of God in West Tennessee and Kentucky had just come to hand by private letters. In his amiable lady we saw and admired the power and loveliness of blessed Christianity, fortifying the mind and cheering the heart, while sweet resignation sat smiling at the approach of death. A few months more and she slept in Jesus, and all was well.

"But there is still another interesting figure, somewhat robust, but not corpulent, a fine manly face, and smiling countenance. Well, that was Dr. J. Tildon, a local preacher. He had been a captain in the Revolution, held a certificate of membership in the CINCINNATI, with Washington's signature as president of the society. He was interesting in conversation.

"That aged lady in black? That was Dr. Tildon's mother. She had lived more than seventy years. She was waiting her change and ripening for heaven.

"And that interesting lady, whose head and hair were naturally white as pure wool, and an eye beaming with intelligence? That was the doctor's lady; she knew when to speak and when to keep silent.

"Here, also, was Dr. William M'Dowell, late of Chillicothe, at that time in the prime of life, a man of most dignified appearance: his raven locks, hanging in ringlets, were beginning to be sprinkled with gray, and the fine Irish bloom was yet glowing on his cheek. He had been a successful travelling preacher, but had retired from the field of toil and privation. This was often a subject of regret to him. His amiable wife was also present, all vivacity of body and mind: she had a smiling, talking eye, and when she spoke it was with wisdom, and what she said was worth attention and memory.

"And this ruddy Englishman, who looked as if he was always in a good humour with himself and everybody else; often laughed heartily, but not at his own wit? That was Brother Mason, the watchmaker, quite gentlemanly in his manners. And that meek, neat lady, of Quaker appearance? That was Sister Mason. In her we saw a pattern of neatness and piety.

"Here, too, was the pious widow of the Rev. B. Talbot. While her countenance well expressed the meekness and sweetness of resignation, it seemed to say, 'Pity me, pity me, O ye my friends; for the hand of the Lord hath touched me.' Sympathies were well expressed in those kind and gentle attentions which are calculated to soothe and cheer the bereaved heart, and no gloom was cast over the company.

"And now I must make you acquainted with my colleague, the Rev. Edward Matthews, a Welshman, and not long from his native land, with the fire, manners, and dialect of his country, a pleasant and companionable man, and zealous in the cause of God. He was modest and reserved, but Mr. Asbury and the Virginians led him out and made him feel at home.

"But it is proper that I should notice one other circumstance, which added much to the religious sociabilities of the day: it was music, sweet, spirit-stirring music. It charmed the ear and warmed the heart. We had six or eight *intellectual* musical instruments in our company, which the Lord himself had strung and tuned. The Methodists used only such in that day. With these we occasionally made melody in our hearts to the Lord. In this exercise Dr. M'Dowell took the lead, for he had the best instrument in the company, and could use it with skill. He sounded the key-note, all the rest chiming. O, it was heart-warming, soul-animating!

"The writer of this reminiscence was also one of the company. But he was the junior of all present; at that time a student of the fourth year in the Methodist Theological Seminary, which had its establishment in all the United States, and a few branches in the western wilds, and a backwoodsman withal; it behoved him, therefore, to be swift to hear and slow to speak. But being now in 'good company,' he resolved to take a lesson or two on good behaviour and Christian politeness, and also gather a few good thoughts on Divinity; for in those day he was all eye and ear, and constantly on the look-out; he was studying men as well as a few good books. In due time we were summoned to the dining-room. Upon approaching the table, the bishop tuned his musical powers, a deep-toned, yet mellow bass, to

'Be present at our table, Lord,
Be here and everywhere adored;
Thy people bless, and grant that we
May feast in paradise with thee.'

The blessing asked, and all were seated—old Virginia for all the world; and for once we partook of food, ate our bread with single-ness of heart; the decanters with wine or stronger drink were neither on the table nor sideboard; but we had a fresh supply of new wine just from the kingdom. From the dining-room we re-turned to the parlour, and again united our musical powers in one of the songs of Zion, then bowed before the sprinkled throne, and found access by one Spirit, through the one and only Mediator, to the God of all consolation. The afternoon passed pleasantly and profitably away on subjects of conversation. We had just entered the nineteenth century. Here were those who had lived and witnessed many of the scenes of more than half of the eighteenth century; the prophecies which (in whole or in part) in the Old and New World, had been fulfilled, and what would probably take place in the fulfilment of prophecy during the century on which we had just entered. Glorious things were anticipated, and we were ready to think that the beast and the false prophet would both be overthrown, and Satan bound and imprisoned. Well,

o

almost half of that century has passed away, and these things
have not yet taken place ; but the Lord hath said that he would
make short work in the earth ;

> 'And what his mouth in truth hath said,
> His own almighty hand shall do.'

But the day was now far spent, the shadows of evening were
lengthening out, and the time for parting came, when all met in
the parlour, and tuned our well-strung instruments in lofty
strains to

> 'The Lord into his garden comes,
> The spices yield a rich perfume,
> The lilies grow and thrive,' etc.

and then the parting prayer and benediction by Mr. Asbury. O,
it was a season not soon to be forgotten, it savoured of heaven !

CHAPTER XX.

Asbury in the far South—Conference at Newbern, North Carolina—Baltimore
Conference—Virginia—Delaware—Philadelphia—Green Mountains, Vermont
—Conference in Boston—Lakes—Moravians at Bethlehem, Pennsylvania—
First Conference north-west of the Ohio—Indian Invasion—Shakers at
Lebanon, Ohio—Philip Gatch's—Cincinnati—Camp-meeting—Additions to
the Hymn Book—Charleston—Western Conference—Conference at Alexan-
dria—Perry Hall in Mourning—General Conference in Baltimore—New
Church in Eutaw-street dedicated—Portrait of Asbury taken by Order of
the General Conference—Whatcoat—Coke's Proposal to divide the Continent
into Two separate Dioceses—Bishop White Affair—M'Kendree elected
Bishop—Western Pioneer—Memorial of New York Conference—Restrictive
Rules—Subject of Slavery—Proposal to strike the Section from the Dis-
cipline—First Two Paragraphs retained—Asbury's Motion—Asbury and
Boehm—Western Travels—Indiana—Regulation on Slavery—Crosses the
Wilderness—Asbury and M'Kendree in a Thirty Dollar Chaise—Rembert's
Chapel—Virginia Conference—Attempt to prejudice Slaveholders against
the Methodists—New York and New England Presbyterians—Cincinnati—
Camp-meeting—" Old Stone" Conference—Baltimore Hospitality—Pittsfield
" Perpetual Hills"—Boston—South called on to assist Boston Methodists—
Lee's History—Comments—Review—Life in the Mountains—Awful Wilder-
ness—Discipline translated into German—West—Governor Worthington—
Virginia—Great Fire in New York—Genesee Conference—Wise Men of
New York Conference—Mad River—Dayton, Ohio—South Carolina.

THE opening of the sixth decade of American Methodism found
the toil-worn Asbury in the far South. His New Year's dinner

was taken in the woods on his route to Columbia, South Carolina. He was redeeming time by riding three hundred miles a week, and preaching on the route. At Newbern, North Carolina, he held Conference, preaching several times during the session. From hence he passed on through Virginia to Baltimore, where he preached on the Sabbath, and opened the Conference on Monday. Upward of a hundred preachers were present ; the increase in the membership within the bounds of the Conference was nearly three thousand. As was his custom he went to Perry Hall, where he had a delightful interview with his old friends and travelling companions of three thousand miles, Hollingsworth and Hitt. After visiting points in Virginia and Delaware, he proceeded to the Conference at Philadelphia. From hence he passed through New Jersey and on to Vermont. When he came to the Green Mountains, he says : "We boldly engaged the Green Mountains, of which we have heard awful accounts. I match it with rude Clinch or rough Alleghany. When we reached the Narrows, Daniel Hitt led the horses ; he preferred my leading them, so on we went ; but I was weak, and not attentive, perhaps, and the horse ran me upon a rock, up went the wheel, hanging balanced over a precipice fifty feet deep, with rocks, trees, and the river between us. Never in my life have I been in such apparent danger, but the Lord saves man and beast." Crossing after this the New Hampshire mountains, he entered the state of Massachusetts, and held Conference in Boston. The New England Conference had then ninety-two preachers on the list. After Conference he went to Lynn, where he preached on Sunday and Monday. His route from this place was through Wilbraham, Springfield, and across the mountains to Pittsfield, from thence to Schenectady, and along the banks of the Mohawk. Here he was so lame as to be obliged to go upon crutches, but he nevertheless continued to preach. He went from hence to Cazenovia, Onondaga, Skaneatelas Lake, Owasco Lake, Cayuga Lake, Seneca Lake, and Lyonstown, and thus from point to point until he reached Genesee and Tioga, and thence on through Pennsylvania until he reached Bethlehem, a place he had long desired to see.

In describing this place, he says : "We found ourselves at the grand tavern at the north end, the property of the 'Moravian Brethren.' The house is large, but a plain building, the entertainment good at a dollar a night for man and horse. On the second bench of the high grounds on the main street, which begins on the hill above, stand the church buildings. On the east and west are rooms appropriate to the institution, and certainly the west end has a grand appearance. On the same street below stands the ' Brethren's ' house, one hundred feet front, five stories high, very plain, and much German taste discoverable everywhere ; add to this the majestic Lehigh, and you have the most striking features of this celebrated place. I asked the young man who managed the tavern if they ever permitted any minister to preach among the ' Brethren.' He could not answer ; he was a servant and knew not how to answer. Next day came the master of ceremonies, the *cicerone* of the establishment, who shows the wonders of the place. I asked him, but was informed that the minister must perform *himselbst*. Daniel Hitt and two gentlemen from York who had given money for the sights shown here for money, went to the Church-meeting. And what did they see and hear ? A man read in German they knew not what, and sung and played upon the four thousand dollar organ, but sermon or prayer they heard not. I doubt much if there is any prayer here, public or private, except the stated prayer of the minister on the Sabbath day. The ' Brethren' have a school for boys at Nazareth, and one for girls at Bethlehem, and they have a store and a tavern. The society have worldly wealth and worldly wisdom, and it is no wonder that men of the world, who would not have their children spoiled by religion, send them to so decent a place."

From this place he directed his course to Lancaster, and without visiting Philadelphia he proceeded across the Alleghany Mountains, and through Ohio to the far-off Scioto, where the first Conference north-west of the Ohio was held in Chillicothe. Sixty-six preachers had assembled from the different and distant parts of the far West and South. Among them were many hardy pioneers who had blazed their way through the wilderness, men of giant hearts and stalwart frames, who had braved a thousand dangers, and who were ready for any hardship and toil the Church might demand. The most of them have passed away, and the few that remain stand here and there like the solitary oak to tell of the glory of the primeval forest in which they stood.

During the session of the Conference Asbury visited the Deer Creek camp-ground, and preached a powerful discourse from the text, " We then, as workers together with him, beseech you also that ye receive not the grace of God in vain." 2 Cor. vi. 1. An immense concourse of people were collected from all parts of the country. Whole Methodist families came from the distance of forty and fifty miles, and some even further. They came in covered waggons, bringing their provisions with them. They did not, like many of the Methodists of the present day, take the cars in the morning, and, whirled along at the rate of thirty miles an hour, reach the encampment in time to hear the eleven o'clock sermon, take dinner at a boarding-tent, and return in the evening, wondering that they had received no spiritual benefit. Had they done so, camp-meetings would not have been attended with the power that characterized them. But they closed up business at home, and made all their arrangements to spend a week at the feast of tabernacles, devoting themselves exclusively to the worship of God, and the result was invariably an increase in spirituality in the hearts of the members, and the conversion of their children. The great wonder is not now that so few are converted at our modern camp-meetings, but that any are converted. This, however, is to be attributed to the fact that there are some who act upon the primitive plan of going prepared, and determined to remain during the continuance of the meeting.

After the business of the Conference was closed, during which they received an addition of thirteen preachers to the ranks of the itinerancy, and elected seven delegates to attend the General Conference, Asbury set out for what he called the frontier settlements on the Great Miami. A great alarm about this time was spread through the country on account of a threatened invasion of the Indians. A council, however, was held, at which Governor Worthington and General M'Arthur met the chiefs, and all hostile demonstrations were quieted. On his way he stopped at Lebanon, where he heard much about the Shakers. At Union Village, about three miles west of Lebanon, the Shakers commenced their operations, and at this day it is, perhaps, the strongest hold of Shakerdom in the West. The society owns a large tract of fine land under a high state of cultivation, and have several family houses within a distance of three or four miles of each other. As there are different grades it is necessary to keep them separate. On the Little Miami, he preached at Philip Gatch's, and from thence proceeded to Cincinnati, where he stopped with Mr. Farris, in company with Solomon and Oliver Langdon. While here he thus expressed himself : " I am young again, and boast of being able to ride six thousand miles on horseback in ten months. My round will embrace the United States, the Territory, and Canada, but O ! childhood, youth, and old age, ye are all vanity." He alludes to the erection of the stone church where Wesley chapel now stands, and thought it a very neat and comfortable house of worship, though the crowd to hear him was so great that they could not find seats for their accommodation.

From Cincinnati he went to the camp-meeting at Mount Geri-zim, Kentucky, where there was a large collection of people, and where he remained several days preaching. Quite a number were converted during the progress of the meeting.

While on this tour he employed a part of his leisure time "in seeking appropriate portions of Scripture for the new hymns designed to enlarge the common hymn book."

Pursuing his course through Tennessee, North Carolina, and Georgia, on Christmas day he reached Charleston, South Carolina, where the next Conference was to be held. On Sabbath he preached at the old church and at Bethel, when he took occasion to notice the life and labours of Kendrick and Dougherty. January 1, 1808, the Conference began. They sat six hours a day, and everything progressed with peace and harmony. The increase within the bounds of this Conference and the Western Conference was three thousand seven hundred. At the close he passed through North Carolina and Virginia to Alexandria, where a Conference was to be held, and thence on to Baltimore.

A letter from the Rev. Asa Kent communicates the following incident connected with the travels of the bishop at this time :

"He was travelling through, I think, the country parts of North Carolina into Virginia, and put up with a brother who kept a house of entertainment for travellers. They had just risen from tea as a neighbour called at the door, and said a duel had just been fought but a few miles distant, and one of the parties had received a ball in his leg.

"Soon a carriage drove up to the door, and some half dozen spruce young men alighted and wished for supper as soon as convenient. Their business was at once understood, and their host brought them into the room and introduced them to the bishop, and they were seated till the table should be laid. He began a free conversation with them and found they were young gentlemen of refined manners and education, and he wanted some method by which he could approach them so as to do them good.

"Supper was announced, and they invited the bishop to eat with them ; but he excused himself, having just left the table ; still they desired it, and he went with them. He supposed that he had designated the principal, second, and surgeon ; but they did not seem to have an idea that their business was known. He implored the blessing of God upon their souls, bodies, food, etc. He took a cup of tea, a beverage not often slighted by him, and excused himself from eating, and proposed telling them some of his reflections for the day. I am sorry that I cannot give the exact words of the Bishop ; the matter is familiar, and I think the substance is found in what follows.:

" ' In passing over these hills and through these valleys to-day, I have been led to reflect upon the mighty changes which have taken place since I first passed through this section of country years ago. Then the settlements were, " like angels' visits, few and far between." The pioneers depended much upon their rifles for support, until they were able to obtain supplies from the soil. Now I am really delighted with the changes which I behold. These hunters were a hardy class of men, and would give thrilling incidents of their exploits in those " days which tried men's souls." But, noble-minded as they were, they were apt, by habit, to fall into a besetting sin—they became reckless of life. The glorious Author of all life has permitted man to take the life of beasts when he needs their skins for use, or their flesh for sustenance. He may also kill wild beasts, or anything that would injure or destroy man, or the labour of his hands ; but some have a rare thirst for blood, even when they have no idea of making any use of either hide, flesh, or tallow. Behold the sportsman as he goes forth for his game. He hears the chirping of a bird ensconced in the foliage of that tree. He stops, and with his keen eye discerns his victim, as she raises her grateful song to the top of her voice. He has no ear for such music, and holds a short consultation upon her life : "She is a fair mark, and I wish to test my skill, and the correctness of my rifle, by putting a ball through her heart." He takes aim, the singing ceases, and the harmless creature falls dead to the earth. He leaves her to rot where she fell, and passes on with much self-complacency. Alas for that man ! God has told him that not a sparrow falls to the ground without his notice. God was there, and saw the working of his mind when he determined upon blood, and the motive which induced him to present the deadly weapon. He has taken what he cannot restore, if it were to save his soul from death. We may try to excuse his thoughtlessness, but that will not suffice ; there is a depravity of nature which must be removed.

" ' There has been a company out hunting in these woods to-day. With cautious steps they approached the place where they expected to find their game, and coming suddenly to an open space, they saw a noble buck standing still, and looking intensely at them. One fired, but instead of sending the ball through his heart it took effect in his leg, and with one bound into the bushes he made his escape. Who can tell what he may suffer from that wound, and it may be, go halting upon that leg all his life ?'

"The bishop said he had watched their agitation as he progressed; their hurry increased, with downcast eyes, until he came to that point. 'Then they rose simultaneously, bowed me a good evening, leaped into their carriage, and were soon out of sight.'"

The next Conference was held at Philadelphia, and from thence he went to the New York Conference at Amenia, and the New England Conference at New London, and from thence returned by way of New York and Philadelphia to Baltimore. While here he visited Perry Hall, which he now found a house of mourning. Mr. Gough, the proprietor, was dead. Of this gentleman Asbury writes: "Harry Dorsey Gough professed more than thirty years ago to be convicted and sanctified; that he did depart from God is well known, but it is equally certain that he was visibly restored; as I was the means of his turning to God, so was I also of his return and restoration. Certain prejudices he had taken up against myself and others I removed. In his last hours, which were painfully afflictive, he was much given up to God. Mr. Gough had inherited a large estate in England, and, having the means, he indulged his taste for gardening and the expensive embellishment of his country seat, Perry Hall, which was always hospitably opened to visitors, particularly those who feared God. Although a man of plain understanding, Mr. Gough was much respected and beloved. As a father, a husband, and a master, he was well worthy of imitation. His charities were as numerous as proper objects to a Christain were likely to make them, and the souls and bodies of the poor were administered to in the manner of a Christian who remembered the precepts and followed the example of his Divine Master."

On July 5, 1806, in Dover, Delaware, Asbury's episcopal colleague, Richard Whatcoat, was called from labour to reward. He was a native of England, where he was converted at an early age and joined the Wesleyan society. After passing through various subordinate offices in the Church, he received license to preach, and was in due time regularly inducted into the ranks of the travelling ministry. Having fully counted the cost of toil and sacrifice connected with the work of an itinerant, he manifested a devotion to the same by the entire consecration of himself. He entered with zeal upon some of the hardest circuits of the Conference, and all his labours were characterized by the most remarkable fidelity. For fifteen years he travelled extensively, and laboured successfully in England, Wales, and Ireland. Some of his circuits required eight weeks to complete the round, and he often preached three times a day. On one circuit which he travelled the people were too poor to render him any support, and rather than deprive of the

Gospel that class for which it was specially designed, he sold his horse and travelled on foot. As a matter of course, wherever he went he was cordially received by the people, who flocked out in crowds to hear one who manifested so much interest in their welfare. He was as successful as he was popular, multitudes being converted through his instrumentality. Like Asbury, and the other noble band of early pioneers to America, his heart was stirred at the descriptions given of this vast field of missionary enterprise, and in 1784 he volunteered his services and came over with Dr. Coke, to enter upon his much loved toil in this western world. From the time of his arrival on these shores, whether as travelling large districts, or with the laborious Asbury, making the tour of the continent, he always inspired and maintained the confidence and esteem of all the preachers. He enjoyed to a remarkable degree the confidence of Wesley, and perhaps no man ever lived who filled up the measure of Wesley's idea of a Methodist more than the self-sacrificing Whatcoat.

At the General Conference of 1800, as the reader will already have seen, he was raised by the suffrages of his brethren to the distinguished office of a bishop, a position which he filled with honour to himself and usefulness to the Church for a period of six years. Though the materials are scarce from which to write a sketch of this great and good man, yet is there enough in the unblemished reputation of his character, and his unceasing devotion to all the interests of the Church, together with the success that crowned his labours, to make a volume. The merest sketch, however, must suffice, and such is all we propose to give. One of his cotemporaries thus speaks of him : " We will not use many words to describe this almost inimitable man. Dead to envy, pride, or praise, he was raised above the world : sober without sadness, cheerful without levity, careful without covetousness, and decent without pride." Like most of the preachers of those days he led a life of poverty, and when he died was not possessed of property sufficient to pay his funeral expenses. Though not possessed of much erudition, his attainments were respectable, and he was a most devoted student of the word and works of God, a study of vastly greater consequence than many things supposed to be essential to the ministerial work. So deeply was he read in the Scriptures, and so faithfully had he treasured up their teachings, that one of his friends called him a walking concordance. His labours as a bishop were only excelled by those of his senior in the episcopal office, and such is the change of circumstances that they

will not likely be equalled again in this country.   During the last
years of his life he suffered much from disease, but in the midst of
all he was regarded as a prodigy of patience.   Excruciating as were
his sufferings,

> "He did not murmur or complain
> Beneath the chastening rod,
> But in the hour of grief and pain
> He hung upon his God."

At Wesley Chapel, Dover, the place of his grave, Bishop Asbury
delivered a funeral discourse from the text, "But thou hast fully
known my doctrine, manner of life, purpose, faith, long-suffering,
charity, patience."   In that discourse the bishop said "he had
known Richard Whatcoat from his own age of fourteen to sixty-
two years most intimately ; and had tried him most accurately, in
the soundness of his faith, in the doctrine of universal depravity
and the complete and general atonement ; the insufficiency of
either moral or ceremonial righteousness for justification, in
opposition to faith alone in the merit and righteousness of Christ ;
the doctrine of regeneration and sanctification.   He spoke of his
holy manner of life, manifest in all places, and before all people, as
a Christian and as a minister ; his long-suffering, a man of great
affliction of body and mind, having been exercised with severe
diseases and great labours ; but this did not abate his charity—his
love of God and man—in all its effects, tempers, words, and
actions ; bearing with resignation and patience great temptations,
bodily labours, and inexpressible pain.   In life and death, placid
and calm ; as he lived, so he died."

Asbury had made his death the occasion of numerous discourses
at the Conferences and elsewhere, and the above tribute to his
memory is sufficient to show how greatly he loved his first
colleague in the episcopacy.

On the 6th of May, 1808, the General Conference opened in
Baltimore.   One hundred and twenty-nine members were present
and took their seats.   On the succeeding Sabbath the new church
in Eutaw-street was dedicated, and the sermon was preached by
Asbury from 2 Corinthians, iii. 12 : "Seeing then that we have
such hope, we use great plainness of speech."   The sermon was
characterized by great directness and force.   During this Conference, at the request of several preachers in England and the
General Conference, Mr. Bruff, an artist, took a likeness of Asbury,
which afterward appeared in the English Methodist Magazine.   It
represented him with flowing white hair, falling in ringlets on his
shoulders.   At this Conference Asbury was left alone in the

presidency, Coke not having returned from England, and Whatcoat having died.

After attending to the necessary preliminaries connected with Conference business, the case of Dr. Coke was taken up. During his last absence he had married a lady of wealth and respectability in England, who proved in every respect a helper in the great work of extending the Gospel abroad. He had suggested as a condition of his return to the United States that the continent be divided into two separate dioceses, he to preside over one and Asbury over the other. He furthermore claimed the full right to give his judgment in the General and Annual Conferences in everything pertaining to the making of laws, stationing of preachers, and sending out missionaries. What the General Conference felt disposed to grant Dr. Coke in relation to the exercise of the rights which he claimed in the Conferences we are not prepared definitely to state, but the proposal to divide the country into two separate and distinct ecclesiastical dioceses they did not for a moment entertain. The Conference were somewhat dissatisfied with the course pursued by Dr. Coke in relation to the Bishop White affair. It seems from the history of the transaction that the proposal of the doctor, made to Bishop White for a union of the Protestant Episcopal and Methodist Episcopal Churches, was of a purely confidential character, and designed only to elicit an opinion as to the propriety and practicability of the measure. In addition to this it was of a personal character, and in no way involved the Methodist Church or the General Conference. The whole affair was doubtless prompted by the purest motives, arising in all probability from the peculiar condition of the Methodist Church at the time. The O'Kelly schism had created a considerable alarm lest the Church should be torn asunder ; and this state of things doubtless moved the doctor to look to the Protestant Episcopal Church, believing that a union with that body without a compromise of principles would prove of essential service to both. No one should hold him accountable for an error of judgment under circumstances of this description. Such eventually was the light in which the subject was viewed by the General Conference, and the following resolutions show that they entertained for him the highest regards :

" 1. *Resolved*, That we do retain a grateful remembrance of the services and labours of Dr. Coke among us, and that the thanks of this Conference are hereby acknowledged to him and to God for all his labours of love toward us from the time he first left his native country to serve us.

" 2. *Resolved*, That Dr. Coke's name shall be retained on our

Minutes of the names of the bishops, in a *Nota Bene: Dr. Coke, at the request of the British Conference, and by consent of our General Conference, resides in Europe.* He is not to exercise the office of superintendent or bishop among us in the United States until he be recalled by the General Conference or by all the Annual Conferences respectively."

Furthermore, in their address to the British Conference, they hold the following language in regard to Dr. Coke : " Your request for the continuance of our beloved brother, Dr. Coke, among you, has been taken into the most serious and solemn deliberation in our Conference, and, in compliance with your request, a vote has passed that he may continue with you until he may be called to us by all the Annual Conferences respectively or the General Conference. We are, however, not insensible of his value, or ungrateful for his past labours of love, and we do sincerely pray that the everlasting God may still be with him, and make him a blessing to hundreds and thousands of immortal souls."

On the twelfth day of the Conference a resolution was passed that the episcopacy be strengthened by the election of an additional bishop. When the ballot was had it was ascertained that the lot had fallen upon William M'Kendree, the western pioneer. He was taken from the well-tried field of itinerant labour, and hence was practically acquainted with, and had a deep experience in the toils and hardships of an itinerant life. On the 17th of May he was ordained by Asbury, and regularly inducted into office. The subsequent life and labours of this bishop showed the wisdom of the choice of the General Conference.

The next question brought before the Conference was the memorial of the New York Conference in relation to a delegated General Conference. In this memorial the Eastern, Western, and South Carolina Conferences concurred, the two former unanimously, the latter giving five dissentient votes. The subject was referred to a committee consisting of two from each of the Annual Conferences. The following are the names of the committee, and the Conferences to which they respectively belonged : New York, Ezekiel Cooper and John Wilson ; New England, Joshua Soule and George Pickering ; Western, William M'Kendree and William Burke ; South Carolina, William Phœbus and Josiah Randall ; Virginia, Philip Bruce and Jesse Lee ; Baltimore, Stephen G. Roszel and Nelson Reed ; Philadelphia, John M'Claskey and Thomas Ware. After seven days' deliberation this committee presented their report, which was read and laid on the table for the space of eight days, when, on motion, it was taken up and discussed.

The report was designed, if adopted, to constitute a section of the Discipline relative to the constitution of the General Conference and its powers and prerogatives. The original paper was finally adopted, with a few slight modifications. As this section has been changed in some parts from time to time, we have thought it proper to give it to our readers as it originally stood in the Discipline :

"The General Conference shall not change or alter any part of our rules of government so as to do away episcopacy, or destroy the plan of our itinerant general superintendency.......It shall have full power to make rules and regulations for our Church under the following restrictions :

" 1. The General Conference shall not revoke, alter, or change our articles of religion, nor establish any new standards or rules of doctrine contrary to our present existing and established standards of doctrine.

" 2. They shall not allow of more than one representative for every five members of the Annual Conferences, nor allow of a less number than one for every seven.

" 3. They shall not revoke or change the General Rules of the United Societies.

" 4. They shall not do away the privileges of our ministers or preachers of trial by a committee, and of an appeal ; neither shall they do away the privileges of our members of trial before the society, or by a committee, and of an appeal.

" 5. They shall not appropriate the produce of the Book Concern or of the Charter Fund to any purpose other than for the benefit of the travelling, supernumerary, superannuated, and worn-out preachers, their wives, widows, and children.

" 6. Provided, nevertheless, that upon the joint recommendation of all the Annual Conferences, then a majority of two-thirds of the General Conference succeeding shall suffice to alter any of the above restrictions."

The subject of slavery was introduced by Stephen G. Roszel, who proposed an amendment, which was lost. John M'Claskey moved that the whole section on the subject be stricken from the Discipline, which was also lost. Mr. Roszel subsequently offered the following, seconded by Thomas Ware, which was carried, namely : " That the first two paragraphs of the section on slavery be retained in the Discipline, and that the General Conference authorize each Annual Conference to form their own regulations relative to buying and selling slaves."

, On motion of Bishop Asbury, which was carried, one thousand copies of the Discipline, with the section and rule on slavery omitted, for the use of the South Carolina Conference, was ordered to be prepared.

At the close of the Conference Asbury felt greatly relieved that his "beloved M'Kendree" had become associated with him in bearing the labours and responsibilities of the episcopacy. After a short respite he started out with Henry Boehm, a German minister, on a tour through Pennsylvania, preaching to English and German congregations in numerous places.

Of this tour Mr. Boehm, the only surviving travelling companion of Asbury, and who still retains a vivid recollection of him, furnishes the following reminiscences :

"For several years Bishop Asbury gave me intimations of his intention to take me with him, one motive of which was to minister to the Germans when an opportunity offered in his tours. At the General Conference at Baltimore, in 1808, he came to the conclusion that I should travel with him. Accordingly I proceeded to Pipe Creek, where I met the bishop at the house of Brother M'Cannon. Here we saw the remains of the house of worship erected in the days of Mr. Strawbridge, of whose person I have some faint recollection when on a visit at my father's, near seventy years ago. We proceeded through Frederick-town, Hagerstown, and Fort Cumberland, preaching frequently by the way ; then toiled across the Alleghany Mountain, the road being very rough. By the time we descended on the west side of the mountain the indefatigable bishop was attacked with inflammatory rheumatism, which deprived him of the use of his feet ; and his companion had to follow the appointments on to Pittsburgh. The last appointment was on Sabbath, and had to be noticed in some of the newspapers ; the bishop in the morning, and his companion in the afternoon in German : this was a heavy cross for a young man, but in the name of the Lord I undertook the work, and succeeded both in the morning and afternoon, as also at five o'clock, in Brother Wrenshall's yard. The Methodist society was small, and had no house of worship in Pittsburgh.

"I now hastened back to the forks of Youghiogany and Monongahela, and found Father Asbury still very lame. During my absence he had provided himself with a pair of crutches, and was actually shaping his course for a start. It was truly, from all human appearance, a hopeless case, but it must be undertaken. We started for Washington ; every step of the horse was painful ; when we arrived at said town I lifted him off his horse, and carried him into the house, to the astonishment of the kind family, when they found that he had travelled on horseback through a shower of rain. We carried the crutches with us, though for the time being they were of no use. Next morning we were on the road, and arrived in safety at Brother Beck's, a family of blessed memory. Here we rested a little while, and then proceeded to Wheeling, tarried with Colonel Zane, one of the early settlers on the banks of the Ohio. I recollect, among many remarks, one very remarkable incident, related to us by the old people. Their house was assaulted by a company of Indians; the wife moulded bullets, while the husband used them with such effect that they happily succeeded in defending themselves against a superior force.

"We crossed the Ohio, and then crossed the Muskingum at Zanesville. In the vicinity of New Lancaster we fell in with brothers Sale and James Quinn, now among the happy dead; the former was presiding elder of the district, then extending from the Big Miami to the Muskingum. Brother Sale accompanied us to Chillicothe and to Xenia, where his family resided. There lived here a worthy family who had removed from Virginia, and laid a lasting foundation for Methodism, namely, Pelham, Bonner, and others.

"We proceeded to Lebanon, an infant village down the Little Miami, to the venerable Philip Gatch's, where we found a camp-meeting. Here I had an opportunity to preach to the Germans, as also in Cincinnati, which was probably the first sermon preached in German by a Methodist minister in that town, containing then about two thousand inhabitants. Notwithstanding the affliction of Bishop Asbury, he preached almost daily when opportunity served, and by the time we arrived at Cincinnati he was much better of his lameness. In this town, likewise, there was a foundation of good materials in the Methodist society, fine, steady, pious members.

"Leaving Cincinnati, we travelled in company with Brother and Sister Lakin to Lawrenceburgh, Indiana Territory, where we tarried with Brother Elijah Sparks. This was quite an infant village. We passed down opposite Kentucky River, where we crossed the Ohio in a leaky scow, and were in considerable danger. We now took our course through Kentucky to Tennessee, to Brother James Gwin's. Here the Western Conference had its session, embracing all west of the Alleghany Mountains, except what the Baltimore Conference included; it likewise took in East Tennessee, with South-West Virginia. What changes since that period! To my great surprise Father Asbury bore up under all the toil and labour of travelling and preaching, together with the care of all the Churches, and notwithstanding, he was a very agreeable companion on the road."

Crossing over to Kentucky they met M'Kendree, and journeyed on to Nashville, and thence to the seat of the Conference. The Conference was in Williamson county, held in the encampment, where the preachers ate and slept in tents. It was a peaceful and prosperous time ; eighty preachers were stationed. At this Conference a regulation was adopted respecting slavery, to the effect that "no member of the society, or preacher, should sell or buy a slave unjustly, inhumanly, or covetously."

From this Conference they started, with fifty travellers in company, across the wilderness. The toils of the journey preyed heavily on Asbury's constitution, but still he toiled on. Arriving at Buncombe, North Carolina, they stopped for rest, and M'Kendree and Boehm preached alternately. Thence they journeyed to South Carolina, stopping at Camden, where they were greatly refreshed by intelligence from Baltimore and elsewhere of glorious revivals of religion. The next point was a camp-meeting in Georgia, where Conference was held. There was an immense concourse of people, many of whom had come a great distance. The number of travelling and local preachers present was about three hundred, and preaching, exhortation, and prayer were kept up without intermission. During this tour Asbury and M'Kendree rode together in a carriage. In the Journal it is thus described : "We are riding in a poor thirty-dollar chaise, in partnership, two bishops of us ; but it must be confessed it tallies well with the weight of our purses. What bishops ! Well, but we have great times ; each Western, Southern, and the Virginia Conference will have a thousand souls truly converted to God, and is not this an equivalent for a light purse, and are we not well paid for starving and toil ? Yes, glory to God !"

Asbury went to Rembert's Chapel to fill an appointment which had been made for Bishop M'Kendree. Mr. Rembert, after whom this chapel was named, was a resident of South Carolina, and his house was a favourite resort of the bishop. In speaking of this Christian gentleman, whose hospitalities he frequently enjoyed, he says : "He is kind and good, rich and liberal, and has done more for the poor Methodists than any man in South Carolina. The Lord grant that he, with his whole household, may find mercy in that day."

The next Conference they attended was the Virginia, which was held in February, 1809. Among the eighty-four preachers present there were only three who were married. While at this Conference

Asbury complained of the course taken by certain people to pre-judice slaveholders against Methodist principles, and thus keep them from having access to the slaves. In this connection he asks the following question : " Would not an *amelioration* in the con-dition and treatment of slaves have produced more practical good to the poor Africans than any attempt at their *emancipation ?* The state of society unhappily does not admit of this ; besides, the blacks are deprived of the means of instruction, and who will take the pains to lead them in the way of salvation, and watch over them that they may not stray, but the Methodists ?"

In consequence of the position taken by the General Conference previously on the subject of slavery, some of the legislative assem-blies of the South had passed laws prohibiting ministers from instructing the slaves except upon certain conditions, and authoriz-ing the peace officers to break up any meetings that might be held in private for their benefit. In regard to the effect of the address of the General Conference upon the citizens of South Carolina, Asbury says : "Nothing could so effectually alarm and arm the citizens of South Carolina against the Methodists. The rich among the people never thought us worthy to preach to them ; they did indeed give their slaves liberty to hear and join our Church, but now it appears the poor Africans will no longer have this indul-gence." Asbury frequently lamented that his way was hedged up, and that he had not the access to the slaves which he so much desired. At the Conference held in Tennessee in 1808, the year immediately preceding the present time, we learn from his Journal that a rule was adopted on the subject of slavery which prohibited any member of the Church, or preacher, from selling or buying a slave "unjustly, inhumanly, or covetously."

The bishops continued on their journey until they reached Balti-more, the old starting point, and from thence passed through Penn-sylvania and New Jersey on to New York. Here Conference was held. One hundred and fifteen preachers were stationed. The ordination of elders took place at John-street, and the occasion was one of great interest to the Church in the city. From hence Asbury sought the rest and quiet of Sherwood vale, where he spent the Sabbath and preached. From this he started with Boehm for his Eastern tour. Passing through New Haven, New London, Newport, Bristol, and Warren, he journeyed on to Boston, where he preached in the old Chapel on Sabbath morning, and in the afternoon in the new. Such was his feebleness here that he was obliged to preach in a sitting posture. From this place he went to New Gloucester, where Conference was held. On Sabbath

P

he preached to an immense congregation consisting of thousands. In Danville, Vermont, he was invited to preach to the court, which was then in session, but his health would not allow the undertaking; a large congregation, however, collected in the Church, and he preached, sitting in one of the pews near the pulpit. From hence he proceeded on his way through Marshfield, Middlesex, Waterbury, and Richmond, to Lake Champlain, and from thence onward to Fort Edward, where he preached in Dr. Lawrence's store to five hundred attentive hearers. Afterward he preached in M'Cready's barn, on Saratoga Lake, and from thence he went to General Clark's where he preached in a barn-room. His next stopping place was Ballston Springs, which he compares to those of Bath, in England : "The water," he says, "has a taste of beer, lemon juice, and salt of tartar." From Ballston he went to Kingsbury, where he took to the woods for a shade and preached to a thousand people. While here he remarks : "I wish to fast as when young, and when fast-day comes the body has a journey of forty miles to make, and do its part in preaching ; but Christ is strength in my weakness." Thus he continued on his journey, until he reached Onondaga, where he preached in the court-house on Saturdry and Sunday to large congregations. Describing his journey from this place in the midst of a storm, he says, "We had an awful time in the woods among rocks, and trees living and dead barring our way."

We cannot trace the bishop in his wanderings from place to place. Suffice it to say he passed on from New York through Pennsylvania, crossed the Alleghany Mountains, stopping at Wheeling, where Colonel Zane had given the Methodists a lot for a house. He preached here in the court-house "with light and power, having an open time." Boehm preached in St. Clairsville, and also at Zanesville, named after the colonel. From thence they went to Lancaster, where he spoke to the assembled people in the court-house, and then on to Chillicothe, Hamilton, Milford, Columbia, and "fair Cincinnati," as the bishop called it. He found the "old stone" enlarged and the society increased. At the camp-meeting held near Cincinnati the bishop preached, as also Blackman, M'Kendree, and Burk. Conference was held this year (1809) at Cincinnati.

From this Conference he and M'Kendree started out for the South, through Kentucky, Tennessee, North and South Carolina, holding meetings and Conferences on the route, and returning by Virginia to Baltimore, where he says : "If we want plenty of good living and new suits of clothes let us come to Baltimore." They evidently did want them, and the Baltimore Methodists showed their religion and good sense in providing for these bachelor bishops. After Conference Asbury went to Perry Hall, and started from thence on his customary route eastward, in company with Bishop M'Kendree, holding Conference in Pittsfield, Massachusetts, at which eighty-four preachers were stationed, and two missionaries sent out, one Michigan, and the other to Canada. From Conference they started out and crossed the "perpetual hills" into New Hampshire, where they held Conference at Winchester, in the Presbyterian Church. A camp-meeting was in progress during the session of the Conference, and there was preaching three times a day by the members.

At Boston Asbury preached in the old chapel on Sabbath morning, and at the new in the evening. On Monday he wrote letters to Baltimore, Georgetown, Alexandria, Norfolk, and Charleston, urging the Churches in these places to take up collections in behalf of the new chapel in Boston, which was greatly embarrassed with debt. Passing through Warren, Bristol, and other places, they came to New London, where for the first time he saw Lee's History of Methodism, concerning which he writes : "It is better than I expected. He has not always presented me under the most favourable aspect, but we are all liable to mistakes. I correct him in one fact. My compelled seclusion at the beginning of the war, in the state of Delaware, was in no wise a season of inactivity. On the contrary, except about two months of retirement from the direst necessity, it was the most active, the most useful, and most afflictive part of my life. If I spent a few dumb Sabbaths ; if I did not for a short time steal after dark, or through the gloom of the woods, as I was accustomed, from house to house to enforce that truth I, an only child, had crossed the ocean to proclaim, I shall not be blamed I hope ; especially when it is known that my patron, the good and respectable Thomas White, who promised me security and secrecy, was himself taken into custody by the light horse patrol ; and if such things happened to him what might I, a fugitive and an Englishman, expect? In these very years we added eighteen hundred members to society, and laid a broad and deep foundation for the wonderful success Methodism has met with in that quarter. The children and childrens' children of those who witnessed my labours and sufferings in that day of peril, now rise up by hundreds to bless me. Where are the witnesses themselves ? Alas ! there remain not five perhaps whom I could summon to attest the truth of this statement."

From Connecticut they returned to New York, where, after

spending the Sabbath, July 8, 1810, they crossed the Hudson River and the Catskills, and directed their course to the Sharon camp-meeting. While passing through this route he remarked that he did not see how the people in the mountains could be kept from starvation, were it not for the saw-mills and lumber with which they abound. From hence they went on through Cazenovia, and attended the session of the Genesee Conference, which was held in connection with a camp-meeting. The formation of this Conference Asbury regarded as one of the most judicious acts of the episcopacy. After Conference they proceeded to Geneva, passing round Seneca Lake, where they went through what Asbury calls "an awful wilderness." They were now in Pennsylvania, on the route to Northumberland, and as they pursued their course, Boehm, who was in company, was thrown from the sulky, but without injury. While in the wilderness Asbury describes the scene : "Thunder and rain, and awful mountains, deep roads and swollen streams." Crossing the Susquehanna they stopped at Middletown, where they dined with a doctor by the name of Romer, who had translated the Discipline into the German language for the benefit of his countrymen. On Sunday Asbury preached in Lancaster, morning and evening. From this place they went to Carlisle, where he drew a plan for a new chapel, seventy by forty-five feet, to cost two thousand dollars. The road between Indian Creek and Connelsville he describes as very bad, and thus writes about it : "I enter my protest, as I have yearly for forty years, against this road." His next appointment was a camp-meeting near Brownsville, where three thousand people heard him preach. From hence he went to Barnesville, Ohio, and from thence to Wills' Creek and Meig's Creek, and on to Marietta, where he preached to a small congregation. His course from this place was across the Ohio, and up the Little Kanawha to a camp-meeting, from whence he returned across the country to Chillicothe.

While at Chillicothe he was requested by Governor Worthington to furnish an inscription for the tombstone of his sister, Mary Tiffin, and he gave the following : "Mary hath chosen that good part which shall not be taken away from her." Luke x. 42. After a short rest he journed across the country to the Little Miami, and on to Cincinnati, where Boehm preached in German on Friday evening. On Sabbath Asbury preached to large and attentive congregations. On the morning of his departure for Kentucky there was a dense fog. He thus describes it : "The great river was covered with a mist until nine o'clock, when the airy curtain rose slowly from the waters, gliding along in expanded and silent majesty." Passing through Kentucky, where he held a Conference, he crossed the mountains into North Carolina, thence to South Carolina, where, at Columbia, they found a kind friend in the person of Mr. Taylor, a member of the United States Senate, who opened his house for the session of the Conference. On Sabbath he and M'Kendree preached. About eighty preachers were present.

On the succeeding Sabbath he preached at Lumberton. His fatigues and exposures had wrought heavily upon him, and he was quite unwell. After preaching he made the following note : " I preached here possibly for the last time. I spoke in great weakness of body, and having offered my service and sacrifice, I must change my course and go to Wilmington. I am happy, my heart is pure, and my eye is single ; but I am sick and weak, and in heaviness by reason of suffering and labour. Sometimes I am ready to cry out, *Lord, take me home to rest.* Courage, my soul ! " Accordingly he directed his course to Wilmington, and having fulfilled his mission in that place, went to Raleigh, where Conference was held. On the Sabbath during Conference he preached in the State House to two thousand people. The next Sabbath we find him at Richmond, Virginia. From thence he returned to Maryland, where, after resting awhile at Perry Hall, he went to Philadelphia. At the session of the Conference he had visits from Drs. Rush and Physick, whose kindness and services he acknowledged with gratitude.

At the Conference held in New York, May, 1811, a great fire occurred, consuming about one hundred houses. Referring to New York at this time, Asbury says : " The Society has increased, our chapels are neat, and their debt is not heavy ; they wish to rebuild John-street Church, and to build a small house at the Two-Mile Stone." From New York he went to Sherwood Vale and to Governor Cortlandt's, at both of which places he preached. He then travelled into Vermont, and, visiting several places, crossed Lake Champlain to Sable River, where he preached to a large congregation. From thence he went to Plattsburgh, and on to the Indian Village, and across the St. Lawrence. In crossing the line separating the United States from Canada, he writes : " My strong affection for the people of the United States came with strange power upon me while I was crossing the line." After visiting several places, and preaching, he returned to the States, making the following remarks : " Well, I have been in Canada, and find it like all stations in the extremities ; there are difficulties to be overcome, and prospects to cheer us. Some of our labourers have not been as faithful and diligent as we could wish." On his return he attended, with M'Kendree, the Genesee Conference, and from thence proceeded to the New York Conference. At this Conference he says: "Some of the wise men of New York Conference have discovered that it will be far better to elect presiding elders in Conference, and give them the power of stationing the preachers. When the election for General Conference came on, there was some disposition manifested to reject the Canadians and the presiding elders. If the preachers take any specific power, right, or privilege from the bishops, which the General Conference may have given them, it is clear that they dissolve the whole contract."

From Conference he travelled through Pennsylvania, taking the ordinary route, and directed his course to Mad River, in the interior of Ohio. At Dayton he preached in the court-house to a thousand people. His next route was through Franklin and Lebanon, where he drew a plan for a new brick church forty by sixty, and thence to Cincinnati, where Conference was held, and where he and M'Kendree preached in the chapel and market-house.

His next trip was through Kentucky and on to Georgia, where he held Conference at Camden. Of this Conference he says: "Scarcely have I seen so much harmony and love. There are eighty-five preachers, and the increase is three thousand three hundred and eight." The next point was Charleston, where he spent the first day of the year 1812 "in meditation, writing and prayer." After preaching at Cumberland and Bethel Chapels he started for various points in North Carolina, and then on to Petersburgh, Virginia, where Conference was held. From hence he went to Maryland and held Conference; then another in Philadelphia, from which place he directed his course to New York, where the General Conference was to be held.

The above is but the merest outline of the bishop's labours in his itinerant journeyings. Anything like a detail would swell his biography into almost as many volumes as he performed continental tours. A vast amount of otherwise interesting matter must necessarily be left untouched on account of its sameness: our object has been to present as far as possible that which is the most interesting in a connected whole, and yet sufficiently full to give the reader an idea of the great labour and self-sacrificing devotion of this extraordinary man. Sweeping over a circuit of thousands of miles, and attending conferences, camp, quarterly, and other meetings, almost without number, it would take entirely too much space to give a detailed account of his journeyings and labours.

CHAPTER XXI.

THE General Conference of 1808 having provided for a delegated General Conference, the Annual Conferences accordingly elected their representatives, who convened in New York on the 1st of May, 1812. After the appointment of several committees, the adoption of rules for their government, and the settling of several preliminaries, among which was one allowing all travelling preachers in full connection who might be present a seat as visitors, Bishop Asbury read to the Conference a letter received from Dr. Coke. This letter was full of fraternal affection, and expressed continued attachment to the cause of American Methodism. It, however, communicated the intention and design of the doctor to go out as a missionary to India. After the reading of this address, which we regret very much has been lost, as it was the last letter of Dr. Coke to his American brethren, Bishop M'Kendree presented the following address :

" *To the General Conference of the Methodist Episcopal Church, now
assembled in the City of New York.*

"DEAR BRETHREN,—My relation to you and the connection in
general seems, in my opinion, to make it necessary that I should
address you in some way, by which you may get possession of
some information perhaps not otherwise to be obtained by many of
you.

"It is now four years since, by your appointment, it became my
duty jointly to superintend our extensive and very important
charge. With anxious solicitude and good wishes I have looked
forward to this General Conference. The appointed time is come,
and the Lord has graciously permitted us to meet according to
appointment, for which I hope we are prepared jointly to praise
and adore his goodness.

"Upon examination, you will find the work of the Lord is
prospering in our hands. Our important charge has greatly increased since the last General Conference ; we have had an increase
of nearly forty thousand members. At present we have about one
hundred and ninety thousand members, upward of two thousand
local, and about seven hundred travelling preachers in our connection, and these widely scattered over seventeen states, besides the
Canadas and several of the territorial settlements.

"Thus situated, it must be expected, in the present state of
things, that the counsel and direction of your united wisdom will
be necessary to preserve the harmony and peace of the body, as
well as co-operation of the travelling and local ministry, in carrying on the blessed work of reformation which the Lord has been
pleased to effect through our instrumentality. To deserve the
confidence of the local ministry and membership, as well as to retain confidence in ourselves and in each other, is undoubtedly our
duty ; and if we consider that those who are to confide in us are a
collection from all classes and descriptions, from all countries of
which the nation is composed, promiscuously scattered over this
vast continent, men who were originally of different educations,
manners, habits, and opinions, we shall see the difficulty as well as
the importance of this part of our charge.

"In order to enjoy the comforts of peace and union among us,
we must 'love one another ;' but this cannot abide where confidence does not exist ; and purity of intention, manifested by proper
actions, is the very foundation and support of confidence ; thus
'united, we stand ;' each member is a support to the body, and
the body supports each member ; but if confidence fails, love will

grow cold, peace will be broken, and 'divided, we fall.' It therefore becomes this body, which, by its example, is to move the passions and direct the course of thousands of ministers, and tens of thousands of members, to pay strict attention to the simplicity of Gospel manners, and to do everything as in the immediate presence of God. If we consider the nature of our business, and the influence of civil governments, and political measures, it will hardly be expected that every individual in so large a body as you form will continually be sufficiently and strictly evangelical in all cases; it is therefore hoped in cases of failure, that the wisdom and firmness of your united prudence as a body will counteract evil effects by a well-ordered and prudent disapprobation and better example. Church and state should never be assimilated.

"Connected as I am with you and the connection in general, I feel it a part of my duty to submit to your consideration the appointment of the Genesee Conference; and perhaps it may be for the general good if in your wisdom you should think proper to take into consideration a division of the work in the western country, and a proper arrangement of the work in general; and the magnitude and extent of the work which the Lord has graciously pleased to prosper in our hands, may make it proper for you to inquire if the work is sufficiently within the oversight of the superintendency, and to make such arrangements and provision as your wisdom may approve. I would also suggest the necessity of keeping in view not only the travelling, but the relation and situation of our local brethren, and to pursue that plan which may render the whole the most useful; and it may also be proper to bring into view any unfinished business (if any) which we had under consideration at our last General Conference. Hitherto, as a body, we have been preserved by our well-digested system of rules, which are as sinews to the body, and form the bonds of our union. But it is evident, both from Scripture and experience, that men, even good men, may depart from first principles and the best of rules; it may therefore be proper for you to pay some attention to the administration, to know the state both of the travelling and local ministry, as it relates to doctrine, discipline, and practice.

"Before I conclude, permit me, my dear brethren, to express a few thoughts concerning the view I have of the relation in which I stand connected with this body. It is only by virtue of a delegated power from the General Conference that I hold the reins of government. I consider myself bound by virtue of the same authority to exercise discipline in perfect conformity to the rules of the Church, to the best of my ability and judgment. I consider myself justly accountable, not for the system of government, but for my administration, and ought, therefore, to be ready to answer in General Conference for past conduct, and be willing to receive information and advice, to perfect future operations, and I wish my brethren to feel themselves perfectly easy and at liberty.

"I shall take the liberty here to present my grateful acknowledgments for the high degree of confidence which my beloved brethren have placed in me, and especially for the able counsel and seasonable support afforded by many, which has, I believe, with the Divine aid, preserved and supported me. Dear brethren, such are the effects of our high responsibility, connected with a consciousness of the insufficiency of my talents for so great a work, that I move with trembling. Your eyes and the eyes of the Lord are upon me for good. We shall rejoice together to see the armies of Israel wisely conducted in all their ranks, carrying the triumphs of the Redeemer's kingdom to the ends of the earth ; and the Lord will rejoice to make his ministers a flame of fire. In you I have confidence, and on you I depend for aid, and above all, I trust in Divine aid. Influenced by these considerations, and with my situation in full view, I cannot entertain a thought of bearing such awful accountability longer than I am persuaded my services are useful to the Church of God, and feel a confidence of being aided by your counsel and support, which is with you to give in any way or form you judge proper. And while I join with you, my dear brethren, in pure Gospel simplicity, to commit and recommend ourselves and our several charges to the special care of the great Head of the Church, I remain, with sentiments of love and confidence, your servant in the Gospel of Christ."

Several parts of this address were referred to select committees, with instructions to report upon them at a subsequent day. The Genesee Conference, which had been constituted during the interim of the General Conference, was recognized as properly and legally organized.

At the opening of the morning session, on the 8th of May, Bishop Asbury rose and addressed the Conference through Bishop M'Kendree. In his address he gave a succinct and interesting narrative of the rise, progress, and present state of Methodism in America, and intimated, as with prophetic ken, its glorious future. His address was truly inspiring, and was received with every demonstration of gratification by the ninety representatives present. When he concluded Bishop M'Kendree rose and replied, thanking him, in behalf of the delegates assembled, and of the Church in general, for his address, and for the fatherly care with which he had watched over the interests of Methodism from the beginning.

The various matters pertaining to the interests of the Church embraced in the address of Asbury were referred to select committees. The bishop expressed a desire to visit his native land, and gaze once more upon the scenes of his youth and early labours ; but as the Conference had decided not to increase the number of bishops, the committee on the episcopacy presented the following : " It is our sincere desire and request that Bishop Asbury would relinquish his thoughts of visiting Europe, and confine his labours to the American connection so long as God may preserve his life." The Conference unanimously concurred in the above resolution, and Asbury, regarding the voice of the Church as indicative of an order of Providence, cheerfully acquiesced in its decision.

The General Conference of 1808 having been impressed with the importance of the collection of reliable material for the purpose of furnishing a complete history of the Church, suggested the propriety of each Annual Conference attending to this matter, by collecting such historic facts and incidents as might come within their reach. Accordingly several historical letters were presented and referred to a committee consisting of Nathan Bangs, Thomas L. Douglass, and Learner Blackman. This was an important movement, and we doubt not that this action led the chairman of that committee to devote more specific attention to the subject than he would otherwise have done, and we rejoice, in common with the great Methodist family, that it resulted in a clear, concise, and comprehensive history of the Church from his pen. We think it proper to remark in this connection, that the History of the Methodist Episcopal Church, by Dr. Bangs, is worthy of the name, and justly deserves the wide and well-earned reputation which it has obtained both in this country and in Europe. If the old definition of history has not become obsolete, which makes it to consist in the simple unadorned narration of facts and events, then does this work come up most fully to all the requirements of that standard. The highest philosophy connected with history is that which makes it speak by the truthful examples it furnishes.

The work having increased to such an extent in the West and South, the bishops united in recommending the General Conference to divide the Western Conference into two, to be called the Ohio and Tennessee Conferences, the former to comprehend the Salt River, Kentucky, Miami, and Muskingum Districts, and the latter to embrace the Holston, Nashville, Cumberland, Wabash, and Illinois Districts. Acting on this recommendation the division was made, and the bishops were empowered, should they deem it necessary, with the concurrence of the Annual Conferences concerned, to organize another Conference farther South.

As yet the Church had no missionary society. It was, indeed, itself missionary in all its operations; but no specific regulations had been adopted for the raising of missionary funds, apart from the efforts of Asbury, who carried his little blank book in his pocket, and solicited subscriptions wherever he went. We have been greatly interested in looking over one of these missionary subscription books. It contains long lists of names, from the east, west, north, and south, of members of the Church, and others friendly to Methodism. Among these we have the autographs of many preachers, some of whom are still living; but the great majority have passed away, and joined the sainted Asbury in the better land.

That ever fruitful theme of discussion and excitement, the subject of slavery, was again brought before the General Conference, by a motion suggesting an inquiry into the nature and moral tendency of the system. It was considered, however, in the judgment of the Conference, that no further action was necessary or desirable, and the motion was accordingly laid on the table without debate. In alluding to this Conference, Asbury says, in his Journal: "There were many and weighty affairs discussed, among which was a motion to strengthen the episcopacy. After a serious struggle of two days, to change the mode of appointing presiding elders, it remains as it was. Means had been used to keep back every presiding elder who was known to be favourable to their appointment by the bishops, and long and earnest speeches have been made to influence the minds of the members. Lee, Shinn, and Snethen were of a side, and these are great men."

This was the last General Conference which Asbury attended. He had seen Methodism in its infancy in America, and like a father had watched over its development until it had arisen to vigorous manhood. He saw the Church as she extended her conquests and influence from the cold provinces of Canada to the sunny savannas of Georgia, and from the shores of the Atlantic to the "father of waters" in the distant West. He had held forth to listening thousands in crowded cities, and at great camp-meetings in the wilderness, and had preached to little flocks in solitary log-cabins, always and everywhere the same affectionate and indefatigable servant of the Church. In alluding further to this General Conference, he said he "saw nothing like unkindness but once, and there were many weighty affairs discussed. A subject before it was the question, If local deacons, after four years of probation, should be elected to the eldership by two-thirds of the Conference, having no slaves, and having them, to manumit them where the laws will allow it, shall they be ordained? This passed by a large majority."

After the session was ended the bishop left New York for " Sherwood Vale," where, as usual, he enjoyed the hospitalities of his old friends. From hence he went to Croton, to visit his friend, Governor Van Cortlandt, whom he called the elder of ninety. While in this neighbourhood he preached at White Plains. From hence he went, in company with his old friend Boehm, to Peekskill and Rhinebeck, on the Hudson. He was now suffering from illness, and at times had high fevers. A sickness that would have laid up most men was endured by this astonishing man in the very midst of heavy labours and long rides. At Albany he met the Conference, and with unremitting attention transacted all the episcopal business. The Dutch Reformed Synod was in session at the same time. During his stay he preached on the site which had been selected for a new church.

From this place he passed on through Connecticut and arrived at Lynn, where the New England Conference held its session. Here he read the proclamation of the President of the United States, declaring war between this country and Great Britain. The church in Lynn, which had a steeple, excited the regret of Asbury on that account, and he admonished the Methodists in relation to some things which he regarded as extravagances, and a departure from that primitive simplicity which he fondly hoped would ever characterize the Church. At Pittsfield he was grieved at hearing of a division of the Church, and a secession therefrom of three hundred and eighty. From this place he visited Lansingburg and Troy, and from thence went to Lyons, the place of the session of the Genesee Conference. There were thirty preachers present, and the business of the Conference was conducted with great concord. He was deterred on account of the war from visiting the frontier work on the Niagara, a thing which he greatly desired to do. From hence he directed his course to Pennsylvania. On his route, as was often the case, he was obliged to stop at a public house. The entertainment he received, we may judge from his Journal, was not of a very agreeable character. He says: " Farewell to Merwines ; I lodge no more there ; a whisky hell, as most of the taverns are."

In crossing the Lehigh he was led to express his admiration of the beautiful country of the Wyoming. In speaking of the Ger-

mans he says : " They are decent in their behaviour, and would be
more so were it not for vile whisky, which is the prime curse of
the United States, and which, I fear, will prove the ruin of all
that is excellent in morals and government." In regard to the
war which was then raging, he remarks : " I feel a deep concern
for the Old and New World. Calamity and suffering are coming
upon them both. I shall make but few remarks on this unhappy
subject, as it is one on which the prudent will be silent, but I
must needs say it is an evil day. I have written many letters of
serious warning to our elders." His next stopping place was a
camp-meeting on Pipe Creek, Maryland. This was a large encampment, having a hundred tents, and a congregation of five thousand.
During this meeting he laboured incessantly night and day, sleeping but about two hours out of the twenty-four. From this meeting
he crossed the south mountain and preached to large congregations
in Cumberland. In crossing the mountain he says : " We had a
strange medley of preachers, drovers, beasts on four legs, and beasts
made by whisky on two, travelling on the turnpike at the same
time." Having descended the western slope of the Alleghanies,
he urged his way to another camp-meeting, where he preached on
Friday and Saturday. The ministry, which had been carefully
instructed to preach to the soldiers, were not faithless on this
occasion.

The commanding officer of a large company of soldiers, on the eve
of starting for Buffalo, sent a note to the clergy on the camp-ground,
requesting that the soldiers might be addressed by one of the
ministers previous to their marching. Bishop Asbury, who was
present, had an answer communicated, informing the commander
that his request should be complied with. Accordingly the officers
and men marched out in rank and file to the encampment, where
they were met and conducted to seats prepared for them. The
bishop gave out the hymn,

> "Soldiers of Christ arise,
> And put your armour on."

He then addressed the throne of grace, and prayed most fervently
for the President of the United States, the Cabinet, the Senate,
and House of Representatives. His text was, " And the soldiers
likewise demanded of him saying, And what shall we do ? And
he said unto them, Do violence to no man, neither accuse any
falsely, and be content with your wages." Luke iii. 14. In his
discourse he dwelt impressively on the evils of war, its destructive
influence upon commerce, the arts of life, and the wealth of nations

but more particularly its pernicious effects in relation to religion and morals. He showed that war should, if possible, be avoided, and it never should be declared only as a dernier resort. If Christian nations should be embroiled in war, they should only act on the defensive. He also enlarged upon the importance of good discipline in an army, and showed that the government or military discipline could at the same time be strict and mild, and that the officers should be kind and generous to their men. In a word, he said that the commanding officer should be as a father to his soldiers, and they should in turn be obedient to all his military commands. He concluded by giving a fatherly advice to the soldiers. After his discourse he descended, and took a position where the company passed in review before him. As the commanding officer approached he placed his hands upon his head and prayed for him most fervently, blessing him in the name of the Lord ; then each of the officers ; and as the soldiers passed he took each one by the hand and gave them a parting blessing. Tears flowed from every eye of the thousands gathered there.

His next point was a camp-meeting on Indian Short Creek, where he found nearly a hundred tents, and thousands of people congregated from the surrounding country. This meeting was attended with unusual interest, and a large number of converts were added to the Church. His route from this was through Barnesville, and thence on to the Wills' Creek neighbourhood, and thence to Zanesville, where, sick and weary, he found rest in the hospitable mansion of Christian Spangler, Esq., one of the early and fast friends of Methodism in Ohio. Having recovered and recruited, he started out to another camp-meeting, on Rush Creek. This also was a powerful meeting, and was kept up day and night, resulting in great good. From hence he passed through Lancaster, and on to Chillicothe, where he visited Judge Van Meter and White Brown. While here he held the Ohio Conference, where he laboured hard, but was much assisted by the elders in the stationing of the preachers. In a computation which he makes of his travels, he says he had journeyed six thousand miles in eight months, had met nine Conferences, and attended ten camp-meetings. The records of itinerancy nowhere in the world can furnish such an example of travel and toil.

In his visit to Cincinnati he was somewhat depressed in spirits at finding the Church low in religion. Kobler, Hunt, Bowman, Burke, and Collins had introduced Methodism into Cincinnati several years before. The first Methodist Church was erected in the year 1806, and was now undergoing an enlargement. Passing over into Kentucky he directed his course to Frankfort, the capital of the State, where he preached in the hall of the House of Representatives. From this place he went to Louisville, situated at the falls of the Ohio, where he preached, and from thence entered the interior and passed on to Nashville, Tennessee. On Sabbath, November 11th, he preached in the new brick church, which he describes as being thirty-four feet square, with galleries. Referring to his former labours here, he says : " Twelve years ago I preached in the old stone-house, taken down since to make a site for the state-house. The latter house exceeds the former in glory, and stands exactly where our house of worship should by right have stood, but we bear all things patiently." Conference was held this year at Gwin's, and there were present a large number of preachers. Forty were ordained to the office of deacon, and ten to the office of elder. The increase in the bounds of the Conference during the year was eight thousand.

His route after this lay through North and South Carolina. At Columbia he preached in the House of Representatives. His next point was Charleston, where Conference was held. He speaks of the harmony which subsisted between the presiding elders and the episcopacy with evident satisfaction. The increase during the year in the bounds of the Connection was eighteen thousand. The bishop lamented the loss of fourteen itinerants by location. His route from Charleston was to Georgetown, and thus on through the Peedee settlements. At the residence of General Lee he was quite unwell, but he rested not. At Fayetteville he had to be carried into church, and, notwithstanding his illness, preached to the congregation assembled. From the meeting he went home to Mr. Russell's, and was thoroughly blistered for a high fever. In two days we find him on the route of travel again, and though he had a fever he rode through a bitter cold thirty miles, and the next day thirty-six, which brought him to Wilmington, North Carolina, where he was again carried into church, that he might minister the word of life. With fever and swelled feet he started out from this place, holding meetings on his way, to Newbern, the seat of the Conference, which was held, as he says, in Sister Tenkard's elegant school-room. This Conference was characterized by "great order, great union, and great dispatch of business." Passing through Halifax, Petersburgh, and Richmond, preaching at these and intermediate points, he arrived at Georgetown, District of Columbia. While here he received an invitation from the British Conference, requesting him to visit that body, and engaging to pay all the expenses of the journey.

At Baltimore he held Conference, which was opened April 24, 1813. The Conference was composed of ninety preachers ; the number of white members was twenty thousand two hundred and seventy-two, and of coloured members seven hundred and ninety-nine. Again we find him, after the session of the Conference, at his much-loved home, Perry Hall. From hence he passed through Delaware, and attended the Conference in Philadelphia. While here he preached at the Academy, St. George's, Ebenezer, and the Tabernacle. His next point was Burlington, New Jersey. It seemed to be a doubt in the mind of the bishop whether Burlington or Trenton would ever become famous for vital religion. Preaching at Lumberton, Allentown, Rahway, and Belleville, he went to Sherwood's, New York, and from thence on to Amenia, where the Conference was held. It was a time of order and peace, though the bishop pleasantly said, "King Gordius had well nigh been among us, but the knots were untied peaceably, and not cut in rashness." Speaking of his colleague's sermon on Sabbath, he remarked : "Bishop M'Kendree preached. It appeared to me as if a ray of Divine glory rested on him. His subject was, 'Great peace have they that love thy law, and nothing shall offend them.'" Before announcing the appointments of the preachers Asbury delivered a valedictory address, in which he assured them that the plan of their future labours was deliberately formed with the aid of the collected wisdom of judicious counsel and much prayer.

The Eastern route now lay before him, and taking up the line of travel he crossed over Connecticut, New Hampshire, and Massachusetts. At Winchester he wrote his last will and testament, making M'Kendree, Hitt, and Boehm his executors. While in New England he remarked : "I believe for one that there has been more true Gospel preaching in the other states than in the five New England states, with all their boasting. I have difficulties to encounter, but I must be silent. In New England we sing, we build houses, we eat, and stand at prayer. Were I to labour forty years more I suppose I should not succeed in getting things right. O rare steeple-houses, bells ! (organs by and by ?) these things are against me, and contrary to the simplicity of Christ." At the session of the Conference at Colchester, a resolution was passed against steeples and pews.

At Providence he was introduced to Governor Jones, who received him with great cordiality. From the East he returned to New York. Conference was held at Westmoreland. In his journey to this place he complained of hunger and heat, and remarked

that the East was not hospitable.   Maryland or the South was to
him the land of hospitality.   A large concourse of people was
assembled at the Conference, and thousands were preached to by
the bishops and preachers.   From hence he started for the West,
and while among the mountains he found a stopping place at a
German Lutheran's, whose son was a preacher, but refused to read
or pray in the family.   "Alas," said Asbury, "so stupid and so
wicked! I would rather be a slave in South Carolina with the
Gospel and a good master!"

While here he prepared a valedictory address to Bishop M'Kendree, who in conjunction with the Genesee Conference, had requested him to give his opinion in relation to the government and
usages of the Methodist Episcopal Church.   The address is quite
lengthy, and enters elaborately into a discussion of the Church
dogma of apostolical succession.   As it never has been published,
we shall make such extracts from it as are considered most important, and possessing the greatest interest at the present day.
Some of the views entertained by the bishop would doubtless have
been modified had he lived to witness the progress of the Church
and the country.   They were, however, wisely adapted to his day,
and will serve to show how narrowly he watched over all the interests of his beloved Methodism.   In regard to the episcopacy
and its duties, he says : " My desire is that there may be four
effective bishops travelling, as from the beginning, through the
whole continent, one to preside alternately in all the Conferences,
(not to change presidents during the sitting of the same Conference,
unless in cases of indisposition,) the other two or three to plan the
stations and perform ordinations, assisted by the elders in both
branches.   The plan of stations should be submitted to the president, time enough for him to give a final decision before the appointments are read to the preachers.

"I would particularly warn you to guard against the growing
evil of locality in bishops, elders, and preachers, or Conferences.
Locality is essential to towns and cities, travelling is as essential
to the country.   Were I to name cities, such as Jerusalem, Antioch, Rome, and all the great cities, both ancient and modern,
what havoc have these made in the Churches?   Alas for us! out
of seven hundred preachers we have about one hundred located in
towns and cities and small circuits, and in some week-day preaching nearly abandoned.

" Guard against two orders of preachers, one for the country
and the other for the cities.   The latter generally settle themselves to purchase ministers, and men of gifts and learning too

often set themselves to sale. I am bold to say that the apostolic order of things was lost in the first century ; and since that time Church government may be compared to the rolling of a snowball, gathering much filth of various kinds. At the time of the Reformation, the reformers beat off only part of the dirt ; and for many centuries more filth has been rolled on to an enormous size. "In the eighteenth century John Wesley formed an Evangelical Society in England. At the first General Conference of the Methodist Episcopal Church, held in Baltimore, Maryland, in 1784, an apostolical form of Church government and order was formed in America. You know that the present ministerial cant is, we cannot now, as in former apostolic days, have such doctrines, such discipline, such convictions, such conversions, such witnesses of sanctification, and such holy men. But I say we can, I say we must, yea, I say we have in part ; and can men claim the rights and privileges of apostles if they are impostors and not true ministers ? Thus, instead of going to preach they stay to preach. Hence schools, colleges, and universities are resorted to in order to make ministers, a practice Christ never commanded. The present Episcopal churches are local and greatly independent. All the numerous orders of Presbyterians, Independents, and Baptists, are local still. If we wish pure Church history, see the Acts of the Apostles, men flying by the impulse of the Spirit and driven by persecution. See Paul, Timothy, Titus, Tychicus, Archippus, Trophimus, Artemas, Luke, Epaphroditus, etc. At present I can only view it in this light, that with many ministers men go into the ministry by their learning, by their parents, or blind priests like themselves, moved by pride, worldly honour, or Satan. Observe well what a situation the apostles found themselves in ! If unfaithful, God would condemn them with a double condemnation, the people ready to starve, stone, or beat them to death. Modern priests seek to please the people that they may not beat or starve them to death. But will not God condemn false teachers to the nethermost hell ? We lay no claim to the Latin, Greek, English, Lutheran, or Protestant Episcopal Church episcopal order. It will be easily seen that we are so unlike each other that we are not even third cousins. Will their bishops ride from five to six thousand miles in nine months for eighty dollars a year, with travelling expenses, less or more ; preach daily when opportunity serves ; meet six camp-meetings in the year ; make arrangements for seven hundred preachers, and ordain one hundred men annually ; ride through all kinds of weather and roads, at our time of life, the one fifty-six and the other sixty-nine years of age ?

" Be sure always to see how the charitable contributions are appropriated. Never sign the journals till everything is correctly recorded. Be rigidly strict in all things ; and should there be a failure in any department, such as you cannot cure, appeal to the General Conference for a final decision. Examine well and with caution admit men into the ministry. It is ours to plead, protest, and oppose designing men from getting into the ministry. It is our fort, stronghold, and glory, and the superior excellency of our economy, that each character must undergo a strict examination every year. Put men into office in whom you can confide. If they disappoint you let them do it but once. Of all wickedness, spiritual wickedness is the greatest, and of all deception, religious deception is the worst. Fear not for the ark ; God will care for his own cause. If we have not men of great talent we have men of good hearts. Preserve a noble independence of soul on all occasions. Be the willing servant of slaves, but the slave to none. Put full confidence in men that merit it ; be not afraid to trust young men, they are not so likely to fail as old men ; young men are willing and they are able to work.

"Ours is not a civil, but a spiritual government, therefore one election is sufficient to secure a man's standing and office, unless in cases of debility, criminality, or corruption in administration.

"The circulation of our travelling and local ministry with their different gifts and diversity of talents is admirably calculated to be singularly useful. Many of our local brethren travel hundreds of miles in the course of the year, and highly enjoy themselves, and feel perfectly at ease and at home in the different circuits and districts, preaching anywhere and everywhere without fear of offending the travelling preachers."

While Asbury was opposed to educating men for the ministry as they would be educated for any other profession, without regard to a Divine call, he was yet altogether in favour of having Methodist preachers thoroughly educated, and gave, in his own diligent attention to study, an example to all his sons in the ministry. Though there were then no colleges or Biblical Institutes in the Church, yet the study of the learned languages was by no means neglected ; and Asbury well knew that he would prove unworthy of his relation as a son of Wesley and a colleague of Coke, did he not advocate to the extent of his ability the importance of a sound and thorough education in matters pertaining to general science and literature, as well as a theological training.

After preaching at Boehm's Chapel he went to a camp-meeting.

This meeting was largely attended. While at the Widow Willis's he entered the following tribute in his Journal :

" From the door I saw the tomb of dear Henry Willis. Rest, man of God ! Thy quiet dust is not called to ride five thousand miles in eight months, to meet ten Conferences in a line of sessions from the district of Maine to the banks of the Cayuga, to the states of Ohio, Tennessee, Mississippi, to Cape Fear, James River, Baltimore, Philadelphia, and the completion of the round. Thou wilt not plan and labour and arrange the stations of seven hundred preachers. Thou wilt not attend camp-meetings and take a daily part in the ministration of the word, and often consume the hours which ought to be devoted to sleep in writing letters upon letters."

From hence he went to the Pipe Creek camp-meeting. While here he said : " We are told there are between forty and fifty converts, and many professors powerfully quickened. The poor Africans, abandoned by all sects to us, were greatly engaged." Crossing the mountains he entered Ohio, and held Conference at Brownsville. Taking Chillicothe and West Union in his route, he entered Kentucky, and visited his old friend Dr. Hinde, in Clark county. " Once more," said he, " I see Dr. Hinde from the other side the flood rejoicing in Jesus. He will never again, I presume, put a blister on his wife's head to draw Methodism out of her heart. This mad prank brought deep conviction by the operation of the Spirit of God upon his soul."

From hence he went to the Tennessee Conference. This Conference was one of peace and prosperity ; the families in the neighbourhood were extensively visited, and much good resulted therefrom. During this Southern route Asbury records the following significant sentence : "On the peaceful banks of the Saluda I write my valedictory address to the presiding elders." As a faithful old patriarch, leaning upon his staff, he addressed the elders of the tribes of the Methodist Israel, being assured that he would ere long be called away from their councils.

After visiting Georgia, encouraging and strengthening the Churches, he returned to Charleston, where he preached in all the Methodist churches. In North Carolina he received intelligence that Dr. Coke had sailed with a company of missionaries for India. In Norfolk, where Conference was held, he was quite afflicted. During his illness he says : " I have been moved about among the families" (so great was the desire to have him) " of the Williamses, the Harrises, the Weavers, the Bennetts, and the Merediths ; and O, what kindness and nursing !" His next point was Richmond,

and from thence to Georgetown. The following note was made
in his Journal : " In the year 1774 I first visited Virginia and
North Carolina ; in the year 1780 I repeated my visit, and since
that time yearly. In the year 1785 I first visited South Carolina
and Georgia, and to these states, except one year, I have since
paid an annual visit until now, 1814.   I suppose I have crossed
the Alleghany Mountains sixty times."

The Baltimore Conference, which held its session in 1814 at
Georgetown, D. C., requested him to preach a funeral discourse on
the death of Otterbein. Speaking of him, Asbury says : " The
holy, the great Otterbein ! Forty years have I known the retiring
modesty of this man of God, towering majestic above his fellows in
learning, wisdom, and grace, yet seeking to be known only of God
and the people of God."   Again he visited Perry Hall, where he
was sick several days, receiving the kind attentions of that hospitable
mansion.   His next Conference was held in Philadelphia.   From
this Conference he wrote a serious and affectionate letter to the
New England Conference, remonstrating on the neglect of family
worship.   He was much afflicted during this time, and for twelve
weeks made no entry in his Journal.   He was burdened with attention and kindness during his illness, and says : " I would not be
loved to death.   Attentions constant, and kindness unceasing, have
pursued me to this place (Greensburgh) and my strength increases
daily.   I look back upon a martyr's life of toil, privation, and
pain, and I am ready for a martyr's death !   My friends in Philadelphia gave me a light four-wheeled carriage ; but God and the
Baltimore Conference made me a richer present ; they gave me
John Wesley Bond for a travelling companion.   Has he his equal
on earth for excellencies of every kind as an aid ?"

On his Western tour he stopped at Pittsburgh, and thence passed
on through Ohio, stopping at Steubenville, Zanesville, Middletown,
Circleville, and other places, where Bond preached.   Asbury was
prevailed upon to preach in Chillicothe, but it was in great weakness and suffering.   The Conference was held at Cincinatti.   At
this place he expected to have met M'Kendree, but the latter had
been thrown from his horse and considerably injured.   Asbury
being unable to preside, his place was occupied by John Sale.
While here gloomy tidings were received in relation to the war ;
the British had entered Maryland, and burned the public buildings
at Washington.

From Cincinnati he went to the Kentucky Conference, which
was held on the camp-ground.   At this meeting the bishop pleasantly remarked : " Our encampment cook is Brother Douglass ;

as for the bishops, they are sick, lame, and in poverty." From hence they passed through North and South Carolina, and attended Conference in Georgia. From this point, returning through North and South Carolina, they went into Virginia. At the Conference held in Lynchburgh he was severely attacked with asthma and spitting of blood. At the Baltimore Conference he was quite feeble, but notwithstanding, preached several times, and attended to the work of stationing the preachers.

Again we find the worn and weary bishop at that place he so much loved, and which he so often visited, Perry Hall. A sense of loneliness, however, came upon him as he remembered the friends of other days who had passed away. The seasons of happiness he had spent with some of the inmates of that hospitable mansion were gone, never to return. This was the last visit of the bishop to this place.

In much feebleness he entered upon his Eastern route, passing through Delaware, Pennsylvania, and New Jersey. At New York he attended the North Church and preached, and from hence went to Croton, visiting the family of Governor Van Cortlandt, who had entered into rest. Conference was held at Albany, and at the request of the members he preached the funeral sermon of Dr. Coke, who had died on the passage to the East Indies, and was buried in the Indian Ocean. We find the following tribute in Asbury's Journal : "Dr. Coke, of blessed mind and soul, of the third branch of Oxonian Methodists, a gentleman, a scholar, and a bishop to us. As a minister of Christ, in zeal, in labour, and in services, the greatest man in the last century."

The Rev. William Thacher, who was a member of the New York Conference, and was present at this session, thus writes in relation to Asbury :

"Bishop Asbury, almost done, is with us again, sustained by Bishop M'Kendree. Bishop Asbury is like the old patriarch, bowing down upon the top of his staff, his bodily strength much prostrated, his speech failed of its usual articulation, and his voice of its animated tone. But little of his presence was afforded us in Conference. Forty-four years' hardships, and indefatigable labour and travelling, and the fatigues and cares of Conferences, has worn him down ; and that which came upon him daily, the care of all the Churches, was never more deeply and heavily felt by man. These things engrossed his whole soul. He was the apostle of American Methodism, and had literally laid down his life for his brethren, ever prepared to divide his last dollar with a needy preacher. He was now in his last year. Desiring an interview with me, he sent me word, and I called to see him at his lodgings, and with a most tender solicitude for me and mine he gave me some kind and affectionate advice, and demonstrated his love for and confidence in me; then, with an overflowing heart, bade me his last parental farewell."

From this Conference Asbury and his companions started for Massachusetts. The Conference was held at Unity, N. H. On his way he was detained two days with affliction in Boston, but was able to preach in the evening previous to leaving. This was his last sermon in Boston. He was unable to preside at the Conference, and his place was supplied by George Pickering. On his return to New York he preached at Ashgrove and at Freeborn Garrettson's. On Sabbath, the 18th of June, 1815, he preached in New York at the Fourth-street Chapel, and at the African Chapel on Tuesday. The church was crowded by both white and coloured people. These were his last ministrations in this city. His text at Fourth-street was Zephaniah i. 12: "And it shall come to pass at that time that I will search Jerusalem with candles, and punish the men that are settled on their lees, that say in their heart, the Lord will not do good, neither will he do evil." There are living those who heard this discourse, and who represent it as pungent and searching, full of awakening power to the Church, but abounding in tenderness.

From New York he went to Philadelphia, where he also delivered his last message to a large and deeply-interested congregation. His next sermon was at Carlisle, and from thence, to use his own expression, he "beat across the mountains." He preached at Somerset, Brightwell's, and Washington. While at the latter place he says: "A Baptist missionary came into town collecting money for foreign lands. We labour for those at home. Feeble as I was, the necessity of bearing testimony to the truth pressed upon me. As our Baptist brother talked and read letters upon missions to foreign lands, I thought I might help with a few words. I related that a few years past a London Methodist member, in conversation, had complained to me that the kingdom and the Church had given so largely to support foreign missions. I observed in reply that the Methodist preachers who had been sent by John Wesley to America, came as missionaries; some returned, others did not; and now behold the consequences of this mission: we have seven hundred travelling, and three thousand local preachers who cost nothing. We will not give up the cause, we will not abandon the world to infidels; nay, we will be their plagues; they will find it herculean work to put us down. We will not give up that which we know to be glorious until we see something more glorious ; nor will we concede an inch to schismatics and heretics, who say ' Do away your forms, and leave your peculiar doctrines, and we will show you something better.' Show it to us first ; we are not ignorant of Satan's devices."

At West Liberty he preached from the text, "The time is short." His next stopping place was Zanesville, in the vicinity of which a camp-meeting was in progress. Within the last three months he had travelled through New Hampshire, Vermont, New York, New Jersey, Pennsylvania, and a portion of Ohio. He visited the encampment, and preached from 2 Cor. v. 2 : "Knowing the terror of the Lord we persuade men." His sermon was unusually interesting and powerful, and several souls were converted through its instrumentality. David Young, one of the most popular among the preachers of that day, was present at this camp-meeting. Though advanced in years and feeble, he is still living in Zanesville, a patriarch of Western Methodism beloved by all. Asbury's next appointment was in Chillicothe. His text was, "And the Lord turned and looked upon Peter." After the sermon intelligence came to him that his friend Eleanor Worthington was ill and desired to see him. He accordingly visited her, and in conversation with her found that she was much exercised on the subject of religion. She was a member of the Episcopal Church, and had doubtless been converted, but lacked that assurance which is the privilege of the children of God. When the bishop told her it was common for persons to be well assured that God had blessed them, her countenance was instantly lighted up, and her heart overflowed with joy. He administered the sacrament of the holy communion, and left her rejoicing in the Lord.

While here he received the intelligence of the overthrow of Bonaparte, and indulged in the following reflections: "The time is coming that all kings and rulers must acknowledge the reign of the King of kings, or feel the rod of the Son of God. But will forms do for the United States of America? Foolish people will think they have a right to govern themselves as they please ; aye, and Satan will help them. Will this do for us? Is not this republic, this land, this people, the Lord's. We acknowledge no other king but the eternal King ; and if our great men will not rule in righteousness, but forget God and Christ, the consequence will be ruin."

At a camp-meeting held near Mechanicsburgh he preached from the text, "The day is far spent, and the night is at hand." Thursday, September 14, he says : "Our Ohio Conference began, and all our fears vanished.   We have great peace, abundance of accommodation, and comfortable seasons in preaching noon and night in the court-house and the chapel.   Great grace, peace, and success have attended our coming together.   We have sixty-eight preachers. Ten delegates have been chosen to attend the next General Conference."   Bishop M'Kendree was present at the Conference, and at its conclusion the two went to Cincinnati.

While in this place Asbury had a long and earnest conversation with M'Kendree in regard to the affairs of the Church.   He gave it as his opinion that the western part of the United States would be the glory of America for the poor and pious, and that it ought to be marked out for five Conferences, and he traced out their boundaries.   Having passed the first allotted period of life, three-score and ten years, and being in ill health, he informed him that it could not be expected that he should visit the extremities every year, sitting in eight Conferences and travelling six thousand miles in eight months.   The labour and anxiety connected with the stationing of the preachers he regarded as too great a tax upon him in his feeble health.   From Cincinnati he went to Lebanon, and preached, at the request of the Conference, a memorial sermon on the occasion of the death of Dr. Coke.   On the following Sabbath he preached his last sermon in Cincinnati, and from thence passed over into Kentucky, preaching at Georgetown and Lexington.   Here Conference was held.   On Sabbath he ordained the deacons, and preached on the occasion of the death of Coke. While here he entered the following in his Journal: "My eyes fail; I will resign the stations to Bishop M'Kendree; I will take away my feet; it is the fittieth year of my ministry, and forty-fifth year of labour in America.   My mind enjoys great peace and divine consolation.   My health is better, which may in part be because I am less deeply interested in the business of Conferences; but whether health, life, or death, good is the will of the Lord.   'I will trust him, yea, I will praise him; he is the strength of my heart, and my portion for ever.'"

CHAPTER XXII.

Educational Advantages—His Devotion to Study—His Knowledge of the Languages—Thorough Course of Reading—Hebrew Bible and Greek Testament his constant Companions—Critical Exegesis—Power of Discrimination —Style of Writing—Imagination and Wit—Specimens—Gracefulness of Style—Specimens—An Appreciative Sense of the Beautiful—A Man of Sympathy—Notices of Books in his Course of Reading—Criticisms—His Skeletons of Sermons—Secret of his success as a Student—Method of Study —His Library—Preparations for the Pulpit—Obituaries in the early Minutes written by Asbury—Epistolary Correspondence—Letters.

ASBURY was not in the strict sense of the word a scholar, and yet he was far from being deficient in education. He did not, like the Wesleys, and Fletcher, and Coke, enjoy the advantages of a collegiate training, his opportunity for literary culture being simply such as was to be found in the primary schools of that day in England ; but at the same time such was his love of study, and his unremitting application, that he amassed an amount of varied learning that was astonishing, when we consider the circumstances under which it was attained. Riding day and night on horseback, and lodging mostly in the cabins of the wilderness, where there were neither books nor facilities for study, and when in the cities and towns holding quarterly meetings, councils, and conferences, and having the care of all the Churches, temporal as well as spiritual, himself originating and acting as agent for all the institutions of the Church, the wonder is that he was able to prosecute with success any department of study. As it was he made himself acquainted with Latin, Greek, and Hebrew, besides taking a thorough course of reading in Theology, Church History and Polity, Civil History and General Literature. His Hebrew Bible and Greek Testament were his daily companions : and though in his preparations for the pulpit he made no show of learning, yet his numerous sketches furnish abundant evidence of the fact that he was skilled in critical exegesis, and " a workman that need not be ashamed, rightly dividing the word of truth," with a power of discrimination rarely attained. His style of writing, as his Journal in three volumes will show, was plain, pointed, direct. He seemed to eschew all figures of speech, and to express his thoughts with sturdy old Anglo-Saxon nervousness. Occasionally a slight sparkle of wit may be found playing like a sunshine over his grave sentences, and sometimes, though rarely, he indulged in a flight of imagination that shows he was not destitute of the elements of a graceful writer. As mere specimens we present the following, which we take from the volume now in our hand.

While on a visit to New Haven, the seat of Yale College, he makes the following remark : " New Haven ! thou seat of science and of sin ! Can thy dry bones live ? ' O Lord ! thou knowest.' " While at Middlebury, the seat of a college, he entered the following : " At Middlebury we find college-craft and priest-craft." At a certain place in the South he said of the people that they had " more gold than grace ;" and describing another place he said, " they had neither dollars nor discipline, being sadly deficient in both." While at the salt-works in Virginia, he exclaimed : " Alas ! there is little salt ' here, and when Sister Russell is gone ¯ there will be none left." Boston, he said, " was famous for poor religion and bad water." Alluding to a congregation there who sold their preacher to another congregation for a thousand dollars, and loaned out the money at thirty per cent., he said : " How would it do to tell the South that priests were among the notions of Yankee traffic." New York, he said, was " as famous for oysters and bad ale" as " Asbury town was for distillation and bad whiskey." Travelling in New Jersey, he remarked : " Since this day week I have ridden over dead sands and among a dead people, and a long space between meals." We might easily multiply specimens of Asbury's wit, which, though rarely if ever indulged while occupying the pulpit, yet would flash out among the preachers in council and Conference at times in the most genial manner. Like Cowper's village pastor, he never stooped from the holy place,

" To court a grin when he should woo a soul."

But we promised some examples of gracefulness of style or beauty of composition. Having attended the session of the New York Conference which was held in John-street in the summer of 1802, he says, " it would require a volume to tell the restless tossings he had, the difficulties and anxieties he felt about the preachers and people here and elsewhere, alternate joy and sorrow ; but I am done, I am gone ! New York, once more farewell !" Having passed the din and strife of the city, and having gained the country, he says : " How sweet to me are all the calm scenes of life which now surround me on every side. The quiet country houses, the fields and orchards bearing the promise of a fruitful year ; the flocks and herds, the hills, and vales, and dewy meads, the gliding streams and murmuring brooks ; and thou, too, solitude, with thy attendants, silence and meditation, how dost thou solace my pensive mind after the tempest of fear, and care, and tumult, and talk of the noisy, bustling city."

While in the South, after riding, as he describes it, six hundred miles over the hills, barrens, swamps, savannas, rivers, and creeks of South Carolina, he says : " At Gause's Manor we were pleasantly situated.   I had a visit to the sea-beach, which to me was a most instructive sight.   The sea reminded me of its great Maker, who stayeth the proud waves thereof; its innumerable productions, the diversified features of its shores, the sand-hills, the marshes, the palmetto, tall and slender ; the sheep and goats frisking in the shade, or browsing in the sun ; or the eye directed to the waters beholds the rolling porpoise, the sea-gulls lifting and letting fall from high the clam, which breaking, furnishes them with food ; the eagle, with hovering wing, watching for his prey ; the white sail of the solitary vessel tossed upon the distant wave ; how interesting a picture do all these objects make !"

His descriptions of the " noble Hudson with its Palisades," the " lofty Catskills with their towering cliffs," the " beautiful Ohio, with its verdant shores," the " wild Potomac," the " lovely Shenandoah," the " thundering Niagara," the " Natural Bridge, under whose arch he longed to preach," the " interminable forests" and " broad prairies," all show that he possessed a lively and appreciative sense of the beautiful.   To those who looked upon him as cold and stoical, and destitute of those more tender and endearing sympathies which constitute the charm of social life, let us hear him as he speaks of the death of a Christian lady in whose hospitable mansion he often found a home : " I was invited to pass a night under the hospitable roof of General Thomas Worthington, at Mount Prospect Hall.   Within sight of this beautiful mansion lies the precious dust of Mary Tiffin.   It was as much as I could do to forbear weeping over her speaking grave.   How mutely eloquent !   Ah, the world knows little of my sorrows—little knows how dear to me are my many friends, and how deeply I feel their loss."

In his Journal we find notices of upward of a hundred books which he read, some of which he made the subject of severe thought and study.   His various criticisms of works which came under his review, show that he was far from being a superficial reader or thinker.   We have often been astonished at the amount of his reading, and have wondered how, in the midst of his numerous and onerous engagements, he found time to perform a tithe of what he accomplished. He was never, in any sense of the word, unemployed, and what is more important, was never "triflingly employed." That the reader may see that he was as accurate in his judgment of books as he was of men, we subjoin some of his criticisms. Of *Edwards on the Affections,* he says : "Excepting the small vein of Calvinism which runs through this book, it is a very good treatise, and worthy the serious attention of young professors of religion." Of *Sherlock's Sermons* he makes the following remark : " The author was doubtless a man of great abilities, but it is a pity he had not been a more evangelical writer. I find some good things in his writings, and others in general harmless, but not very interesting." After he had finished reading the lives of *Haliburton, De Renty,* and *Walsh,* he thus characterizes them : " One of the Church of Scotland, another of the Church of Rome, and the latter a Methodist preacher, but the work of God is one in all. To set aside a few particulars, how harmonious does the work of God appear in men of different nations and Churches." Having read two volumes of *Sermons by Rev. Mr. Knox,* of the West Indies, he says : " I am much pleased with his defence of revealed religion. Through the whole work there is something sublime and spiritual, so catholic too, and free from peculiar doctrines. I esteem him as one of the best writers among the Presbyterians I have yet met with......I approve the spirit and principles of the man ; he appears to be of the spirit of Mr. M'Gaw ; he gives some favourable hints of restoration, that natural evil should purge out moral evil ; but gives it not as his own opinion, but as that of others. In another place he says : ' Perhaps the heathen world shall have an after trial ;' if in time, it is true. So it sometimes is, that if a man is a rigid Calvinist, and turns, he must go quite round ; but general redemption and conditional salvation is the plan." Concerning a work written by *Rev. Silas Mercer, a Baptist,* he says : "I have been wonderfully entertained with it. He has anathematized the whole race of kings from Saul to George the Third. He is republicanism run mad. Why afraid of religious establishments in these days of enlightened liberty ? Silas has beaten the pope, who only on certain occasions, and for certain reasons, absolves subjects from allegiance to their sovereigns : and if the nations of Europe believed the sweeping doctrines of Silas, they would be right in decapitating every crowned head, and destroying every existing form of Church government. If plunging baptism be the only true ordinance, and there can be no true Church without it, it is not quite clear that even Christ had a Church until the Baptists plunged for it." *Comber on Ordination* elicited the following critique : " Much pomp was annexed to the clerical order, though plausible in its way. I believe the episcopal mode of ordination to be more proper than the presbyterial, or ordination by presbyters, but I wish there were primitive qualifications in all who handle sacred things." The *Confession of Faith* and the *Assembly's Catechism :* " There are some good and other very strong things in it. These books are calculated to convert the judgment and make the people systematical Christians." *Fletcher's Checks :* " The style and spirit in which Mr. Fletcher writes at once bespeak the scholar, the logician, and divine." *Robertson's History of Scotland :* " O what treachery and policy attendeth courts, and how does court policy, without design, give way to a reformation. This has been the case in England and Scotland. The fate of the unfortunate Mary Queen of Scots was affecting. The admired Queen Elizabeth does not appear to advantage in the Scotch history." *Dr. Chandler's Appeal to the Public :* " I think, upon the whole, he is right. Why may not the Protestant Episcopal Church have as much indulgence in America as any other society." *Potter's Church Government :* " I have read and transcribed portions of this work, but I must prefer the episcopal mode of Church government to the presbyterian. If the modern bishops were all as the ancient ones, all would be right, and there wants nothing but the spirit of the thing." *Clagget against Chubb :* " He writes well for a layman, but I suspect he would write as much against us whom he terms Arminians. Chubb is quite wrong. Clagget is no way smooth and entertaining, though he has truth and argument on his side." *The Valley of Lilies, by Thomas a Kempis :* This is much in the style of his Christian's Pattern, or Imitation of Christ. I wonder Mr. Wesley has never abridged this work." *Haweis's Church History :* " This is perhaps among the best I have seen, but his partiality to good old Calvinism is very apparent. I find it is the author's opinion that the evangelists were chief superintending episcopal men, (ay, so say I,) and that they prescribed forms of discipline and systematized codes of doctrine. After the death of the apostles, it would appear that the elders elected the most excellent men to superintend. This course was doubtless the most expedient and excellent. Every candid inquirer after truth will ackowledge, upon reading Church history, that it was a great and serious evil when philosophy and human learning were taught as a preparation for a Gospel ministry." *Marshall's Life of Washington :* " Critics may, for aught I know, find fault (especially on the other side of the water) with the style and general execution of this work. I like both. The early history of the country very properly precedes, and is connected with the life of the great man who has been so justly styled the father of his country. There is nothing in the work beneath the man of honour; there are no malevolent sentiments or bitter expressions derogatory to the character of a Christian. The author deserves credit for the pains he has taken to furnish authorities and authentic records in the notes to his work. If any author in America has done better than Marshall, it is Belknap, perhaps." *Mungo Park's Travels in Africa :* "Certain parts are so extraordinary that it appears like a romance. If true he experienced astonishing hardships. It would seem by this narrative, that the Africans are in a state so wretched that any sufferings with the Gospel would be submitted to in preference. But I have my doubts." *Ostervald's Christian Theology :* In Cave's Lives of the Fathers, and in the writings of the ancients, it will appear that the Churches of Alexandria and elsewhere had large congregations and many elders; that the apostles might appoint and ordain bishops. Mr. Ostervald, who, it appears, is a candid and well-informed man, has gone as far as might be expected for a Presbyterian. For myself I see but a hair's breadth difference between the sentiments of the respectable and learned author of Christian Theology and the practice of the Methodist Episcopal Church. There is not, nor indeed in my mind can there be a perfect equality between a constant president and those over whom he always presides." *Simpson's Plea for Religion :* "The author has drawn aside the purple curtain of the Church of Rome, and the black robes of the antichristian Church of England, to lay bare the abuses of bad systems and the vices of mitered heads. He has raised his warning voice against the corruption of manners and morals in all orders, which will, he predicts, without a speedy reformation, cause the downfall of all ecclesiastical establishments. He has magnanimously renounced his living as a minister, which his conscience would permit him no longer to hold. He said he knew not where to go, but the Lord has taken him to the ' Church of the first-born.' O what a warning is given to all Churches, to all ministers, to all Christians, and to thee, O my soul !" *Blair's Sermons :* "I find some very beautiful things in these sermons; they contain good moral philosophy. His sermon on Gentleness is worthy the taste of Queen Charlotte, and if money were anything toward paying for knowledge, I should think that sermon worth two hundred pounds sterling, which, some say, the queen gave him." *Prince's Christian History :* This book is Methodism in all its parts. I have great desire to print an abridgment of it to show the apostate children what their fathers were." *Gordon's History of the American Revolution* : "Here we view the suffering straits of the American army, and what is greatly interesting, Washington taking his farewell of the officers of the American army." *Saurin's Sermons:* "Long, elaborate, learned, doctrinal, practical, historical, and explanatory." *Thompson's Seasons :* "I find a little wheat and a great deal of chaff. I have read great authors, so called, and wondered where they found their finery of words and phrases. Much of this might be pilfered from the 'Seasons,' without injury to the real merit of the work ; and doubtless it has been plucked by literary robbers." *Wesley's Journal :* "I am now convinced of the great difficulty of journalizing. Mr. Wesley was doubtless a man of very general knowledge, learning, and reading, to which we may add a lively wit and humour ; yet I think I see too much credulity, long, flat narrations and coarse letters taken from others, in his Journal ; but when I come to his own thoughts they are lively, sentimental, interesting, and instructing. The journal of a minister of the Gospel should be theological, only it will be well to wink at many things we see and hear, since men's feelings grow more and more refined."

Besides his readings, Asbury's sketches or skeletons of sermons, if collected together, would make a volume of rare value for their exegetical and practical character. Above all the books for reading and study, the Bible, which he read in the original languages, occupied the highest place ; and no day, when his health would permit, was suffered to pass without its thorough and systematic study. This was the great armory from whence he drew the weapons of his warfare, and in the successful wielding of which he was enabled to demolish the strongholds of the adversary. Following in the footsteps of Wesley, he urged upon the preachers the importance of study ; and many, from his own example, who, when they entered the itinerancy, were utterly deficient in education, not only made themselves acquainted with their own language and literature, but made themselves acquainted with the classics of Greece and Rome, as well as the literature of Palestine. All honor to those self-made men who, without a college, and almost without a salary, pushed their way to the cabins of the wilderness, and in the midst of all their toils and embarrassments worked their way into the domain of letters.

The secret of Asbury's success as a student consisted in his rigid adherence to a systematic method ; and it is rarely if ever that any one excels who does not adopt and adhere to a systematic course of study. Discipline is everything to body and mind, and the most insurmountable difficulties are overcome by patient perseverance. To labor and to wait may be a difficult task for the impulsive and ambitious to learn ; but there is no royal road, no patent-righted, labour-saving way to profound attainment in any department of learning. His method, when not travelling, was to rise at four o'clock every morning ; spend two hours in prayer and meditation, two hours in reading and study, and one in recreation and conversation. Ten hours out of sixteen were spent in reading the Hebrew Bible and other books, and writing. He retired to his room at eight o'clock when not at meeting or in council, and spent an hour in meditation and prayer before retiring to rest.

Being obliged, for the most part, to depend for a library on the resources of his saddle-bags, which consisted of his Hebrew Bible, Greek Testament, Book of Discipline, and a few other books, his preparations for the pulpit were not drawn from commentaries, sketches, and pulpit assistants, but from original sources. Reading his text in the original, and thus going to the very fountain of inspiration, he was enabled to bring out of this rich and inexhaustible treasury things, if not novel, at least constructed after the model of the Holy Scriptures. His sermons were mostly of a textual, and rarely, like many discourses of the present day, of a topical character, and which stand frequently as nearly related to one passage of Scripture as another.

Examining the numerous sketches of his sermons given in his Journal, we are struck with the naturalness of his divisions of the subject-matter of the texts ; and those who have heard him preach assure us that he followed the advice of the Discipline, which he administered to the letter, in "always making out what he took in hand," "always suiting his subject to his audience, and choosing the plainest texts." In fact, "to convince, to offer Christ, to invite, and to build up," were prominent points, rarely, if ever lost sight of in his discourses. In this respect he was a model preacher.

We cannot close this chapter without calling the attention of the reader to two more features in connection with the literary attainments of Asbury. It is conceded pretty generally by those who were competent to give information on this subject, that most of the obituaries found in the older Minutes of the Conferences were from his pen. As biographical sketches they are models of excellence. In these we find no attempt at eulogy or elaboration. The strong points in the character of each were seized and delineated with a master hand. We have presented in the early part of our book a few of these as specimens of what we conceive to be a rare biographical style.

The other remarkable quality in the literary character of Asbury which is worthy of notice, is his admirable epistolary style. His correspondence was voluminous, and his letters possess an interest beyond their personal value, in the vast amount of information they contain on matters not only pertaining to the Church and her interests, but to the country at large. His numerous letters to Thomas Morrell, who was stationed at John-street Church, and which were published several years since in the Christian Advocate and Journal, are full of interesting facts and incidents pertaining to the current history of Methodism.

CHAPTER XXIII.

His last Round—Unceasing Toil—The ruling Passion—Entry in his Journal—Journey through North and South Carolina—Arrival at Richmond, Virginia—Dissuaded from Preaching—Determined to preach once more—Is carried into the Church—Beautiful Morning—His Text on the Occasion—His Audience—An impressive Scene—Close of the Discourse—Anxiety to reach Baltimore—Farewell—Arrives at the Residence of his old Friend, Mr. George Arnold—Illness increased—Unable to proceed further—His Sufferings—Sabbath - Family called together for Religious Service—Bond, his travelling Companion, reads and expounds the Scriptures—Conclusion of Services—While sitting in his Chair the Spirit of Asbury passed away—His Funeral—Burial—Request of the Citizens of Baltimore made to the General Conference—His Remains removed to Eutaw-street Church—Vast Procession—Funeral Oration pronounced by Bishop M'Kendree—Epitaph—Resolutions of the Baltimore Conference in 1856 in relation to the Erection of a Monument in Mount Olivet Cemetery—Reflections.

THE veteran pioneer had taken his last round, and had attended his last Conference. Forty-five years of incessant toil in cities and villages, and in the log-cabins and wildernesses of the far West and South, travelling round the continent with but few exceptions every year, subject to every kind of itinerant hardship and privation, bore heavily upon his physical constitution, and we find him as if impelled by a ruling passion strong as life, and undismayed by the approach of death, urging his weary way from appointment to appointment. He needed rest and relief from all cares and anxieties, but like one who was determined to rest not until the grave should unveil its bosom to receive him, he continued to travel and preach. When he could no longer walk to the house of God, he was borne in the arms of his brethren; and when he could no longer stand in the holy place to deliver his dying message to the assembled flocks over which he had been a faithful and affectionate overseer for upward of forty years, he sat, as the beloved of the Apocalypse, and poured out the treasures of his loving, overflowing heart to the weeping multitudes, who sorrowed most at the thought "that they should see his face no more." In the midst of his last labours he says in his Journal : " I die daily, am made perfect by labour and suffering, and fill up still what is behind. There is no time or opportunity to take medicine in the day-time, I must do it at night. I am wasting away."

By slow and difficult stages he passed with his faithful Bond through South and North Carolina, preaching at different points until he reached Richmond, Virginia. His anxiety to preach once more in Richmond was so great, that notwithstanding the entreaties and endeavours of his friends to dissuade him therefrom, seeing his extreme debility, he overcame all their efforts, saying, "I must once more deliver my public testimony in this place." When the hour for preaching arrived he was taken in a close carriage to the old Methodist Church. On arriving he was borne in the arms of his friends into the church and placed upon a table prepared for the purpose, whereon he was seated. The "Old Church," whose walls had so often echoed to his voice, was crowded to its utmost capacity.

It was a bright and beautiful Sabbath of spring in the year 1816. Nature, which in the South at a more early season puts on her flowery robe and decks herself in garlands of beauty, on this morning wore her most smiling aspect. The air was freighted with the perfume of bright spring flowers, and earth and sky conjoined to make the Sabbath a delight. But that day, so full of joyousness and hope, like the aged messenger of God who saw its opening glories, was destined, like himself, to pass away. How befitting the language of the poet :

> "Sweet day, so calm, so bright,
> Bridal of earth and sky,
> The dew shall weep thy fall to-night,
> For thou, alas ! must die."

After singing, reading the Scriptures, and prayer, the bishop announced, in tremulous tones, his text : "For he will finish the work and cut it short in righteousness : because a short work will the Lord make upon the earth." Impressed with the consciousness that his work was done, and that he was like one who was waiting for the voice of the bridegroom, the text was well chosen. Before and around him were his brethen and friends of former years. With tearful eyes and throbbing hearts they were listening to the last sermon of their beloved father in God. Slowly and measuredly the solemn truths fell from his trembling lips. Carried away by his feelings he exceeded his strength, and was obliged to pause frequently from sheer exhaustion. Feeble as he was he preached for nearly an hour, during which time a deep and awful stillness pervaded the entire assembly, only broken by the sobs of sympathetic hearers. To the vast audience gathered on this occasion the scene before them must have been sublimely impressive. For the last time they were listening to the voice of their beloved bishop, who had gone in and out before them in his continental visits for so many years. When he closed his discourse he was much exhausted, and was borne back to his carriage and taken to his lodgings.

Almost any other person would have desisted from travelling in such an ill state of health, but the spirit of Asbury could brook no delay; besides, he was particularly anxious to reach Baltimore to be present at the session of the General Conference in May. Accordingly, taking his last farewell of the brethren and friends in Richmond, he proceeded on his journey in the care of his ever-faithful Bond. Having arrived at the residence of his old and long-tried friend, Mr. George Arnold, about twenty miles south of Fredericksburg, in Virginia, his illness increased so that he was unable to proceed.

On the evening of the twenty-ninth of March his carriage stopped at the door of this his last earthly resting-place, and he was borne into the house never more to leave it until his worn and weary body should be carried to the tomb. He suffered much during the night and the succeeding day, notwithstanding everything was done that affection could do to mitigate his distress. When Sabbath came he requested the family to be called together at the usual hour for religious services. His travelling companion read and expounded the twenty-first chapter of Revelation, during which time Asbury was calm and devotional. His end was near, and his faith doubtless enabled him to catch a glimpse of the holy city which John saw coming down out of heaven, and to hear the voice assuring him that God would wipe away the tears from sorrow's weeping eye. The sun of his life was declining, but there were no clouds in the evening heavens. All was calm, and clear, and bright.

The services were closed, and Bond, perceiving that the venerable bishop was sinking in his chair, hastened to support him; and while he held up his reclining head, the spirit of the patriarch passed away in peace to its God, and thus,

> " Like some broad river widening t'ward the sea,
> Calmly and grandly life join'd eternity."

His funeral was attended by a large assemblage of citizens from the surrounding neighbourhood, and with appropriate religious services his body was deposited in the family burying-ground of Mr. Arnold.

At the session of the General Conference a request was presented by the people of Baltimore, that his remains be removed, and deposited in a vault prepared for that purpose in the Eutaw Church, immediately beneath the pulpit. The occasion of the re-interment was one of thrilling interest, not only to the members of the General Conference, but to the inhabitants of the entire city. An immense concourse assembled at the Light-street Church, from whence his remains were taken to the Eutaw Church. At the head of the vast procession was Bishop M'Kendree, the colleague of the departed Asbury, and the only surviving bishop of the Church. Next followed the members of the General Conference ; and lastly the members of the Church and citizens in thousands. Amid the tears of the multitude, M'Kendree pronounced the funeral address ; and with the solemn and impressive ceremonies connected with the burial service, the sacred relics were deposited in their resting-place. Over the vault the following epitaph was inscribed :

Sacred to the Memory of
REV. FRANCIS ASBURY,
BISHOP OF THE METHODIST EPISCOPAL CHURCH.

He was born in England, August 20, 1745 ;
Entered the Ministry at the age of seventeen ;
Came a Missionary to America 1771 ;
Was ordained Bishop in this city December 27, 1784 ;
Annually visited the Conferences in the United States ;
With much zeal continued to " preach the word "
For more than half a century ;
and
Literally ended his labours with his life,
Near *Fredericksburg*, Virginia,
In the full triumph of faith, on the 31st of March, 1816,
Aged 70 years, 7 months, and 11 days.
His remains were deposited in this vault May 10, 1816,
By the General Conference then sitting in this city.
His journals will exhibit to posterity
His labours, his difficulties, his sufferings,
His patience, his perseverance, his love to God and Man.

In March, 1856, the Baltimore Conference passed the following resolutions :

"*Resolved,* That we highly appreciate the intention of the Trustees of the Methodist Episcopal Church in the city and precincts of Baltimore, to erect a monument which may designate to future generations the burial place of the venerable ASBURY, and also record the gratitude of the Church for the blessings which have resulted from the labours of that faithful servant of Christ, to whom, under God, American Methodism is so deeply indebted for her wonderful progress and prosperity.

Resolved, That we present this subject to our various congregations as soon after we reach our several appointments as may be convenient, and that we request the donations of those of the members and friends of our Church who may feel disposed to contribute to this memorial."

The trustees of Mount Olivet Cemetery having selected and contributed a site for this monument, the resolutions were designed to carry out their benevolent undertaking, and it is presumed that ere long a monument worthy of the Pioneer Bishop will be erected by the Baltimore Methodists, to "designate to future generations the burial-place of the venerable Asbury."

The reader has seen in the preceding pages that the life of Asbury was one of continued incident, from his youth through all the period of his laborious and useful career. What the London "Athenæum" says of the tireless itinerant, Wesley, in Great Britain—that if "under the horsehoof of Attila the grass never grew, so the grass never grew under the tread of John Wesley" —may with equal propriety be affirmed of the indefatigable Francis Asbury in America.

Well did Methodism find its way into the States. It had no ruffles or lawn that it feared to soil, no powdered locks that it feared to disorder, no buckles it was afraid to tarnish. It lodged roughly and fared scantily. It tramped up muddy ridges, it swam or forded rivers to the waist, it slept on leaves or raw deer skin, or pillowed its head on saddle bags, it bivouacked among wolves or Indians; now it suffered from ticks or mosquitoes; it was attacked by dogs, it was hooted and it was pelted; the hurricane blew down trees across its path; it lost its way in the woods, it was stricken by fever and wasted by pestilence, it was fined, maltreated, and imprisoned, but it throve. Through the ample woods of the West, taking long windings to avoid the swamps, skulking out of sight of Indians, following by the dim light of some backwoodsman's blaze, drifting along great silent rivers to some poor settler's hut, giving even the shirt off its back, worn, weary, rain-drenched, yet pursuing its noble mission, and making footpaths for love and fondness, Methodism went on till it had crossed the frontier of states.   The only distinction of its bishops was one of bodily toil or personal labour.   They traversed six thousand miles a year through a country that had no inns, no roads, where they and their horses, when they had any, were hungry and shelterless.   If they wanted a dinner they had to hunt it, and then cook it by a fire that would not blaze, and the rain and wind often put it out.   It was a feast day when they dined on raccoon or bear steaks, and jolted on a road full of ruts in a forty-dollar chaise.   Perhaps even Methodism would not do ill to recall the history of some of those early pioneers.   Methodism is now a power in the States.   Its loyalty is no longer called in question, as at the time of the Declaration of Independence.   West and South it is paramount.

Foremost in that band of tireless itinerants was Francis Asbury, the pioneer bishop of the Methodist Church in America.   Always and everywhere with harness on ready for the spiritual warfare, he may be said almost to have created the Church in its present form, and during his long and active life kept all its departments in motion.   He ordained upward of three thousand preachers, and preached seventeen thousand sermons, besides attending to the varied and multitudinous duties connected with his peculiar relation to the Church and his episcopal office.   Though dead he yet lives in the affections of the great Methodist public, North and South, numbering upward of a million.   So effectually has he stamped his powerful mind upon the masses of Methodism all over this vast continent, from the hills of the Aroostook to the slopes of the Pacific, that no time or change can efface the impression. What the name of Washington is to the patriot American—a charm and a watchword in whatever pertains to American liberty, the name of Asbury is to the American Methodist in whatever concerns the genius and mission of Methodism.

London :
BOWDEN and BRAWN, Printers, 13, Princes Street, Holborn.